C. W. Post,

~ The Hour and The Man

Arms:

*Or on a Fess between three Arches, Gules; a
Lion passant, Or, between two Bezants, Or.*

Crest:

*On a Wreath of the Colours, a demi Lion, Or,
resting the sinister paw on a Bezant, Or, charged
with an Arch, Gules, as in the Arms.*

Authority:
College of Arms
Queen Victoria Street
London, E. C. 4
(1962).

IN ME MEA SPES OMNIS

Post

C. W. Post,

~The Hour and The Man

A Biography

with

Genealogical Supplement

by

NETTIE LEITCH MAJOR

Illustrated

PRESS OF JUDD & DETWEILER, INC.

WASHINGTON, D. C.

NINETEEN HUNDRED AND SIXTY-THREE

PRINTED IN UNITED STATES OF AMERICA

DEDICATION

THIS BOOK is respectfully dedicated to
MARJORIE MERRIWEATHER POST MAY
whose kind and considerate cooperation
made the presentation possible.

NETTIE LEITCH MAJOR

Sir Oswald Birley portrait

Charles William Post

Althaeus P. Cole

Ella Letitia Merriweather
(*Mrs. C. W. Post*)

Contents

*Ancestors and Descendants of Charles William Post (1854–1914)
and Ella L. Merriweather Post (1853–1912)*

xi

List of Illustrations

Foreword

THIS IS THE first full-length biography of C. W. Post. In reading the manuscript I was struck by the eloquent portrayal of Post as a successful business executive, fertile inventor, world traveler, generous philanthropist, colonizer, and rebel against hypocrisy. He was a unique and complete man—a crusader for causes in which he believed, an excellent public speaker, and a remarkable embodiment of the practical American spirit. As an eminent leader of his generation, he touched life at many points and achieved much. The interesting genealogical section of the book shows the splendid New England background from which he came. His parents were both persons of strong character and ability, and their qualities can be traced through his life.

The interpretation of C. W. Post found here emphasizes the intense activity of his entire life. It was a high-tension life of boundless vigor, courage, and selflessness. The quality of his character as a man of principle and simplicity stands out in strong relief. It is demonstrated that he hitched his wagon to stars in various parts of the firmament. As a man of action with a wide range of interests, he could quickly grasp the essence of a problem and find the satisfactory solution leading to genuine accomplishments. His efforts were not always successful, but he took that in his stride.

C. W. Post was an innovator in many areas, and his influence on our nation has been multiplied by the charm and personality which won him many friends. Here was a citizen of our democracy who took his duties to it more seriously than most of us do.

In this penetrating study of his life, C. W. Post is revealed not as a mere visionary, but as a stalwart figure of genius whose shadow extended beyond his own era. Its authoritative nature stems from the fact that it is based on extensive, painstaking research in the Post family archives; in Springfield, Illinois, and elsewhere. Many of these primary sources and contemporary published accounts had not previously been used. Extraordinary value is attached to this volume by the inclusion of a wealth of interesting illustrations, most of them

hitherto unpublished. Special thanks for the use of the archival material are due Mrs. Herbert May, the inspiring daughter of C. W. Post
and herself subject of the final chapter.

The author has made a distinct contribution to American biography
and is to be congratulated on her literary craftsmanship. This story
of a life is not embroidered with sensation or fiction; it is unembellished,
unadorned and unvarnished. It abounds in fact and authentic anecdote. The reader will utter the words of Oliver Twist, "Please, sir, I
want some more."

G. WALDO DUNNINGTON

Northwestern State College of Louisiana
Natchitoches, La., USA
26 March 1963

Introduction

THIS IS NOT so much the story of a man, but of a life. It is not a memorial to a person, but to a purpose. For the man held it to be most important to live a life and make it true to its purpose. Those who knew Charlie Post—the strong heart, the kind friend, the patient, wise and just counselor, who dreamed so fairly and wrought so manfully—have mostly passed from the scene.

Perhaps it is true that a biography, however brief, cannot avoid bias on the part of the author. If this be the case, then the author pleads guilty of prejudice in favor of the subject. The startling personality of a magnificent man has been revealed as the result of extensive research in countless newspaper files, public records, private correspondence and interviews with the few remaining who knew Charles Post. He was an exceptionally devoted Christian and one of the most able men of his day. While making a place for himself in the world he did not resort to the ruthless tactics so common in the era through which he emerged. The frailties of human nature crop into the lives of the best of us, and C. W. Post had his portion. We have made no other attempt than to recall an industrial transition in American economy where one man played a vital and important role.

This is not an all-encompassing story of the founder of *Postum, Grape-Nuts*, and *Post Toasties* (forerunners of *General Foods Corporation*), but an account of the little-known accomplishments in Post's life. It is intended to reveal a great humanitarian, an inventor, and the amazing facets of an amazing man.

It has been said—"there is no history without genealogy, and no genealogy without history." How true that becomes when we study the lives of the makers of history. The fibers assembled into the whole cloth are woven from the threads of ancestry. The fibers woven into the cloth that made Charlie Post were plucked from ancestral threads of merit. In addition to the highlights of his private life and public works, we are including a genealogical supplement of his ancestry back to the immigrant Stephen Post who came to Connecticut in the year 1634.

Following the life of C. W. Post, there is a chapter on his daughter, Marjorie Merriweather Post May. His story would not be complete without an introduction to the splendid woman grown from "the little girl of the past." If the reader should feel that the writer appears to be hypnotized by the presence of Mrs. May, or glamorized by her personality, the reader is correct. However, the author has written her true impressions, and inquiry among contemporaries reveals there are no other reactions. The writer's gratitude is expressed to the wonderful daughter of C. W. Post for her constant interest and splendid cooperation.

Special appreciation is due Dr. G. Waldo Dunnington for his assistance and suggestions with the manuscript. To Mrs. Delia Pierson of Judd & Detweiler (printers), very sincere thanks are given for her untiring aid and infinite patience with the writer in editing and for her guidance through the maze of publication details.

It is hoped that many people will come to know C. W. Post through the challenges of his life and the Christian principles he followed.

NETTIE LEITCH MAJOR

Washington, D. C.
June 1963

C. W. Post,

—The Hour and The Man

Chapter 1

~

Charles William Post
(1854–1914)

Aᴛ ᴛʜᴇ ᴛᴜʀɴ of this century the people of Battle Creek frequently greeted a tall, immaculately groomed Westerner wearing a broad, white Stetson hat. Generally he hurried along after a friendly word or two, while at other times he stopped long enough to slowly work off, with characteristic simplicity and directness, one of an unlimited number of stories which he seemed to have on tap to point the subject. This was a far different Charlie Post from the man who had arrived in Battle Creek a few years prior. The town was not yet what his contribution would make it. In less than five years the townspeople had been made aware of an energetic, ingenious citizen whose love of beauty was to transform the lives of the working classes. He would soon become known in Great Britain as the man whose persistent endeavor finally induced the Englishman to dismiss kidneys and bacon from the breakfast menu and adopt the American prepared cereal. British workmen would issue a resolution of thanks to him as the one who outlined at least a portion of their plans for the Free Labor Party, which protected its members from overt acts of Socialists and Anarchists. In his own country Senators and Congressmen would respect this man's insight; his subtle, irresistible power to crush the political life out of an unworthy officeholder. While speaking in a well-modulated, quiet voice, Post's searching but impenetrable grey-blue eyes looked deep into the soul of the listener. The entire country was to become aware of a tough fighter who excelled in any game played by the rules. He was to come through an era that crushed the weak and toughened the strong. The plow through heavy seas of industry and labor would be rough sailing, but it would not leave mangled bodies in its wake. This, in itself, was singular in the days of ruthless business tactics.

When a trainload of health-seekers disgorged at Battle Creek, on a bleak, raw day in February of 1891, there was no particular reason to notice the pale, wan man on the stretcher. His wife, Ella, and little three-year-old daughter, Marjorie, hopefully followed the ailing man; the Battle Creek Sanitarium seemed the last chance for him, everything else had been tried. Most of these health-seekers were en route to the Sanitarium; some few would wander aimlessly about the town seeking any miracle cure offered by the various other cure-all businesses in the town. The Sanitarium had attracted national attention for a number of years as a medium for regaining health through proper health-foods, meatless meals, mental science, calisthenics, water-therapy and current fads. Its fame and success was such that all other types of cure-all exponents had set up for business in the town. The "Grahamite dieters" were perpetuating the memory of Sylvester Graham by strict reliance on Graham flour and Graham crackers. Vegetarians came into popularity in ancient times and are still among us. Health resorts, spas, and sanitariums had been popular since long before the days when George Washington tried the waters at Berkeley Springs. But fads, cure-alls and dietary wonders caught the public fancy then as well as now. With the great success of Dr. John Harvey Kellogg at the Sanitarium, various healers, mesmerists, exponents of gymnastics, and medicine men descended on Battle Creek with the idea of siphoning off some of the profits from the Sanitarium. This was a town dedicated to *health*, for very little else had placed it on the map. Had there been one person around in 1891 who knew the power or potential of this newly arrived patient, perhaps Battle Creek would have been better prepared for the imminent upheaval which soon was to transform the village into a wild melee of manufacturing "health foods." The Sanitarium, under the direction of Dr. Kellogg, was operated by the Seventh Day Adventists. Dr. Kellogg and his brother, W. K. Kellogg, had not yet successfully marketed a health food—it took Charles William Post, the very man who was to be given up by the Sanitarium as a hopeless case, to show them the way.

Up to this date, the American housewife had not been emancipated from the kitchen. Breakfast alone involved long hours of preparation. Oatmeal had become the standard American breakfast, but it then required an extremely long, slow-cooking process. Many housewives placed the pan in water, shoved it to the back of the kitchen range and cooked the oatmeal into the night. A few prepared, packaged foods had been introduced on the market, most of them not palatable and some downright unpopular. The American male was accustomed to a hearty breakfast of meat, potatoes, or flap-jacks, and he readily relegated dry cereals to the barn as "hay for horses."

These were the unsanitary days, when open barrels of crackers, pickles, flour, sugar and such, stood around the grocery store, and meats hung from hooks in the open—all a picnic ground for air-borne life. Milk was delivered from a large can, emptied into the housewife's pitcher at the door, the lid of the can being the indifferent measurer —pint, quart, gallon or whatever was needed. There were no cereals endorsed by champions until Charlie Post thought of the idea. When today's TV-conscious, club-going housewife reaches up on the shelf for a packet of *Post Tens*, and breakfast is ready, she may give thanks to C. W. Post for his ingenuity. It began with *Postum*, 1895, *Grape-Nuts*, 1897, *Post Toasties*, 1906, and a hard fight for pure-food laws. Post's twin gifts of razor-sharp business ability and deep esthetic appreciation united in a driving force not far short of genius. Today, *General Foods Corporation* is a monument to the inventive ability, imagination, advertising genius and financial acumen of that "sick man" who learned so much from defeat.

Let us take a long and detailed look at C. W. Post, probe into what went on before the Battle Creek days, and then see the results of his advent upon the scene. Battle Creek, and the Kelloggs, did not know that this man had a past history of inventive ability, with a driving, unrelenting force within him. Nothing had stopped him save stomach ills and nervous disorders. He was to cure himself and pass the knowledge gained on to the world through the new and untried field of national advertising, and live to hear himself called the "grandfather of advertising in America." While Post did not "invent" advertising, he was the first to know what to do with it as a tremendous implement of force.

Charles William Post was born October 26, 1854, at Springfield, Illinois, to Charles Rollin and Caroline (Lathrop) Post, of hale and hearty Colonial New England stock. (See genealogical supplement.) He was "Charlie" to the family but he became known internationally and intimately as "C. W." The emaciated man who arrived at Battle Creek in 1891 had grown up a stalwart and athletic youth, with great pride in an erect military carriage. Even during long, discouraging sick spells there was no slump in physique. Photographs herein show his general appearance, but they cannot tell one that he was six-feet-one-inch tall, weighing from one hundred sixty-five to one hundred seventy pounds for most of his mature life. He once proudly wrote to a friend: "The Post men are all tall and erect, my father is six-feet-two and perfectly erect in advanced years, and he tops me by one inch." The powerfully penetrating grey-blue eyes prompted one plant manager to comment: "There is no use to lie to C. W., the man sees straight through you." His grooming was the epitome of good taste, with strict attention to the cut and fit of his clothes. Perfectionism was the very trait which drove him day and night to the conclusion of any program or project. One characteristic best remembered by his associates was the soft spoken voice and quiet demeanor, which completely belied the hot words and directness of his penned epistles. Factory workers long remembered C. W. sauntering through the plant where he would stop the workers long enough to engage them with amusing stories, of which he seemed to have an endless supply. He had the keen insight of knowing when to become personal with the workers and when not to divert them; a moment or two of relaxation would often prod sagging production or smooth down ruffled feelings. The gentle, quiet voice and manner did not mean that another style of language was unknown for, if sufficiently provoked to do so, he could give off a string of expletives in almost poetic fashion that would wither the soul of a mule. In fact, in Texas, he once bought a brace of mules from an old mule-skinner to discover that they understood only one kind of language and would not respond to any other style. He was readily equal to the demands.

As fame and fortune rose, a natural curiosity turned toward the man. While the complete story has never been written, extensive newspaper coverage, articles, editorials, magazine and short features were published during his lifetime. Most of the stories were slanted toward the "romantic" reasons for success, without an iota of research into facts. Some of the more imaginative writers claimed Post was driven to success through the memory of childhood poverty, yet nothing could be further from the truth. This fallacy is pointed out in the supplemental chapter on his father, a substantial businessman, who maintained one of the nicest residences of Springfield, Illinois, while Charlie Post was growing up. There is ample reason to excuse the fantasy since contemporaries were startled by the amazing ability which was to enable him to build a cereal empire in a few short years. Other writers called the success story "luck"—perhaps this type of explanation makes better reading material; however, before this writer are account books, letter-copy books, correspondence, and private files covering his entire life and that of his parents. It would seem that luck had very little to do with Post's success. A careful analysis and research into public and court records, with private files made available, show that imagination, ability, downright hard work and constant application to purpose, day and night, are the real answers to that success.

Perhaps it would clarify the picture somewhat if matters concerned here were taken in chronological order. Fortune first smiled on Charlie Post in the selection of parents, both of whom outlived him. Rollin and Carrie were reared in families of good educational background and aesthetic appreciation. While their own childhoods were not outstandingly affluent, there was never a lack of funds for all general purposes of life. Carrie was an able writer of prose and verse. Her deep religious feelings, her joys and sorrows, her friendships, each brought forth a sentimental little verse on any subject at hand. The poems were published during her lifetime under the title *Aunt Carrie's Poems* (1909). Several of C. W.'s ancestors, uncles and cousins, were outstanding men of the pulpit and teachers. Many of his cousins were known as forceful ministers of the Gospel, particularly recognized in the field of erudition. This special ability in speech and style of delivery was perhaps the fountain of phrases so aptly turned by C. W. in his homey advertising copy, letters, and speeches.

Rollin Post migrated from his birthplace in Cornwall, Vermont, at age seven, with parents, brothers and sisters, to Marietta, Ohio. After a short time there, the family settled at Waverly, Illinois, where Rollin grew to maturity. In early manhood, he was a farmer at Waverly in the days when the American economy was geared to agricultural pursuits. When the gold-rush craze reached the area, Rollin became a Forty-niner, where he did rather well at trading with the gold-rushers, while at the same time making a surprise strike of a gold pocket. An alert business mind quickly discerned the high profits gained from furnishing scarce supplies to the gold-seekers; by this enterprise he made sufficient capital to return to Illinois and settle in business.[1]

As times rolled toward an industrial economy, Rollin turned his attention toward "supply and demand." By 1852 the Chicago and Alton Railroad had reached Springfield, Illinois. Rollin decided upon that location for his future business as a dealer in agricultural implements and grain. It was into this Springfield setting that C. W. made his appearance in the world. Little of public interest surrounded the family during his early childhood beyond the normal routine of a happy, average American family. The Posts lived not far from Abraham Lincoln; Rollin was long to remember and recount his activities as one of the honor guard to accompany Lincoln's body back to Springfield. The Posts seemed better able than the majority of their neighbors to afford summer vacations to the Eastern Seaboard. Carrie took her little boys back to Hartford and to Massachusetts to visit her remaining family and friends when Charlie was four years old and subsequently as he and his two brothers were growing up. The old original letters of Carrie to Rollin are extant and each reveals the facts of this statement. These letters in question partially serve to refute later newspaper stories of childhood poverty as written about C. W. Post after he had become the "cereal king."

The three Post boys, Charlie, Carroll and Aurrie, were educated in the public schools of Springfield, their education being augmented by their mother's private tutoring. At age thirteen, Charlie entered Illinois Industrial College at Urbana, the forerunner of the University

---

[1] See Gold Rush account in life of Rollin herein.

1860-1888   Springfield, Ill.

C. W. Post's boyhood home, and birthplace of Marjorie Merriweather Post
(Now the Carrie Post and King's Daughters' Home)

This business was started in Springfield, Illinois, before the birth of C. W. Post. The drawing was made about 1860. The first grain shipped over the Chicago & Alton R. R. was shipped from this business house at the corner of 10th & Adams Streets in Springfield. After the three sons grew to maturity the business became known as C. R. Post & Sons.

Charles Rollin Post
(On return from Gold Rush, 1851)

Charles Rollin Post
(Sixty years later)

of Illinois. He had shown aptitude for mechanical engineering and other crafts but, after two years of indifferent grades in his subjects, he pled with his mother for permission to start out on his own. She recognized the fact that the boundless energy, which he maintained most of his life, could not be confined to a classroom and she reluctantly agreed. After the Urbana days, Charlie joined the Springfield Zouaves, or Governor's Guards, and many years later attended a reunion of his old troop. During the Chicago fire in October of 1871, Charlie went with his company to Chicago, where he served under General Phil Sheridan during the time the city was under martial law. This was a memorable experience for a boy not yet seventeen years of age, an adventure which doubtless kindled the spark of wanderlust. On returning to Springfield, he and an old boyhood chum, Charlie Moodie, made up their minds that they should see the new "wild and woolly West." They wandered down into Oklahoma Territory, western Kansas and the cowboy country, trying their luck as cowhands. Obviously the spirit of adventure was short-lived, for they soon returned to Springfield with bright ideas and high hopes. It was Charlie Post who observed that this new country had everything it needed in grain, fertile soil, space, cattle, and ambition, everything save manufactured goods. The boys persuaded Mrs. Post to lend them one thousand dollars to open a hardware store at Independence, Kansas. It is certainly to the credit of these young men that they did not squander the money but doubled the amount within two years, and Charlie repaid his mother. Kansas did not quite suit Charlie Post, hence he sold out to his partner and returned home to Springfield with very definite plans for the future. The first on the agenda was to marry the girl with whom he had grown up. On November 4, 1874, Charles William Post and Ella Letitia Merriweather [2] were married at the home of her uncle at Pawnee, Illinois, her parents having died a few years before this.

[2] Ella Letitia Merriweather was the daughter of John Hood Merriweather, a native of Maryland, and Elizabeth Hummel, of Ohio. See supplement for genealogical data.

Caroline and C. Rollin Post

Aurelian Atwater Post   *Charles William Post*

C. Rollin Post and Great-Granddaughters, 1918

Adelaide Brevoort Close   *Eleanor Post Close*

Age 2

C. W. Post

Age 36

C. W. Post

C. W. Post and Marjorie

Age 20

Ella Letitia Merriweather
(Mrs. C. W. Post)

Chapter 2

~

The Young Married Man

In the 1870's traveling salesmen were in a relatively new profession, and excellent money was garnered on the commission basis. The income could be unlimited for one willing to endure the rigors of road life, train-hopping, bad food, and much loss of sleep. Charlie Post felt that this kind of livelihood would bring better income and an opportunity to study the fast growing, agricultural belt in the West and Southwest. The new bride was ensconced with the Post family in the big, rambling Victorian house on Sixth Street in Springfield.[1] A contract was made to travel westward for the Climax Corn Planter Company, to introduce their new method in the western area. This association had lasted about two years when the B. D. Buford Company, Rock Island, Illinois, made Post a more attractive offer. Bufords were large manufacturers of agricultural implements, offering the territory of Kansas, Iowa, Nebraska, and on west, to be worked out of their headquarters at the old Blossom House in Kansas City, Missouri. The territory extended as far southwest as Dodge City, then the terminal of the Santa Fe railroad, as wild and woolly a town as one had been led to believe. Charlie Post's ability to make warm friends upon casual meeting is exemplified in letters received from the beginning of his travel days until his death. He was interested in his fellow man and, with that interested attention peculiar to so few, he won gratitude and friendship as he traveled. A sample of this is shown by an autographed picture and letter from Walt Whitman in the year 1880. The letter was addressed to Charles W. Post, care of the B. D. Buford Company, at Kansas City, dated February 8, 1880, from 431 Stevens Street, Camden, New Jersey, and reads:

[1] Now the Carrie Post and King's Daughters' Home.

12

"Dear Young Man—I thought today I would send you a little picture to show you I had not forgotten you or those meetings in St. Louis. I have been back here about a month and am tolerably well. How are you getting along? Let me know if you get the picture all right.—Walt Whitman."

The picture and letter are in the hands of C. W. Post's daughter. They indicate the companionship and pleasure found in the company of Post upon casual meeting.

The commercial traveling days of one-night stands, bad water, and worse food, were the beginning of the first break in Post's health, causing digestive disturbances that plagued him intermittently for the balance of his life. The road experiences gained, however, were invaluable in shaping the image of the perfect salesman yet to be, giving him far greater awareness of the needs and potential of the new West than was afforded to the average man of that day. Two factors removed Post from road life—first, the rigors of travel, but fundamentally, sound business sense and the awareness that the manufacturer rather than the salesman stood to make the greater gains.

In a lesser degree, Post had the kind of inventive ability peculiar to Thomas Jefferson and Benjamin Franklin; curiosity and a healthy imagination prodded him to make necessities, improvements on existing implements, or amusing contrivances. His more practical early inventions were items of farm machinery. Along with these ideas, Post invented a particular kind of paddle to generate electricity by water power. The paddle proved very successful and was brought into use many times during the various Texas ventures a few years later when Post found it necessary to furnish electric power for street lighting.

About 1880, the budding inventor abandoned road life and returned to Springfield with the firm resolve to manufacture a seed-planter he had previously designed with a long-time friend, A. L. Ide (Ide & Sons, Engine Builders); the two of them were granted a patent in 1879.[2] Subsequent patents for a sulky plow, cultivators, a harrow, and a hay-stacker were solely those of C. W. His interest in this field was nurtured in childhood when his father had a warehouse at the corner of 10th & Adams Streets as a dealer in plows, cultivators, reap-

[2] U. S. Patent Office: Seed-planter, March 4, 1879; Cultivator, Pt. #256044, 1882; Sulky Plow, Pt. #268280, 1882; Cultivator, #279980, 1883; Cultivator, #294806, 1884; Harrow, #363762, 1887; Hay-Stacker, #424128, 1890.

ers and grain from 1860 forward. Behind the Sixth Street residence was a little shop, in conjunction with the stable, where the Post boys learned to make various implements for their own use. Charlie spent long hours in the old workshop, laboring over mechanical drawings, designing and making farm implement improvements. After several years as a traveler through the West, he was thoroughly familiar with the needs of the farmers. Before he left the road, the firm of Coleman, Post & Read had been established to make the seed-planter by hand while Charlie traveled his territory to help finance operating costs. By 1881, with the help of outside interested capital, they established the Illinois Agricultural Works, Inc. (successors to Coleman, Post & Read), to manufacture Post Capitol City Cultivators mechanically. The new company was incorporated with a capital stock of $300,-000.00. The officers were L. H. Coleman, President; S. Mendenhall, Treasurer; and C. W. Post, General Manager. Aurrie and Carroll Post, with their father, Rollin, each had an interest and active part in the business. Carroll was road salesman, C. W. supervised the shop, the mechanics and all clerical details. He held $50,000, face value, of the capital stock. This was held in his wife's name since it represented the investment of her funds as security for a bank loan to establish the new business. The implement business was a success from the outset. It continued to prosper until a local banker who made the loans became far too interested in taking control of the fast-growing business. The machinations of the banker became quite apparent to C. W. when an attempt was made by the banker to involve Rollin and Carrie Post on a note without their son's knowledge. The father and mother had been induced to sign a mortgage loan on the homestead as additional security for the bank loan. Post's subsequent quarrels and lawsuits with the banker ran on for a number of years, in fact until 1899, long after he was settled at Battle Creek. It is believed that this quarrel and involvement over the implement business were possibly the cause of the first extreme breakdown in C. W. Post's health and nervous system.

While the chores of the implement business were heavy on Charlie's shoulders, he still found time and energy to work out a player piano for his wife. He and Ella cut out the music rolls by hand with a penknife on the kitchen table, indicating in itself a firm knowledge of music as well as inventive ability. In 1863, Fourneau, a Frenchman,[3] devised the "player piano," as it was to become known in America. From that time on there was a rapid succession of players, some good, some bad. However, the most active period was not until 1896 when thousands of such instruments were put on the market by leading piano manufacturers. Prior to that, no really successful player was marketed. Somewhere in his travels, C. W. had evidently seen a player but, dissatisfied with the mechanics of it, he had designed his own. There are no extant records to indicate just what C. W. accomplished; however, his daughter recalls the piano and the popularity of the family "parlor" because of it.

About the same time, C. W. set out to make a bicycle whereby both wheels were of the same size. This style was later known as the "Safety," the successor to the "Ordinary" which had the large front wheel and small rear wheel. The Safety was invented in 1873 by H. J. Lawson but was not marketed until 1885 by the Rover Company. Post made his model about 1880 or 1881, and it seems doubtful that he could have seen the model patented by Lawson. In any event, Post's new bicycle created considerable comment on the streets of Springfield. He retained the drawings and the working model until the Columbia Bicycle Company introduced its model, at which time he bundled up all plans and drawings and dispatched them off to the manufacturer with his compliments.

All of these activities, together with the problems of the Springfield banker, placed him under great nervous strain and overwork. It was a killing pace. Mother nature took a hand in the matter in August of 1885 when he was felled by a complete collapse from nervous exhaustion and confined to home for many months with no business activity whatsoever permitted. Without his knowledge and guidance in the plant, the business soon felt the loss of his astute management and skill. Liquidation of the firm began with the bank taking over $120,000 of assets against which there was only $60,000 of indebtedness. Post's letter-book and private files in the hands of his daughter show that not one investor lost five cents. It was sometime before Post could

[3] *The Player Piano*, by D. Miller, pub. n.d., Library of Congress, #M.L.1059.W.45.

give the matter the attention it deserved, in fact, not until he had long been settled at Fort Worth. In his characteristic way of setting the record straight, he wrote, on November 20, 1889, from Fort Worth, to the *Daily Illinois State Register*, an answer to its account of the "Post Liquidation":

"C. R. Post and Sons did not fail as you state. On the contrary, they sold out and paid everyone who had a just debt, in cash in full 100 cents on the dollar, and do not owe one penny on their old business. This can be easily seen and shown to any who care to investigate, and we will pay a premium on any bona fide paper of C. R. Post, or sons."

This letter is long and gives complete, detailed coverage of the matter. He further explained that, in order to pay the debts, the family liquidated all holdings in Springfield and, thus, after five years of hard work, the Posts were left very little for themselves; mostly unsold agricultural implements and the homestead against which there was a mortgage. C. W.'s letter to the newspaper set forth the pitfalls of engaging financial backing of banks and stockholders against the advice of friends and his own better judgment. This was quite obviously a rancoring "lesson" which stayed with him for the rest of his life and somewhat explains why he insisted upon sole control of the vast cereal empire he later built.

Recounted in a letter Post wrote in 1888 to his friend A. L. Ide, of Springfield, is the following:

"You will perhaps remember that I have an old and warm friend in your town who is in the banking and getting business. He loves to make it warm for me whenever he can, but lately I have been roasting the old boy a bit—I got a judgment against him, and am now trying to collect."

There was a sidelight to this quarrel, one which shows Post's ability to forgive and forget, in spite of the long-time difficulties and bitter exchanges. Some years later at Battle Creek, C. W. was told by a mutual friend that the banker was in very poor health and financial difficulties. He immediately sent a substantial sum of money to the banker's wife, with a warm and friendly note, recalling only pleasant news and fond memories from childhood days.

The recuperation period at Springfield, following C. W.'s complete nervous collapse, was extremely slow and discouraging. Many months

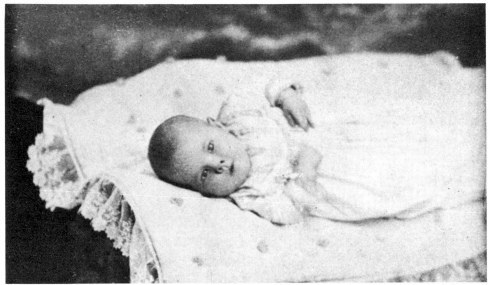

Age 3 months

Age 3

Age 5

(*In a snowstorm*)

Marjorie Merriweather Post

were to pass before he was able to turn attention to further pursuits. Advice came from doctors and family that the winters in Illinois were not the best for him and that perhaps the South or Southwest climate would be beneficial. In the fall, before Marjorie Merriweather Post was born (March 15, 1887), C. W. and his brother Carroll made a long exploring trip through Texas, seeking a likely location for a business and a beneficial climate. The brothers decided on Fort Worth since that area afforded many new fields of opportunity. An offer was made to them by Fort Worth real estate men in September of 1886 for the development of East Fort Worth, or Sylvania Addition, now known as Riverside. They returned to Springfield with well-laid plans, C. W. to await with Ella the expected baby; Carroll to take the rest of the family to Texas at once. Subsequently, Rollin, Carrie, Carroll and Mollie, Aurrie, Uncle Herbert Post, and Cousin Willis Post, were the advance guard. The family settled on a ranch of about 200 acres on the outskirts of Fort Worth, for which they contracted by further mortgage on the Springfield property and the agricultural implements left on hand. C. W. stayed in Springfield until Marjorie was nine months old, at which time he felt that his wife and baby could stand the move and that his own health was better. They left Springfield in November of 1887, and spent the winter at Santa Ana, California, where the climate seemed to put the finishing touches on Charlie's recuperation. By February of 1888, they were settled at Fort Worth at the New Ellis Hotel, where they remained until joining the family on the ranch. By this time, Post & Company had been organized and its offices were established.

References:

City Directory of Fort Worth, 1888: Willis H. Post, Carroll L. Post, Aurrie A. Post, 300 East 4th St. (Post & Co.); Charles W. Post, Secretary, East Fort Worth Co., 504 Main St., Real Estate, with Charles R. Post.

———— *ibid*, 1890: A. A. Post, 912 Main St.; C. R. Post, Post & Co., A. A. Post, W. H. Post, real estate loans, office 610 Main St., upstairs; C. L. Post (Sylvester-Post Cutlery Co.) res. Broadway btw. Jennings & St. Louis; C. R. Post, res. W. Broadway; C. W. Post, Post & Co., also Secretary East Town Company, res. Broadway.

———— *ibid*, 1892–93: A. A. Post, 912 Main St.; Charles R. Post, Willis H. Post, mfg. agents; Herbert Post, wholesale merchant, pecans, res. 413 E. 4th St.

Fort Worth Gazette, Dec. 19, 1889: "Fort Worth Woolen Mills and C. W. Post Trustee are to erect a woolen mill on Alamosa Heights on the line of the Fort Worth & New Orleans R.R."

———— *ibid,* June 14, 1888: "The beautiful groves of Sylvania will be penetrated and traversed by a first-class street car line as promptly as the material can be delivered and the work done, C. W. Post, Secretary, East Fort Worth Town Company."

———— *ibid,* Dec. 2, 1890: "Supplies of paper made from cotton seed hulls show a fine texture and very superior quality. The projectors of the paper will have some paper that is made of 90% cotton and hulls, samples of the pulp and the finished paper can be seen at the office of Mr. C. W. Post, 610 Main."

Chapter 3

~

Fort Worth Ventures

CHARACTERISTICALLY, C. W. Post threw himself into work as soon as a desk and office space were available. He and Carroll set up a sub-division on their land site, homes were built, streets laid out, landscaping put in, water, masonry, and electricity, all were included. In addition to this, a woolen mill was built for the manufacture of blankets, and a paper mill was erected for manufacturing paper from the hulls of cottonseed. The latter two businesses were incorporated, with the family holding all the stock, and for a number of years afterwards a small profit was garnered from these businesses. The sub-division being some distance from town in those horse-and-buggy days, a locomotive and coach, with picnic excursion atmosphere, were hired from the Houston & Texas Railway at $40.00 per day to convey prospective buyers to the new property.

Since Post's letter-book gives the documentation for the facts set forth, perhaps a letter-book should be explained to those who have never seen one. Those were the days before typewriters were in general use, and before carbon paper was readily available. It was customary to write a business or personal letter with strong ink in longhand. Blank books of thin tissue were available for the purpose of "copy." After the letter had been written in ink, the original page of the letter was placed under the moistened tissue sheet, then extreme pressure was applied (by a letter press, or by hand in some cases). This transferred some of the ink of the original letter to the underside of the tissue, thus reflecting an exact copy through the tissue sheet. If too much moisture was applied to the tissue a general smearing occurred, and if not enough moisture was used, then the copy was too

20

Dec. 19 - 89

R. A. Highsmith Esq.
Vernon Texas

Dr. Sir

Yours of 16th to E. M. Rowe regarding Alamosa Heights recd & noted. They lie South & East of the Hospital on the high land where the H & T. C. Ry climbs after crossing Sycamore Creek. The City is in plain view & is the handsomest suburbs about Ft. Worth. The details are so many and the enquiries, both in person & by mail are sufficient in number to warrant a printed sheet which is now in Press. a copy will be sent you. The lots are going fast & to our shrewdest investors.

Yours Truly
C. W. Prest. Trustee.

[mirror-reversed handwritten letter — illegible]

pale to be read properly. Post's letter-book reflects extreme care in the handling of his copy, and every letter therein is in his own hand. This operation in itself was a time-consuming ordeal.

In the subdivision, such details as masonry, electricity, water supply and planning, all came from his individual ideas. Obviously he had a firm knowledge of electricity, for he wrote:

"I oppose the plan of incandescent lamps for general street lighting—and I am to be called as consultant on electric systems. I want you to get for me a list of plants complete. I am willing to undertake the setting if I know just what every piece of iron and steel would cost here that would only take a shovel, trowel, wrench, and pair of tongs to put together."

At another time, shortly after this letter (April 1888), C. W. wrote:

". . . see if you can discover why our engine is the most delicately governed, and the most accurate runner made—it is adopted by the most celebrated Electrical Engineers from Tom Edison down as giving the steadiest light that it is possible to get out of a Dynamo, etc. I have just closed a contract with an Electric Company for their steam plant. They sent a committee of three of their Directors north and east to visit various plants and Electric Rys., with a view of finding the best. Since contracting they have acknowledged that our engine gave the best results for steady running, economy and durability. We like the compliment."

This letter is long and involved, but closes as follows:

". . . we are today furnishing more engines to Electric Companies than any two other builders in America. Our St. Louis Agents are Messrs. J. H. Seigrist, Jr., and Co."

Apparently this business was in joint partnership with his Springfield friend, A. L. Ide, since much of the correspondence is between them. Once, when an agent misquoted a price making it far too low, Post wrote to Ide that it was not too important, saying: " . . . let's not quarrel over the picking of the bone until we GET the bone." It becomes apparent in studying C. W.'s letters, that the electric systems to which he referred were a combination of representing a manufacturing concern, and his own plans and ideas for generating electric power. Several times he mentioned the electric paddle which originated in the Springfield days. Unfortunately we have only the letters written by Post and not those received by him from various correspondents at that period. With the full responsibilities of the sub-division, which involved all phases of home building and electric power, street lighting, transportation, and countless details, obviously he thought he had enough energy to represent various manufacturers as well. One letter, in reply to an inquiry from a Chicago firm, gives an insight into this situation. C. W. indicated that he could take on their system since he now had a contract to supply College Park Electric Belt Line, Sherman, Texas, on a boiler system for electric power:

"I was formerly a manufacturer, '80 to '87, am up in mechanics, but partly in electricity; with knowledge of the principal points and the more important details, I can sell the goods. Was commercial traveler in Kansas, Colorado, New Mexico, Missouri, Iowa and west from 1873 to '80, and should know something of how to handle western trade and people. Don't want to take on your business unless it pays well. I pay my own expenses and when I get left, I do my own howling in private."

Interspersed among the many business letters are numerous ones showing C. W.'s necessary involvements with family matters, the Springfield liquidation, the many exchanges with his banker "friend," and the conscientious handling of his wife's holdings. Ella Merriweather inherited a small estate in cash from her parents when she became 21, and investments were made for her in Springfield, Fort Smith, Arkansas, and Fort Worth. In each instance, C. W. made it very clear that this was the property of his wife and would remain in her name for her use though he was in charge of the financial involvements of her investments.

These incidents are cited to show just how involved C. W. Post could become, the many duties he would undertake, and the constant pull on his strength and energy. Judging by the letter-book alone, it appears he left very little time for rest or relaxation, though so recently recuperating from a severe nervous breakdown. Toward the spring of 1889 the pace began to tell, and the family felt it was time for him to stop and relax. They insisted on a long trip to the Eastern Seaboard, with a needed vacation among his mother's remaining relatives and friends at Hartford, Boston, and seaside resorts. He spent several months in the East, and much time was spent around Boston, all of which greatly improved his general physical condition.

While on that trip, C. W. took a number of snapshots which he intended using in the Fort Worth property developments. The film had been left with a Boston firm for developing, but apparently it was lost or the film was switched or stolen. Not mincing words, his anger flared in a letter to the Boston firm: "Give my compliments to the damn thief, and if you ever catch him, all I can say is this, I wish I had him in Texas for just seven minutes."

His own health never seemed to worry him as much as that of any member of the family. He showed grave concern about his wife's health, which had not been too robust at any time. He wrote Dr. H. B. Buck of Springfield (who had brought daughter Marjorie into the world) that his wife was en route there and that he hoped Dr. Buck *would have her well in no time.* Buck remained a close family friend and physician, as well as co-partner in many Texas investments. One of C. W.'s letters to Buck, in January of 1890, outlines the varied personal and business activities:

". . . I have certainly had my hands full lately and have wished many times you were here to bear a hand. Between selling and collecting woolen mill lots, getting side-track and depot, etc., matters arranged, the Street Ry. through the Ranch, and sales of some of our holdings, besides 1001 little things to fill in the chinks. That brings to mind the little new town we propose to go into. The company owns 640 acres for a town with 20 shares. Wilkinson Com's of In. of Ft. W. & Rio G. (*sic*) is projector and retain 5 shares. He and one Nye of this city, with you, Sam Nesbit and myself own $13/_{20}$ or a control. Shares had been selling at $250 each. They have advanced $500, and I would not today sell at that. Each Shareholder gets 125 lots part business and part residence. We bind Wilkinson to keep 5 shares and not to become interested in any other town site until Dec. 30, 1894, unless we previously sell out at Emerald Grove, and you can imagine he is in a position to settle his colonies right around the town where his interest lies. It is really a big little thing. I expect to go down with the excursion about February 20th and want you to come down and go along. It will cost practically nothing; we will make some money and have a good time. I think you will agree you generally don't lose on trips with me, and really I have been feeling lately that our little partnership is going quite smoothly, both parties improving. You were to look after my physical improvement while I was to look after your financial improvement. The results show very favorably thus far. I have been enjoying unusual good health lately and seem to be able to stand a great deal more work. Our new neighbor who joins us on the south and also owns the Brinkerhoff & O. (Oliver ?—*Editor*) piece is a Denverite and an estimable and cultivated gentleman as well as a first class judge of prop-

Chas. W. Post, 1890.

An Original Etching by C. W. Post, at Fort Worth, Texas.

erty. He is ready now to plat and will put his lots on the market at $200 for the lowest price on the upland. The lots are 25x125 and about 10 to an acre. Our upland is enough more desirable than his for many reasons. If you were here to attend to this and have our bottom land sowed to Bermuda grass and made smooth and pretty I am quite sure those lots right on the St. Ry. and the graveled road would bring $150 to $200 each, and you see that is at the rate of $1500 to $2000 per acre and is well worth working for. I have sold 422 Woolen Mill lots since Dec. 12 at $50 each, which is $500 per acre for land we bought 1½ years ago at about $23 per acre. I have paid for your share in Emerald Grove $250, Wilkinson is going down at once to build a store, windmill, and have the town well dug. I took the liberty of speaking for you because it had to be done in a hurry, but remember if I ever buy anything for you and you don't want it, I will take it myself."

In spite of the high hopes and optimistic outlook, the Emerald Grove proposal was a failure within a matter of weeks after this letter. Within two weeks C. W. wrote Buck that Wilkinson *had* sold out without advice to him, and Brinkerhoff and Oliver sold at about $450 per acre, which in turn dropped the valuation proposed for Emerald Grove development.

With the handling of the myriad details, heretofore set forth, Post even managed such matters as purchase of every item from boilers to pipe and size of thread, elbow joints included, showing a firm knowledge of what he was doing. The "paper" matters, involving mortgages and deeds, were passing over his desk though his legal counsel was the firm of Ross, Herd, and Ross. This connection resulted in a life-long friendship with H. B. Herd which continued in an intimate way until the day he died. From the standpoint of personal life, C. W. had not remained long at the Ellis Hotel; the little family joined his parents at the ranch on the outskirts of Fort Worth. There he endeavored to build a fine herd of cattle, giving attention to many improvements and landscaping. His involvements were so complex that it seems a man of robust health could not have long endured the strain. Even various patents from the farm implement days in Springfield required a watchful eye. An excerpt from one letter stresses a serious problem:

"There are three firms manufacturing cultivators that are plain infringements of my own patents. Two of them acknowledge it."

It seems wise to interject here a correction of one fact so often misquoted about C. W.'s early days at Battle Creek, whereby most writers concluded that the invention of a certain type suspender was born of necessity for a livelihood during the early recuperation period there. The letter-book proves beyond doubt that the "Scientific Suspender" was born at Fort Worth and had been put on the market almost two years before Post left for the Sanitarium. C. W., from early manhood to the grave, was meticulous in personal appearance; grooming was almost a fetish with him; coat and trousers had to be "just so." He was completely dissatisfied with any suspender then on the market, for none seemed to hold his trousers perfectly and allow proper freedom of movement. Experiments continued until one evolved which accomplished the results desired. A letter, dated in February 1889, two years before he went to Battle Creek, outlines and dates the suspender. It was to a dealer, to whom Post was endeavoring to sell the idea of handling the new suspender, as opposed to another model:

"*His* only good point is that of attaching at the pivotal point of the trousers, but he attempts to support same by one button which cannot be done and permit the trousers to hang and set properly, you will observe that when the wearer sits down or in a position where the rear of the trousers are drawn down, his suspending straps must elongate or slip and rub over the shoulders. My device can be used with a webbing that is non-elastic and the position of the supporting strap is not changed in operation as the cords and pulleys permit a rocking movement upon an imaginary pivot, one end of that cord being one time very long and other end short another time, vice versa. It is 'the touch' that makes my suspender successful and practical. The others have failed to find the missing ingredient. Have some buttons sewed 3 inches each way from the side seams of your trousers and put these suspenders on. I am of the belief that if made of good stiff elastic they would be better for all purposes, but just as they are they are vastly better than any suspender on the market. Sew the buttons on and the suspenders are yours!"

With this letter a complete diagram is handdrawn thereon. Shortly after this a wood-cut was ordered from St. Louis, showing front and side view of a man wearing these suspenders. The wood-cuts were to be used for advertising in *Harper's Weekly* and *Century Magazine*. In November of 1889, on the 25th, he wrote to a concern in Boston, stating:

"The concern has been launched! It will be the Scientific Suspender Co., Causeway, Boston—ads will be in January in *Century, Scribners, Puck's* Christmas

Edition, and others, just a small space to begin on—am going to St. Louis in a few days for dies and special tools."

Launched it was; however, there was only a flurry of activity, samples were dispensed around the country, ground work laid, contacts made, with a minor amount of sales. The ads to which he referred are not in evidence in such magazines extant; however, this could easily be the first advertising ever placed by Post, who was to lead the field of advertising. It was not until the Battle Creek recuperation period that the suspender business really got off the ground.[1]

The Fort Worth days were shortly to close for C. W. Post, though it remained the home of his parents and brother Aurrie for the balance of their lives. Heavy financial commitments in real estate, the "1001" details, and intense nervous energy, all added up to another and more serious nervous collapse. But one dream was spawned during those Texas days, a dream to which he clung henceforth, the dream of a model community of ideal homes set into perfect landscaping. The dream did come to fruition—first, with his model homes for workers at Battle Creek, and, finally, with the building of Post City, Texas, now the county seat of Garza County—but this is another story and will be dealt with in due course of events.

Just what day and exactly when C. W. Post collapsed at Fort Worth is not recorded, nor exactly remembered, for his letter-book copies stop abruptly with letters written in February of 1890. Records are clear that he and his little family arrived at Battle Creek in February of 1891. It was at the insistence of the entire family that he was carried to Battle Creek to try the wonders of the publicized Sanitarium, though hearts were heavy and hopes were dim.

[1] C. W. Post, Fort Worth, Pat. #508048, Suspender (1891) assigned to Scientific Suspender Co., Battle Creek, Nov. 7, 1893. U. S. Pat. Office.

Chapter 4

~

The Road to Wellville

BATTLE CREEK was little more than a village when Charlie Post came to town. The first land in what is now Battle Creek was claimed in 1831 by Jonathan J. Guernsey of Cattaraugus, New York, who built the first log house in the town. Sands McCamly platted off the town into lots and named the first four or five streets on July 30, 1836. Old Barney Tavern was built in 1842. Nichols and Shepard were in the threshing machine business as early as March 2, 1852. Elijah Pendill was the first mayor, serving from 1859 through 1861, and again in 1862. The original Sanitarium was built in 1866, with a second and much expanded one built about 1878. Aside from the threshing machine business and a few other small businesses, there was little more than the Sanitarium and a generous sprinkling of "health-faddists" around the town in February of 1891.

The Sanitarium, where guests could tone up their systems with a series of parlor talks and a specialized diet offered by Dr. John Harvey Kellogg, along with many kinds of therapy, had attracted nationwide attention. Not yet had the Sanitarium offered special foods of any attraction to the public, beyond its *Caramel Coffee* and a few trials with a cereal similar to cracked wheat and known as *Granola*. This was an infringement on *Granula*, Dr. James Jackson's controversial "wheat-rocks" manufactured at Dansville, New York, which resulted in a lawsuit against Kellogg, who then changed the name of his product to *Granose*. Neither the coffee-substitute nor the wheat-food was marketed by Kellogg with any success until several years after C. W. Post stirred-up Battle Creek with his *Postum*.

Post was a patient at the Sanitarium from February 16 until November 9, 1891. Nothing Dr. Kellogg tried seemed to do much good. Ella Post wheeled her husband about the grounds, a very emaciated and ill man. There were those who remembered him as a melancholy guest at the Sanitarium—on summer days he lay wanly under the shade trees reflecting on the supposed few months left to him. Ella Post and daughter Marjorie were then living in a small cottage near the Sanitarium. One day Dr. Kellogg called Mrs. Post into his office and sadly told her:

"Ella, I think you should know that C. W. has very little time left, he is not going to get well. I have done everything I know to do."

About this time a cousin of Mrs. Post's wrote to her about a friend who had been cured through Christian Science. Ella immediately made further inquiry and pursued the matter until a telegram was received from her cousin that a Christian Science practitioner, Mrs. Elizabeth Gregory, was located in Battle Creek. C. W. was finally persuaded that he should explore the matter and his wife wheeled him to Mrs. Gregory's residence for a consultation. After attentively listening to the practitioner, he said:

"Mrs. Gregory, I am staying right here under your care."

Somewhat amazed, Mrs. Gregory replied:

"But Mr. Post, you can't do that, I have five children and a small house, there is not room for you."

Mrs. Gregory reckoned without foreknowledge of the determination of the man. Some shuffling of the children was done, and Mr. Post was made comfortable in one of the small bedrooms. At her dinner table that evening he at first held back and made no attempt to eat, he had been without solid food for many months. Mrs. Gregory noticed his reluctance toward food and spoke firmly to him:

"Mr. Post, go ahead and eat your dinner. There is nothing here that will harm you except fear. Eat slowly, eat anything you want, it is what you need, you have been without food far too long."

With some misgiving C. W. consumed a fairly solid meal. At bedtime Mrs. Gregory again admonished him about his fear of food. She quietly informed him that he might become hungry in the night, if so, there would be cold chicken and other snacks available in the icebox at any hour; he was only to help himself. C. W. retired to his room that evening thoroughly convinced that nagging pains would soon start, but he fell into a sound sleep without disturbances. In the night he awoke feeling hungry for the first time in many months. He took advantage of Mrs. Gregory's offer and raided the icebox, returned to bed and slept throughout the balance of the night without difficulty. The following morning he partook of a very hearty breakfast of pancakes and sausage. He began walking about, and within a matter of a few weeks had regained most of the lost weight. His case was recorded as one of instantaneous healing. Never again did he countenance fear of foods for himself; but he was a wise man and realized that others could not be so fortunate. Almost at once C. W. began formulating plans to create an institution wherein he could apply this new-found knowledge, and to combine it with nutritional foods for those who had like disorders. Many years later he commented about his recovery:

"I thought it over a good deal and I came to believe it would be cowardly to quit then, with so much to do and so much responsibility, and I made up my mind I would not quit, but would finish the work I ought to do. I suppose I was a sight, but the only way I knew to get well was to BE well, however ill I looked, and I began walking around like a man who had business to attend to."

The town limits of Battle Creek of that day were very narrow. Post went to the outskirts of the city, eastward from town, and bought a picturesque farm homestead, entering into a contract for the Beardslee property on March 23, 1892. The property consisted of ten acres, on which there was a nice comfortable farm home and barn; from the higher levels the ground sloped roughly down into tangled raspberry bushes and a wooded area. In this farmhouse, C. W. established the institution in which he was to apply the curative truths which had been effective for him. Thus was started *La Vita Inn, Inc.*, shortly to reach prominence as a place for cure through dietary and mental influence, as word went about town that C. W. Post, given up by the Sanitarium, was getting well. In June of 1892 additional acreage was acquired and the property was partially divided into building lots, the sale of which brought sufficient cash for reduction of the mortgage. Mrs. Post's funds from her private holdings were placed as security, and in the beginning the *La Vita Inn* stock was held by Ella Post, 1998 shares; C. W. Post, one share; and J. L. Beilhart, one share. The financial problems were not easy, but there was sufficient cash coming through from liquidation of Fort Worth property, woolen mill lots, paper mill products, and the implement patents, so that furnishing and establishing the Inn was accomplished. In September of 1893 the Inn was re-incorporated under new articles of association, at which time Ella Post transferred all her stock to daughter Marjorie with C. W. Post as Trustee. Consequently, with the advent of *Postum*, under the aegis of C. W. Post, Manager of *La Vita Inn Co., Inc.*, Marjorie Post was the sole owner under her father's trusteeship. *Postum* had been developed at the Inn as part of its corporation; therefore, *Postum Cereal Coffee, Ltd.*, was, technically, a subsidiary of *La Vita Inn, Inc.*

In the meantime, C. W. omnivorously began to read medical books in batches and to digest every written word of the healers and spiritual advisers. As soon as the Inn began to fill with patients, he began the experiments for a hot food-drink, knowing full well that many people could not digest starches and that coffee was a poison to them. Not then did he have any ideas of marketing a product; the need was great for his own consumption and that of his guests, and nothing more.

It was here in the new Inn that the *Scientific Suspender* business once again took form. A small staff of girls was employed to make the suspenders on the premises, in a wide variety of colors, white satin for weddings, hand embroidered in orange blossoms, and many other fanciful models. A very nice little income was derived from this source, and it remained steady until such time as other projects were too overwhelmingly successful to continue the suspender business.

In the beginning, Post devoted his time, between food experiments in the kitchen of the farmhouse, to the study of dietetics and the power of mental suggestion. During the first two years of the Inn, a Swiss chemist was employed to assist in working out a formula for the food-drink; however, Post became thoroughly disgusted with the results and henceforth personally took over the experiments.

In the meantime, every spare moment was devoted to proving the theories of the science of mind over matter. Science was so successful for his own case and others on whom he tried the theories that he decided to write a book. *I Am Well*[1] was copyrighted in 1894, but today is extremely hard to locate, though it had substantial distribution. The title page gives an over-all picture of its purpose: *The Modern Practice, Natural Suggestion,* or *Scientia Vitae,* by C. W. Post, Worded for Plain People, published by *La Vita Inn Company.* Perhaps a few quotations from his book will give an idea of the *new man.*

"I come to your side with the deep compassion of a mother for her helpless child, I have been through the seven times heated furnace (7 years) of physical disease and mental distress. Kill off the old man (self) and let the new Being come up. Know yourself as Spirit, Mind, not Body . . . the writer of these pages desires to say nothing of himself other than as a simple instrument through which Divine Principle chooses to manifest itself by precept and example—seek an easy position where you will not be disturbed, relax every muscle, close your eyes and go into silence where mind is plastic to the breathings of Spirit, where God talks to son."

Paragraph headings run along such as: "THE SENSITIZING ELEMENT OF BODY IS THE HUMAN INTELLECT; CEASE ENMITY, ADVERSE CRITICISM AND EVIL THOUGHTS OF ALL KINDS; STOMACH IS GENERALLY FIRST TO BE ATTACKED BY THE SLIGHTEST MENTAL DISTURBANCES." The work quotes freely from Henry Ward Beecher and popular ministers of the day, with wide quotations from Scripture. There is reflected extensive reading and studying of medical journals and the general history of medicine. Obviously he had probed deeply into Galen, Hippocrates, and on up through Dr. Benjamin Rush to contemporary medicine, with emphasis on the theories of past health faddists. There can be no doubt that Post was informed in a general way about his subject, had read widely and well, and continued to delve thoroughly into the study of nutrition and dietary matters.

There remains a copy of a letter, dated February 26, 1900, addressed to one E. D. Clark of Chicago, wherein Post outlined some of his beliefs; in this letter Clark was thanked for his comments on Post's subsequent booklet, *The Second Man.*[2]

[1] Library of Congress—RZ.401.P.84.
[2] Library of Congress—RZ.401.P.85.

"After careful consideration of the facts, I feel no hesitancy in saying that we are as truly spiritual today as we shall ever be in life, not in so high a degree, but truly spiritual. That the body is slowly transformed, exactly in accordance with the conditions of our consciousness. The life shown in us in its present form, clothed with materiality, gradually evolves, and as it evolves, the so-called material structure changes in its essence until, gradually, the body itself, its very character and tissues partake more and more of a spiritual character, gradually changing from the gross to the more refined. I dislike much wandering in the realm of imagination, but I very much like the sense of reliance upon the supreme and beneficent life, resting upon it, and believing in it and conducting ourselves in accordance with our most perfect sense of its high ideals. I can not conceive of value surrounding the simple acquisition of money and property for the sole purpose of accumulating. There is so much beyond it; as an illustration, I feel that to organize the forces on the plane where we live, make the ways of mankind more comfortable, add to the total sum of human happiness; if you manage a hotel, manage a hotel so as to merit and receive the approval of your fellows. While I was in Washington last, I had the pleasure of some visits with Thomas Y. Hudson, the famous author of the *Law of Psychic Phenomena*. He is sending me his new book, published by A. C. McClurg & Co., I think entitled *The Divine Pedigree of Man*. He is an analytical writer, and highly esteemed among the medical fraternity. Another book, *Through Nature to God*, by Jno. Fiske, the famous historian of Cambridge, would please you, if I have the title correct."

These were the thoughts of Post as expressed in 1900, close on the heels of complete recovery, and at a time when his cereal business had reached very substantial success. Aside from his books on the subject of health, an actual record for the years 1891 to 1895 is not extant; however, a letter written somewhat later does clarify the cure and transition period. The letter was written to F. C. Nunemacher, Louisville, September 12, 1910, long after Post had become a millionaire and the famous cereal king:

"It is rather distressing to hear you are ill. I suffered a nervous breakdown some years ago and can sympathize with a man in that condition, although as I look back now I discover that it was all for the best. By the way, it may be interesting to you to know that I did not get well, after suffering eight years, until I was healed by Christian Science. Wouldn't that put a crimp in your thinker? If it does, it might do you some good. I attribute my success and good health to the knowledge that I began to gather at that time. This does not mean that I am a strict Christian Scientist, for I am not, but I was healed under the method of treatment and have been a close investigator ever since, and use their principles for my own betterment. I do not mean to preach a sermon, I can only add that I sincerely wish you could become conscious of your right to health and to gather the good things that come along with it. You have pluck and you can pull all kinds of loads when you set yourself right."

Those were the words of a man who had reached health, fame and fortune; they clearly indicate that the new power of the man had not spoiled him nor displaced thoughts of his fellow man.

At the Inn, from 1892 until 1894, Post worked out many experiments with grain, trying for a satisfactory hot food-drink. Post only knew that he thoroughly disliked the Sanitarium's *Caramel Coffee*, as did many others who could not drink pure coffee, and that he must find a satisfactory hot drink. He felt there should be something better than the old coffee substitutes served during the Civil War days, or those used by the isolated ranchers in Texas. In the early Texas days, on hunting and exploring trips into remote areas, Post noted that the ranch wives served a hot drink made from wheat berries combined with chicory. The chicory did not please him, but the wheat berries seemed a sound basis; consequently, countless concoctions were brewed, stewed, and various methods tried until one day the food-drink was born. The formula eventually evolved is given here in his own words from the letter-book copy (and the process was *not* similar to *Caramel Coffee*):

"... roasting wheat berries 22½ per cent, glutenous bran 67½ per cent, and good New Orleans molasses 10 percent . . . bran and molasses mixed together and browned in open pans. Then brown the wheat in especially prepared roaster which lets out the steam and vapors in a small stream at one end of a cylinder. A good part of the distillation is retained and the oil works back into the berries. The result (is) due to chemical action and produces an article of food-drink of nourishing value."

The account of this formula and method of cooking was written in the fall of 1896 after cooking improvements had been made. Originally the roasting took place in the kitchen stove, but needed space for care of patients at *La Vita Inn* forced the operation to the barn. Some few years later, after *Postum* had become famous, a sign was painted over that old barn—"Started Here January 1, 1895." The first operations in the barn were a little more simple than the above method; Post devised a roasting trough about ten feet long, with a fire burning under it, Shorty Bristol (his only helper) stood there raking back and forth with a hoe to prevent the burning of the bran and wheat. There was a coffee grinder for equipment, two old sheet iron stoves, supplies of wheat and bran in two bushel sacks, molasses, ten jugs at a time. A bit of fanciful writing has been done about this modest beginning, modest enough without added fancy. Some claimed that his wife and daughter were his only helpers and the materials had been bought on credit. To begin with, the little daughter would scarcely have been big enough to be much help in 1895, though somewhat later when operations took substantial turns, she would dash in from school and Shorty would allow her to push the hoe back and forth until her father made an appearance. Overhead was an old haymow where the packaging began, and Marjorie lost little time in learning to play there by helping to glue the ends of the little *Postum* cartons. To this day her nose wrinkles up when recalling the old smelly glue pot, but it was fun at age eight.

C. W. Post knew he *had* something now. Operations in the barn were in full swing; Shorty Bristol took care of the chores, and patients were delighted with the new drink. The born salesman in C. W. began to itch to put the product before the whole country. Personal contact sales were out of the question—why not advertise! This method would be the normal and expected reaction today, but this was 1894, and to advertise a foodstuff was rare indeed. True—some products were advertised; however, they were mostly soaps, stove polish and patent medicine. The 1890 editions of *Scribners, Harper's Weekly* and *Puck* show fair-sized ads of very modest copy for *Royal Baking Powder, Durkee's Salad Dressing, Chase & Sanborn Coffee, Snider's Catsup, Epp's Cocoa, Tetley's Tea, Baker's Cocoa;* and if the reader remembers these—*Lowney's Chocolates, Pear's Soap* and *Cleaver's Transparent Soap*—he has been around a long time. This writer was somewhat amazed to learn some of the products mentioned had been on the market before 1890, though *Baker's Chocolate* pre-dates our own Revolutionary War period. Generally speaking, foodstuff was not advertised beyond those included here, and certainly no breakfast or cereal foods show in the ads. While C. W. Post has been called the "grandfather of advertising," he did not originate advertising though he did become the largest single advertiser in the country and pos-

Original Barn

In this barn the first Postum *was made. The building has been converted to a Medical Clinic and remains on the plant grounds of* Post Division, General Foods Corporation, *Battle Creek.*

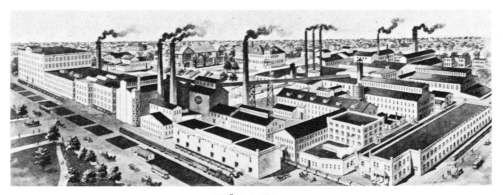

White City

The plant as it was shown in 1905 advertising booklets for Postum Cereal *products. In the center background may be seen the fine Elizabethan office building which housed the executive offices.*

sibly throughout the world. He led the way for more diversified and flamboyant ad copy by what he preferred to call "plain words for plain people."

In a speech at Battle Creek, some years later, Post recounted the beginning of the marketing of *Postum*. He went to Grand Rapids, a neighboring town, and approached E. J. Herrick, the best known grocer in the area. Post stated:

"He told me it was absolutely useless to try and do anything with the product, showing me some big bales of packages of *Caramel Coffee* made by the Sanitarium, which he had bought a dozen years before. He said, 'some years I sell one package, and some years none. You see, there is absolutely no demand, and you better go home and go into something there is some reason for.' But I had my own thoughts on the subject."

Post then guaranteed Herrick that he could create the demand which *would* sell the product for the grocer, and persuaded a skeptical Herrick to take the goods on consignment, paying for it only as sold. That much accomplished, Post thereupon went straight to the office of Willis H. Turner, editor of the *Grand Rapids Evening Press*. The drink was brewed right in Turner's office, Turner tried it, liked it, and called in the staff to sample it. There was general agreement, and ads were placed in that newspaper for the new food-drink. Post conceived the idea and trained a demonstrator to brew the *Postum* in Herrick's store as a free sample offering to all customers. To the amazement and delight of the grocer this demonstration resulted in "bargain basement" crowds. In less than one week Herrick was frantically reordering *Postum*. The revolutionary idea by which Post introduced his product into a cynical grocery market was a prophetic sign of his selling future. Confident though he was, C. W. was unprepared for the resultant demands.

Chapter 5

~

The Food-Drink Story

AMONG THE PAPERS of C. W. Post, dating from 1895 through 1899, some interesting facts are revealed concerning the introduction of *Postum*. Erroneously, in recent years, some writers have claimed Post snooped around the Battle Creek Sanitarium and stole the formula for the food-drink from the Kelloggs, who were resentful henceforth. Certain it is that there was no love lost judging by the remarks attributed to the Kelloggs. Post did not stoop to deny accusations he knew to be false and that could be proved to be false. There was no similarity in the cooking process, nor formula, of *Postum* to that of *Caramel Coffee*, though both were based on grain. Furthermore, to Post belongs the entire credit for public acceptance of cereal coffee, and for marketing methods untried by the Kelloggs. C. W.'s emergence into the field of advertising was as a "first" in the introduction of foods through that particular medium. He brought to his work none of the theories of the advertising schools. He had a story to tell, and he told what he knew. Where advertising usage had run to set forms and lofty phrases, he coined truth and philosophy in epigram. The very typography of his advertising told the mental attitude of the man who had thought things out and was driving straight to the point.

Post's letter-book contains a copy of a letter to his brother Aurrie, dated January 9, 1896, which clearly indicates Post's strong convictions of the power of advertising long before actual proof made itself apparent to him:

"My bills for advertising are enough to intimidate a man. Last month one bill was $981.78; but I am convinced it will re-pay me two-fold."

Within the same letter-book a clear explanation of his conclusions on the value of advertising is given in a letter to W. Blenkiron, London, dated January 30, 1896:

"On this side, [of the Atlantic] all manufacturers who are succeeding with any new specialty have been forced to observe a gradual change in the method of doing business. Formerly, we depended somewhat upon the ability of the merchant to whom we sold to favorably represent our goods and secure an introduction and trade for them; but at this time, if we rely upon the old method, the business will fail. We are compelled to address advertising to, and place it before, the consumer, who, by his demand, compels the patronage of the dealer. It is our belief that this revolution in business is not confined to the United States, but that it permeates a larger part of the civilized world today. As an illustration, take the trade of *Pear's Soap,* their headquarters being in your city, they expend a great many thousand pounds each year in talking direct to the people about their specialty. Whenever they reduce the amount of their advertising to any appreciable extent it is quickly shown in the pulse of the trade. . . ."

At the date when these letters were written foods were not advertised to any extent, if at all. Certainly Post could not have then been aware of, nor could he have had concrete evidence of, the results of advertising a prepared food. It would not be long after this date when he would become known as the "million-dollar advertiser."

It is well to look into Post's explanations of the coffee substitutes of the past, and his full description of his new product. A letter written October 12, 1896, to Elliott & Hopkins, patent attorneys, Chicago, outlines the story, to wit:

"For many years a drink has been made from browned bran mixed with molasses. During the war and perhaps for many generations prior, grain of various kinds were browned and a decoction made therefrom which looked more or less like coffee. All of these products have a more or less flat taste and cannot be called palatable. The bran product makes an article that contains considerable amounts of nourishment, for the reason that the phosphates, gluten, etc., hang to the outer shell of the wheat and by boiling fifteen minutes one can secure a liquid that contains considerable nourishment and of the right kind for depleted nerve centers, but as stated heretofore, that does not make a palatable beverage and would not do to undertake to build a business upon. We experimented over a period of something like twelve months, seeking to make a combination of cereals that would give the elements of nourishment and produce something that was pleasant to taste and eye. It was discovered that preparation of the whole wheat berry in one manner of cooking and of glutenous bran with New Orleans molasses prepared by another method of cooking and blending of these three elements in proper proportions produced the desirable results. We have an article that became famous in a very short time, and feel that we should be protected from a lot of infringers that seek to rob us of the enjoyment of a business that is based on the discovery of a new article of commerce. This is not a 'substitute' for anything. It is a pure food-drink, and stands on its own basis as a separate and distinct article. It is to be stated that there are reasons why one part of the product shall be cooked in closed roasters and the other part of the product in semi-closed pans, in order to confine, to a degree, the distillations and let the oil work back into the product, but we do not know as such process would be considered novel or patentable, but it still remains that these products, together with a discovery of how to blend the different elements, has resulted in the manufacture of a very popular article, and we should be protected by the United States Patent Office. . . .”

A few days later Post acknowledged a letter from the patent attorney as follows:

“Acting upon your advice, I will request you to prepare the patent papers, and you can arrange the facts in proper way to meet the favorable consideration from the patent office. . . .”

This is then followed by a description of the process and the roasters:

“We then brown the wheat in especially prepared closed roasters which let out steam and vapors that arise from the cooking wheat, in a small stream at one end of the cylinder. This is so arranged that a good part of the distillation is retained, and the oil works back into the berries. *We are the first to make this combination,* and this combination produced a new article, which has the taste and appearance of coffee without its injurious ingredients. It is really a new combination of matter, inasmuch as the heat and moisture of the bran produce a malt-like *diastase* and this product, coupled with the proper proportions of browned wheat which is of course principally starch transformed by heat into a more carbonacious product, gives us a new beverage of high food value, estimated by the State Analyst of Michigan to contain 51% food value. I hand you herewith letters received from prominent physicians and we have many such strong letters recommending *Postum.*”

On the 28th of October, Post followed up the patent attorney's communication with complete information and diagram of the roaster itself, enclosing a hand-drawn sketch:

“. . . the red ink shows the inside cylinder which contains the wheat, and the holes below are to admit draft to the fire which is supposed to be underneath the cylinder but is inside the roaster, or stove, it might be called. There is a large semi-circular hood that folds down over the top of this stove and keeps the heat in around the cylinder. The cylinder opens with a door on its face, and inside the cylinder are flanges projecting inwardly which are intended to divert the wheat when it falls, as a result of the circular motion, and carry it from one end to the other, so that if certain spots are hotter than others, the travel of wheat will prevent burning. This cylinder has an opening out through the axle at the back and which permits the escape of the vapors, but it is allowed to stand in the tight cylinder long enough before it escapes to penetrate the kernels with the oil. While it is true we originated the roaster in our own factory, it is also true that the same general construction obtains in common coffee roasters, but in coffee roasters the cylinders are perforated with thousands of small holes to permit this vaporous product to escape. In our machine, the cylinders are tight, for the purpose specified. The main thing in our case is the *new compound, product, or thing which comes into existence....*" [1]

In the meantime, before the patent was granted, Post was rapidly building a volume of business. Account sheets show the advertising amounted to just $200 in 1895, but it sold $5,000 worth of *Postum* before the year was ended. Advertising expense for January 1896 was listed at $981.76; but by May the sales were at the rate of $3,000 per month and by October had zoomed to $6,000 per month. These are not entirely modest figures when one considers that *Postum* was merely a year old, a new item on the market, a long-profit item with minimum production costs. The product was then selling for 15¢ per package, and considering the dollar ratio of 1896, a nice little business was well on its way. But, startling enough, by September of 1897, account sheets show *Postum* sales as $262,279.64, with yearly profit reaching $1,460,009.00 by September 1909. By that date, *Grape-Nuts* and *Post Toasties* were rolling up individual profits and surpassing *Postum*. Before 1900 turned the century corner, C.W.'s advertising was running into very substantial figures, reaching a million dollars yearly before 1904.

Post was extremely fortunate to have received unsolicited praise for his cereal drink. The advent of the product met an untapped field at a time when health and food fads were opinions rife with the American public; as indeed the public is always an untapped field for food fads. Witness the success of *Metrecal* and "900 Calorie Diets" within the last few years! The remarkable popularity of *Postum* with the general public and the medical profession was due to the important place it filled in the dietary field. At that time, many eminent

[1] Patent #574492, Cooking Utensil, Jan. 5, 1897, U. S. Patent Office.

medical authorities held that coffee was a harmful beverage, especially deleterious to people with "coffee nerves." Post was fortunate, too, that he found a beverage so close in aroma and taste to the real thing. The chemist, with his mystic tubes and processes, came to the fore in behalf of *Postum*. Dr. Bennett F. Davenport, of Boston, a medical and chemical authority of foremost rank of that day, drank and analyzed *Postum*. He made a sworn statement that he purchased his sample in the open market, and that his opinion had not been solicited nor bought. He reported that an analysis showed "moisture 5.85 (per cent); mineral, bone forming substance, 4.61; cellulose energy and fat producing substance, 8.70; fat, or energy and heat producing substance, 1.60; protein or flesh forming substance, 13.13; nonnitrogenous extracts, such as starch, sugar, gums, etc., 66.11." Dr. Davenport further stated that:

"The daily introduction of the drug (coffee) simply nullifies the best efforts of the physician. It is easy to command dismissal of coffee, but difficult to secure obedience, unless the patient is put upon Postum Cereal Food Coffee, for that furnishes the morning beverage without the drug. . . ."

Based upon opinions such as these, and upon testimonial letters received at the plant, C. W. Post intensified his advertising copy on the theme of "jangled nerves," and won converts by the hundreds of thousands.

In spite of the words of praise, or because of them, imitators were able to give considerable trouble to Post. The situation became a serious one and threatened the success of the new food-drink. The cheap imitations rapidly concocted by ambitious speculators, with no attempt to manufacture an original product, had to be exposed. It was not until a number of years later that Post explained what had taken place and how he was able to save his own business and at the same time educate the public to know the real product from the vast number of imitations which suddenly appeared on the market shortly after *Postum* became known as a success. At a speech before the National Association of Manufacturers in 1910, Post recounted the whole story, to wit:

"After *Postum* attracted nation-wide attention as a cereal coffee, imitators started up all over the country. The imitators in many cases were shrewd business men who had planned to let me go along building up a demand for a cereal coffee and spending my money to advertise. They manufactured an imitation product at a very much lower price to the consumer and paid the retailer a higher percentage of profit than *Postum*. That second year, the grocers' shelves were stored with sometimes six or eight different kinds of imitations; and when a customer inquired for *Postum* he was told 'We sometimes sell it but we have a better article for less money.' Naturally my business soon felt the effect and felt it seriously. I paid out that year something over $100,000 for newspaper announcements regarding imitations and kept explaining the real value of *Postum*. It was a hard fight and it looked as though we might be driven out of business. I was urged by friends to mix a cheap grade of coffee into *Postum* in order to give it a stronger coffee taste, for that was the method used by imitators.

"I had worked upwards of a year experimenting to make an article purely from the field grain and, although tempted to save the business by what seemed a harmless subterfuge, I refused to adulterate *Postum* in any way whatsoever.

"For the best part of that year those imitators succeeded in deceiving the people with a mixture of cheap coffee, and it became plain that radical measures must be adopted or my business would fail. Thereupon I organized a separate company, got out a new paper box and put up a cereal coffee named *Monk's Brew* for sale at five cents per package, just one-fifth of the price of *Postum*. The paper boxes announced that the cereal coffee contained therein was equal to any cereal coffee manufactured, and the statement was true because those *Monk's Brew* boxes were placed under the filling machine and filled with genuine *Postum*.

"This was sent out to the wholesale and retail grocers with the statement that, as they seemed to want a cheap cereal coffee, we were ready to furnish it. The price was so much lower than any other that the imitators were ruined. It was one of the most complete commercial massacres I have ever seen. The imitators, almost without exception, were absolutely annihilated and the curious thing about it was that it brought discredit, not only upon all of the imitators, but even *Monk's Brew* would not sell at five cents a package.

"This campaign left only one cereal coffee in the market with any demand, and that was *Postum*, well advertised and thoroughly understood by the buying public. We took back from the grocers literally carloads of *Monk's Brew*, which would not sell even at five cents. When those packages came into our factories they were cut open, the contents carefully examined to see that they were in good condition, and poured from the five-cent packages directly into the twenty-five-cent packages, because it was all genuine *Postum*, and sent out again to the trade, where they sold rapidly at five times the price offered under the unknown name of *Monk's Brew*.

"During the year of this contest, I lost about $46,000, but after the field had cleared, the next year the profit went to $385,000, and the next year a greater increase, and so on up to now.

"This illustrates that it pays to manufacture your article upon strictest lines of integrity, where you can court the investigation of the most skilled expert in the field, and next, that the unadvertised article, not known to the people, may have merit, but it will not sell."

Advertising was an infant crawling about the edges when C. W. Post began to teach it to walk erect. He was the novice unhampered by tradition, unaware of the "do and don't" formulas. There was no Madison Avenue expert to tell him whether he was wrong or right in his approach. His early training as a road salesman gave him that intimate touch of selling his wares face-to-face; this was his approach with ad copy—he "sold" his goods to one man at a time through copy that reached the vast unknown audience. Each consumer became aware of the man behind the product, his crusades for good causes, a real personality and friend to the consumer. The housewife came to know him as a friend who had her interests at heart. Upon seeing *Postum* on the shelf there was a subconscious reaction of contact with a friend. This was the intimate touch he was able to bring to the fore. One does not acquire any personal feeling about a corporation. The average housewife buys her supplies from habit, generally speaking, or through the word of a trusted friend. Post was able to make himself known as a trusted friend to the average housewife, thereby creating her buying habits. He was able to maintain this condition, and it prevailed so long as he lived. He used the same theories and approach to crack the foreign markets, and it worked just as well in South America and England as it did in his own country. The little booklet, *The Road to Wellville,* was in each package; it was the personal message to his consumer. This kind of entrenchment was hard to defeat in his lifetime, and W. K. Kellogg was not able to beat it so long as Post lived. It was not until after the death of C. W. Post that Kellogg made inroads on the sales volume of breakfast foods, and with a very similar approach, the personal signature of W. K. Kellogg on every package. The technique seems to obtain in this second half of the twentieth century.

Post bought page, or half-page, newspaper spreads in certain stipulated areas for the expression of a personal opinion on any controversial subject—without mention of his products. At the same time, modest space was bought within the same paper for an ad covering *Postum* products, but in no way referring one to the other. Before this was done, the jobbers in that area would have been well supplied with the products in preparation for the demand Post knew would follow. Post became personally known at the same time his products became easy to find on the grocer's shelf. It was the small-town approach placed on a sectional scale, then expanded around the country on a national scale. It all began in a section around Chicago and in Michigan areas, through newspapers and magazines of those sections, but a rapid jump was made into New York City, and extended up and down the seaboard, thence out through the West. Examination of hundreds of newspapers and periodicals from 1890's up to about 1910 indicates that C. W. Post was the first to buy newspaper space for the sole purpose of expressing a personal opinion to the people. It has been done many times since, but it appears quite likely that he was the first to use the method. His Post-Check Currency (to follow herein) was one of the early crusades, as were his "open shop" battles. The Pure Food crusade was a sincere effort to protect the family of his buying public —health was at stake. Several extant clippings concerning the Pure Food controversy are found in Post's scrapbooks. By 1906 his products were well entrenched in New England, and two newspapers from that section covered the Pure Food story and Post's participation. The *Herald*, New Britain, Connecticut, and the *Standard*, Bridgeport, Connecticut, both dated March 5, 1906, gave the same story, to wit:

"C. W. Post has started an original crusade for the Pure Food Bill now before the House. He has inserted in many newspapers a long story on the benefits of a pure food law, and also gives the language of the Bill. Then he urges the readers to send this petition to the members of Congress, and judging by the vast number that is being received by the Connecticut members, the newspaper readers are following his advice."

At that date, the Bill was already passed by the Senate and was before the House Committee on Agriculture. Several hearings were held and the government experts, especially Professor Wiley, explained to the committee how almost everything eaten and drunk was adulterated. The Bill provided for a general supervision of all canned goods and many other foods. The objection to the Bill was that the Department of Agriculture would have authority, through its experts, to determine what was adulterated and what was not. The Senate changed this and did not give sole authority to the Department. The difference of opinion seemed to be between the Secretary of Agriculture and the state food and dairy commissioners and also the Association of Agriculture Chemists. These groups claimed that the Department of Agriculture frequently made mistakes in determining food standards. The hue and cry was instituted due to false labeling of many products, such as whisky, patent medicine, canned and other foods. The crusade gained great momentum upon the appearance of Post's ads; this was followed by the Federation of Labor endorsement with the promise to take the warning to union members unless a Bill was enacted along sound lines. This was one of the times when C. W. and the Federation were in total agreement on a given subject.

Post did not depend solely upon the written word in order to place his products before the people; he likewise made himself available in various communities. In the fall of 1896 (evidenced by a letter-copy to his father), he made a long lecture tour through New England on the subject of the powers of mental suggestion and proper diet. Among other places, he lectured in Boston, Greenacre, Waltham and Pittsfield. He addressed the Emerson-Browning Literary Club and the Procopedia Club of Boston. This same year he was made a member of the London Society for Physical Research. In this manner Post became personally known as an intelligent, forthright man, and at the same time the community would be made aware of a manufacturer of certain cereal foods.

By 1904, Post was considered an authority on advertising when a meeting of advertising men was gathered at the Post Tavern at Battle Creek. The meeting was of sufficient importance to have been covered by English newspapers, judging by extant clippings from the *Kent Messenger and Maidstone Telegraph*, the *Bristol Times and Mirror* and other papers of England, each dated in November of 1904. Full coverage was given the following pronouncements of Post at the Battle Creek meeting:

"The sunshine that makes a business plant grow is advertising. Growing a business nowadays is something like growing an apple tree. You may select good seed, plant it in a good soil, water and work with it, but the tree will not produce fruit until another and most powerful energizing element is brought to bear. You must have sunshine and lots of it. Can you ripen apples in the dark? Can you grow a profitable business plant without sunshine of public favor produced by advertising? Our *Postum* plant is a good illustration of that law. It was a short time ago when I put a few men at work in the carriage-house of the barn you see today, where we began making *Postum*. The seed then planted, less than nine years ago, was a new kind of apple seed, and it was not altogether certain how the people would like our apples.... We knew we had a good apple tree of finest quality ... to turn the tree into a productive and profitable tree was another question. It needed sunshine, the kind of sunshine that is spread by newspapers and magazines. It is absolutely certain that without the publicity thus given—sunshine—the business never would have developed. A stranger told me once on a train that Post made a start by peddling *Postum* from house to house with a basket. [*Editor:* A 1962 story in this regard at least gave him credit for a pushcart.] That story is like many others that people like to read and which lack elements of truth. Many of you here today were around eight years ago right here in Battle Creek and of course *you* know this was not my start. A salesman, by word of mouth, can only convince one person at a time, whereas a salesman who knows how to talk to a vast audience could address that audience through columns of daily newspapers.... Some thoughtful man might say, once you get a trade established people will continue to purchase, even if the advertising is stopped; but there are always bright men to steal your apples, and if you give them a chance they will come in and take the fruit, sure."

Most of the advertising copy, at the outset, was written by Post, with his "plain words for plain people." Early in the advertising days, he tried an ungrammatical phrase as an attention item, which was met by howls from other advertisers. At that time, a college professor wrote to Post that some of the announcements contained grammatical inaccuracies and suggested that he employ a trained literary man to write them. Post made his answer by way of more paid advertising of the same nature. He had this to say:

"If most of our millions of customers were literary sharps and thought more of the graceful turn of a sentence and the painfully correct stringing out of nouns, verbs, adjectives and pronouns, parenthetical phrases, etc., as related one to the other, such a man might win approval, but approval of what? The merit of the article advertised? Oh no, the approval would be accorded the beautifully constructed sentences, and we have none of those for sale. The people, as a whole, will know what I have for sale, they will know what I mean."

The people did know what he meant—they bought. The constant slogan was *There's A Reason;* then would be outlined all the reasons why *Postum* was better for the human body and mind than coffee. One particularly blazing ad, in bold, black type, arrested the readers of newspapers all over the country.

"CAN YOU CUT OUT THE 'YELLOW' STREAK? All got one, you know. Some small, some large. The more 'yellow' in your make-up, the less yellow gold in your character and pocket-book.

"Is your yellow streak the coffee habit? Does it reduce your working force, kill your energy, push you into the big crowd of mongrels, deaden what thoroughbred blood you may have, and neutralize all your efforts to make money and fame?

"It does that very thing for thousands who don't suspect it. Languid, half sick, stomach and bowel troubles, heart weak and hardly half alive, you cannot succeed under such fearful handicaps nowadays, when the world only yields the crown for the best efforts of keen people.

"Try leaving off coffee for 10 days. Build back to a clean, clear-cut mind and healthy body by *Postum Coffee.* That's the true route to health, and with bounding exuberant health you acquire 'Energy plus.'

"Then, to 'do things' is easy. *There's A Reason. Have a try.*"

Naturally this direct challenge did not go unnoticed nor make him a friend to the coffee importers and roasters. On one occasion this ad appeared on the same page with a well-known coffee, resulting in an investigation by the coffee combine, to ascertain whether Post's friendship with the publisher of the magazine in question caused the placement of the ad on the same page, or whether it was accidental. The matter was never resolved.

Several stories published about Post in later years made the claim that the C. H. Fuller Agency of Chicago had staked Post to his first advertising. This was true; however, with financial conditions not so flat as fanciful stories made them, it seems unlikely that much risk was taken. The amount of advertising placed and resulting sales have been stated heretofore from the actual account sheets, which would not indicate any indebtedness of a very large sum to Fuller, although the latter did handle the advertising for several years until Post established his own agency. Post's letter-book includes the following letter to the Fuller Agency, dated May 10, 1897, showing the strides made by Post just two years after the advent of *Postum*:

"I would like a letter to James Gordon Bennett, Paris, if you can arrange the matter. I shall want to take up some subjects over there pertaining to the Exposition, and will want to get right in next to the headquarters of the exposition management, and I am sure Mr. Bennett would be of service. I leave Tuesday the 3rd and sail on the 7th."

The proposed trip to Paris was undertaken for a two-fold purpose; to place *Postum* in the Paris Exposition, but the prime reason was the pursuit of further knowledge in dietary matters and current curative powers as exploited by a number of European men of prominence of the day. C. W. spent that entire summer traveling in England, Switzerland, and France where he obtained firsthand knowledge from M. Jean Baptiste Charcot, French physician and authority on hypnotism. The trip was extended to Bavaria for study of Father Sebastian Kneipp's water-cure (hydropathy). Father Kneipp had long been an advocate of the internal and external use of water as a cure for just about anything ailing mankind. The Bavarian retreat had become a mecca for the ailing, the halt and the lame. His "barefoot walks in the morning dew (or rain)" were a popular fad which reached our own country. Post experimented right on the scene; however, the whole idea was abandoned after a few trials. He concluded that wet feet were more likely to cause other ill effects for his family, and perhaps worse for his *La Vita Inn* patients. Other water-cures, as used by Father Kneipp, were similar to those used by Dr. John Harvey Kellogg, such as several enemas per day, complete tub immersion and the like, all of which Post had found unsatisfactory while a patient at the Battle Creek Sanitarium. He leaned far more heavily on the theories of "mind over matter" as a curative truth when combined with the proper diet.

This concerted effort to acquire more and more knowledge was being brought about due to additional food experiments then under way at the little plant, where a constant search was being made for new cereal foods. The years of 1895, 1896, and 1897, were the most involved for Post since returning to "Wellville." *Postum* was well under way, the *Scientific Suspender* was a nice business, *La Vita Inn* was beginning to turn away patients for the want of space to accommodate them. With all such activities, Post kept a constant finger on the pulse of national current events and world affairs. Among his letter-copies of this period is one of interest which was addressed to a London Advertising Agency, when placing suspender advertising in that area; this was in the fall of 1896:

"The froth of some newspapers about the possibility of war between the U. S. and England—this is foolish, but there are foolish people in all countries when interests, sympathies, motives and even life blood are in a wide way identical. The fierce animosity engendered many years ago by too widespread ignorance has disappeared with the disappearance of that class, it is plain that the English-speaking people can always arrange their differences upon a peaceable footing. Business is good in our country and money rather easy. This is our Presidential election year, which means a great deal of cheap fun as well as enthusiasm."

Things were looking up in general for C. W. Post, experiments in the little plant were at last evolving a new food product. By the end of 1898, Post was ready to tell the public about a new cereal food. He had found his coffee replacement; now he was ready with a product that would resolve breakfast problems, a cereal food that could be digested easily without a starchy substance—*Grape-Nuts* became a reality.

Chapter 6

~

It Makes Red Blood

GRAPE-NUTS, THE NEW HEALTH FOOD, was introduced to the market for the first time in January of 1898, and to this day it is Post's only product not successfully copied by a competitor. The formula began with yeast, whole wheat and malted barley flour, baked in loaves just as homemade bread. It was then sliced, re-baked slowly for twenty-four hours, then ground. The process reduced the starches to dextrose, or grape-sugar, and resulted in a nut-like substance and flavor with grape-sugar content. A *Grape-Nuts* ad for 1899 read as follows:

"A certain man knew he could do certain things but he could not digest the food necessary to keep him in bodily health and brain power to do the work. He needed the carbohydrates that supply energy, so he set out to study and in two years has perfected the scientific *Grape-Nuts*, the most scientific food in the world. Get a famous little booklet in each package—*The Road to Wellville*—There's A Reason—Think it over."

Post began an advertising program with the new product which extended into very great expense and heavy burdens. In the first year the product was slow getting off the ground; however, very great momentum was gained by 1899, and each following year showed a trend toward outdistancing *Postum*. Each ad carried the assurance that it was a "scientific" food—it made red blood, or it made red blood *redder*. To illustrate the genius of the man, he advertised that it made "steadier nerves"—and he hammered away on the fact that the blood was benefited. What he was talking about was Vitamin B, which *Grape-Nuts* contains; yet it was not until 1911 that a German scientist, by the name of Casimer Funk, working at the Lisner Institute in London, isolated the first vitamin known to medical science.

51

Postum Cereal *plant on the outskirts of Battle Creek as it appeared about 1900. In the background may be seen the model homes for workers known as* Post Addition *or* Postumville.

Model homes for workers erected around 1900 adjacent to the plant gate.

Post's earliest ads for *Grape-Nuts* show that he was thoroughly aware of its strong nutritional values but was unaware of the fact that he was pinpointing a vitamin.

By 1899 the new food was so amazingly successful, the little booklet in such demand, the whole picture one which the entire country began to scrutinize so closely, that Battle Creek soon felt the surge toward its scene. As time moved forward through such startling success, Post was challenged many times for making "health cure claims" for this "scientific health food that makes red blood," and for claiming it a cure for appendicitis. This writer cannot find an advertisement in the old publications wherein Post advertised that it *would* cure appendicitis, though he was accused of such false claims. The ads do not read in that vein; they state that appendicitis was caused by starches, and Post claimed no starches present in *Grape-Nuts*. In the era in which this was taking place, many doctors did conclude appendicitis was caused through lack of digesting carbohydrates. Post took advantage of their current findings and played the ads to that tune. The product was subjected to rigid tests by competitors and disclaimers, but *Grape-Nuts* stood up. Though *Collier's Weekly* later based its accusations against him on false claims about curing appendicitis (see later herein), Post could show that no such claims had been made. *Collier's* further accused him of using advertising endorsements of medical men who did not exist. By thorough research into news items of the day, and by letters preserved in Post's personal files (held by his daughter), many medical endorsements were sent to the company in favor of the product. From the private scrapbooks of news items and magazine articles the following undated clipping (*ca.* 1899), *The London Lancet*, organ of medicine and surgery, made laudatory mention of *Grape-Nuts* with these comments:

"The features worthy of note in this are the excellent proportions of proteid, mineral matters; and soluable analysis shows that it is a nutritive of high order, since it contains the constituents of a complete food in very satisfactory and rich proportions and in an easily assimilable state."

The "cause" of appendicitis has gone through many changes of opinion through the years, even to "seeds" causing attacks. At the time *Grape-Nuts* was reaping its early harvest, starches were the "cause"

COMPLEXION SWEETS

HAV'NT you heard that Raisins clear the complexion?

Well, if you'll look on the outside of old Raisins you'll see the cause, in the little brown crystals that exude through the skins, and taste like honey.

Now these crystals are Fruit-sugar, and that's the kind of sugar "Dextro Candy" is made from.

This sugar differs from Cane or Beet sugar in that it is, by Nature, practically digested before you eat it, so that it doesn't tax the Liver or Stomach.

It, therefore, goes right into the Blood, without delay, to make energy and strength just as fluid beef or chicken broth might.

It is far better food than Pie, Cake, or Pudding, and it is always ready for Dessert, on a moment's notice.

Even a confirmed dyspeptic may eat as much Dextro Candy as he likes, without discomfort, and with lots of benefit to his health and strength.

You can get from your Grocer, for 25 cents, a box as big as a "Grape-Nut" package, and Druggists as well as Grocers, sell a larger quantity in a beautiful Art box for presentation purposes, at 50 cents.

Made by the pure food factories that produce "Grape-Nuts," at Battle Creek, Michigan.

Dextro Candy
Pre-Digested

Sleep Nights!

The drug, caffeine, in coffee keeps many persons awake nights when they ought to be asleep.

If you've found only that one annoying fault with coffee (there are others) isn't it time to quit it and use

POSTUM

There are no drugs of any kind in this pure food-drink.

Thousands of former coffee drinkers have found that the change to Postum has brought sound, refreshing sleep, steady nerves, and bright days.

"There's a Reason"

Worth While.
A Breakfast Food.

FULLY COOKED AND READY TO SERVE DIRECT FROM THE PACKET.

Pre-digested, and therefore easily assimilated.

Rich in brain and nerve re-building elements.

A favourite with the children and the finest food in the world for them.

Containing more nourishment in each pound **that the human system will absorb** than several pounds of meat, bread, potatoes, etc.

That's

Grape=Nuts

There's a Reason.

Get Out of the Shell.

If you are "at odds with your food" stop the use of greasy, poorly cooked, pasty, starchy foods and take on

Grape=Nuts

the toothsome, nutritious breakfast food made of wheat and barley.

It requires no cooking, is ready for instant serving, keeps indefinitely, and has a delicate sweet, winning flavour, most delicious.

Grape-Nuts is fully digested in less than one hour. Its crisp particles are charming, and the chewing required helps in the digestion of other foods.

To four teaspoonfuls of Grape-Nuts add a little cream or milk, and, if desired, fruit, fresh or stewed.

Postum Cereal Company *advertising sketches approved by C. W. Post for 1905.*

Postum *Roasting Room*
Battle Creek, 1905

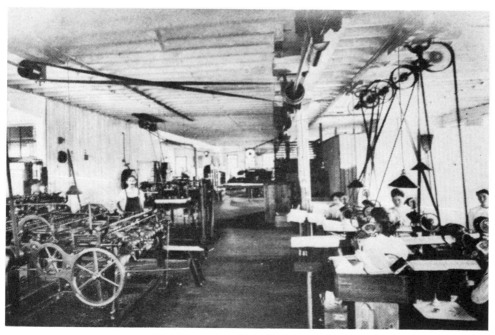

Folding and Stitching Room
for Road to Wellville *booklet, 1905.*

Grape-Nuts *Flour Milling Room*
Battle Creek, 1905

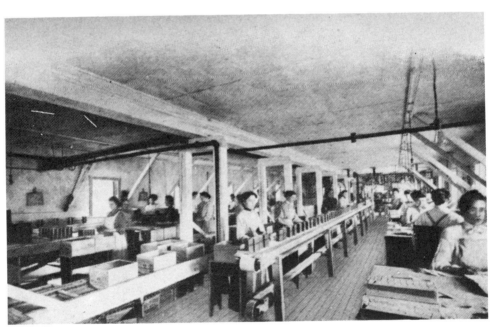

Grape-Nuts *Packing Room*
Battle Creek, 1905

—thus Post used the current reason for his claims about prevention. He was hardly more guilty of a false claim than any doctor might have been at that time.

At the end of the first year for *Grape-Nuts*, the sales reached only $47,167.00 against which there was an expensive advertising program and necessary plant expansion. The expenses began to be great. During this year (1898), Post toyed with the idea of selling out the business to the American Cereal Company, in cash, plus stock in that Company. Several months of negotiations took place, through Jno. S. Donnelly & Company of Chicago [Post's letter-book]. His personal comments at the time would indicate he was feeling somewhat fatigued from the heavy work load of a fast growing business, together with the introduction of this new product with resultant expense. Obviously he thought seriously about selling, judging by the number of letters exchanged with Donnelly; however, negotiations were dropped when *Grape-Nuts* took a sudden strong upward turn. Additional advertising was placed and extensive plant expansion begun. Account sheets show that, by 1909, *Grape-Nuts* was outpacing *Postum* two to one.

Though success was rapidly coming his way, Post never relied on it as a certainty. He kept a total awareness of the reactions of the people, his fingers always on the pulse of the public, and he never relaxed the vigil. One interesting incident with regard to the introduction of *Grape-Nuts* to the people of England is shown by the following excerpts from his speech before the National Association of Manufacturers (*ca.* 1912):

"Many years ago the newspaper advertiser was looked upon by the public with a certain amount of incredulity, but today it is a thoroughly, well established fact that no large concern can long exist in manufacturing and advertising an article that is not based upon absolute merit—or without understanding by the public of what you have to sell.

"After going to England for a number of years, it was thought best to start the introduction of *Grape-Nuts*, and I felt reasonably safe. After shipping a large quantity of *Grape-Nuts* over, and establishing the goods in the shops, space was purchased in the great London dailies and other forms of advertising were adopted. I was particularly impressed with the value of the London buses traversing up and down the crowded streets, the Strand, Fleet Street, Piccadilly, Regent, and so on. So I purchased the right to four or five hundred buses, and handsome blue, enamel signs, with orange colored letters, were placed on the buses. These signs were about nine feet long by twenty-two inches high and occupied a commanding position on the bus. The announcement was simply 'Grape-Nuts' and at the end of the sign, in small letters, the word *FOOD* was placed there so that the Englishman might know what the term meant. But, one evening on going from the office to my apartment, I heard two men talking behind me on top of one of the buses. One said: 'James, have you noticed this new baby-food being advertised, the one called by a curious name, *Grape-Nuts*? I never heard that grapes had any nut particle and why should it be for babies?' Looking around to see if these men were sensible, or escaped lunatics, I discovered they looked quite sane and quite English. I immediately clambered down off the bus and took to the sidewalk to see if I could read as the Englishmen would read the sign. A woman and child were coming along, I surprised her by speaking up: 'Can you tell me, madam, about what this new food called *Grape-Nuts* is for?' She said, 'Why, yes, it is a baby-food.' I said 'How do you know that?' 'Why,' she replied, 'it is quite plain. There is one of the signs now, it says *Grape-Nuts Food*, and of course Food is baby-food.' All I could say was 'Thank you,' and walk away. Then I discovered that the word FOOD, which is a generic term in America, had been used in England for years to define baby-food, such as *Mellin's Food, Ridge's Food,* and so on. These had been advertised so many years in England that the English mind never considered that the word FOOD stood for anything except baby-foods. There was but one thing to do. Take off the expensive signs, destroy them, and start over. The new signs read: 'Grape-Nuts A Ready Cooked Breakfast.' And that's how the signs read even today, and the English public has been taught to understand and to accept a pre-cooked breakfast. Now, had I remained in my office in America, never making personal contact with the vast buying public, I might have spent thousands of pounds a year in a fruitless attempt to induce the English public to use a new food."

Such an incident as this close observation should indicate to any examiner of Post's career that the man was singular in his dedication to purpose. It becomes quite apparent that satisfactory research has never been done in order to clarify the picture of early Battle Creek struggles . . . a climbing to the top by those who would cash-in on the success of Charles W. Post. There is no known incident, hinted or proved, whereby Post ever took an unfair advantage of another man's position. He never struck below-the-belt. At such times as the *Postum Company* might have suffered by the dark hand of an enemy, he could then fight with no holds barred. He believed first in the democratic principles of allowing every man to speak for himself. Strong convictions were placed before the public; if they backed him it was a fight to the finish. If they did not whole-heartedly support his views, a retraction was made.

Within the past decade various publications have stressed the Kellogg vs. Post story upon the grounds that Post was walking in the footsteps of Kellogg and his food products. The actual facts may be better substantiated by consulting a feature story of the *New York World*, Sept. 7, 1902. *The World* sent its crack reporter to Battle Creek to cover the story of Food Town, the amazing sudden growth of the city, and to get the inside story of the personalities of Battle Creek fame. *The World's* considerable space devoted to this story not once mentions a food product connected with Dr. John Harvey Kellogg or the Sanitarium. Dr. Kellogg was credited with being a "noted surgeon known throughout the world for his skill and genius at the operating table; he is at the head of the strange religious sect known as the Seventh Day Adventists." There is a singular fact noticeable in *The World's* story that "the fees for surgery and the wide circulation of his medical books are said to bring him a very handsome income." No mention was made of any material gains made by Kellogg from health foods as early as 1902, which, of course, were the facts at that date. It was not until W. K. Kellogg took over the food products of his brother (*ca.* 1905) that the Kellogg name became at all prominent in cereal foods.

The World did not devote space to Post alone in the food business, it used considerable coverage of A. C. Wisner, the picturesque wizard of *Malta-Vita* (a flaked breakfast food), which materialized shortly after *Grape-Nuts* and *Postum*. A few years prior, Wisner, a native of Athens, Ohio, had been a schoolteacher in Oregon. No one seems to have recounted how or when Wisner found Battle Creek; however, *Malta-Vita* was incorporated in 1900 by Wisner with almost no capital of his own, based upon a stock sales scheme. One year later the firm almost foundered and Wisner believed that, if he could control the company, he could grab a share of the spiraling food business. He was able to interest his friend Neil S. Phelps (who later built Phelps Medical and Surgical Sanatorium) in backing him with support for a bank loan. Somehow the two of them convinced a local banker that they could gain financial backing from private individuals and make a dent in the cereal business. They were able to float the bank loan for a short period of time only. Mr. Wisner went to Chicago with a firm belief he could convince a few able men of finance that he had the potential of an industry in the palm of his hand. Apparently he was a salesman par excellence. He secured the backing of H. N. Higinbotham, a Chicago millionaire; J. M. Studebaker, the famous Wagon Maker of South Bend; Samuel W. Allerton and Howard H. Gross of Chicago. Wisner returned to Battle Creek with sufficient financial support to take over control of *Malta-Vita*. By the end of 1902 the plant was operating twenty-four hours a day, including Sundays, with sales running to $2,000,000, and this within one year of his gaining complete control. A. C. Wisner had that peculiar knack of turning everything he touched into gold. Shortly after *Malta-Vita* was put on a firm footing, a perfect stranger approached him with problems concerning the building of a small railroad in Louisiana to connect with one of the big trunk lines. The projector found himself with his road incomplete and without funds. Wisner went to Louisiana to examine the road and the integrity of the builder. Without much hesitation he told the builder he would back the project up to $10,000. When the road was completed Wisner went to Wall Street, sold the road for one million dollars, paid off the road indebtedness, handed his new partner $260,000, and put $250,000 into his own pocket. Wisner was also the founder of *The Pilgrim*, a very up-to-date magazine now and then delivering ultra-radical opinions on things political and social. He offered William Jennings Bryan $25,000 to become editor of it, but the offer was refused by Bryan.

Another memorable figure was Neil S. Phelps, the son of a Battle Creek pioneer. Upon graduating from college he migrated to California where he taught school and finally set up a college of his own. When a fire swept away his property he returned to Battle Creek almost penniless. He and a man named Ellis, also without funds, formed a partnership and began the publication of commercial forms for use in business colleges. Eventually they set up a printing shop and extended their business to printing textbooks and other fine publications. The Phelps Sanatorium was built at a cost of $350,000, constructed entirely of field boulders. This was the same building purchased by C. W. Post in 1912, for $450,000, as a Home for the Trades and Workers Union.

Charlie Post, with *Postum* and *Grape-Nuts*, turned Battle Creek into a mecca for those who would gamble in industry, with Battle Creek the chief benefactor. By the time *The World* covered the Battle Creek story, Post had wide plant expansions known as *White City*; and in addition he had built a downtown office building, Post Theatre and Post Tavern.

At this point, comment might be made concerning a publication known as *Cornflake Crusade* (published 1957, by Gerald Carson), a highly amusing story wherein the author states Post was able to make patients well by looking them in the eye. Perhaps there could have been some truth in this statement, judging by comments made concerning his deeply penetrating eyes, but most assuredly there is a great deal of fancy therein concerning C. W. personally. The book gives excellent research into the background story of Battle Creek's sudden spring to fame, and to the Kelloggs in particular. The story is well done concerning the melee that turned up at Battle Creek, after fame and fortune hit Post and his products. Every "get-rich-quick artist" in the country, with any food ideas, descended on the town and started his own business. Most of them were bold enough to trespass on the well-entrenched names. By 1902 there were some thirty or forty incorporated competitors on the scene—primarily stock-sales schemes. Among them were *Grape-Sugar Flakes, Neutritia, Malt Too,* and on *ad infinitum,* encompassing some rather ridiculous names. Suffice it to say, most of them disappeared into nothingness while Post and Kellogg managed to struggle it out for top place.

The profit and loss account sheets in Post's copy-book show a *net* profit from *Postum* and *Grape-Nuts* at the end of 1903 in the sum of $1,099,405.65, after plant expansion, advertising, and all other expenses had been deducted. This was a very nice little business in less than eight years, but certainly far below the net results attained within the following few years. C. W. kept the early accounts in meticulous fashion, down to and including a $1.00 tax on Marjorie's dog.

The activities and pressure of a fast-growing business did not prevent Post from indulging in varied outside interests; he kept his mind alert and hands busy with all things political and personal. Before 1897, he had formed a close tie with the Honorable Theodore Roosevelt, which extended into the days of Post's fight with labor leaders (a subject to follow herewith). While on his trip to England in 1897, C. W. investigated the cost of a merchant ship. He had been offered various vessels for sale there, but apparently could not handle the expense at that time. With the thought that the vessels might interest our government, Post enclosed the bills of particulars in a letter to the then Assistant Secretary of the Navy. This reflects Post's reactions to the ominous conditions prior to the Spanish American War:

"I am pleased to observe by the telegram dispatched that your friends are trying to dissuade you from retiring from your present position. I know that some of your friends in the West, at least, feel that your past experience and training are of great value to the country just at present. I, for one, feel it would be a very great mistake for you to make the change the press dispatches announce you had in contemplation. There are many good men in the West who want War, and do not hesitate to say so, and we want it good and hard too. I trust the history of the old Spanish Armada will be repeated."

The years from 1895 through 1900 were perhaps the most eventful and all-encompassing for Post since he had reached manhood. He was approaching the period in life when his feet would be directed down many paths into industry, national prominence, political awareness and world travel. Regardless of how involved he became, he never neglected the smallest detail in search for perfection. Reminiscent of the old Springfield days, C. W. kept up his interest in the player piano and music rolls; the latter now were purchased from a manufacturer and no longer necessary to be cut out by hand at home. He wrote Wilcox and White, Meriden, Connecticut, concerning their music:

"I can not refrain from calling your attention again to the fact that while some of the pieces of music are cut so that they render music in perfect time when unrolled regularly, there are others that seem to have been cut by a different workman, where the pieces are greatly distorted if the music is unrolled regularly. This is true of the *Magic Flute, When You and I Were Young, Maggie, Sweet Marie,* and the *Robin Hood Selections.* On the other hand, some of that class are perfectly cut—then suddenly there is an awkard break in the time where perhaps the notes drag dismally, or start off at a furious pace, far and away from the intent of the composer. This is embarrassing when one has guests. . . ."

This is another example of the man who had time for every detail and neglected none. During this involved period, Post wrote a booklet,

The Second Man, a treatise on the theories of mind over matter. On October 6, 1899, the *Battle Creek Paper Company* was established for the manufacture of cartons and paper containers, and 1900 was the first year for export sales to Great Britain. There were still countless details involving the Fort Worth ventures, as well as experiments under way for further health foods. But the problems involved in another field so plagued him that for several years he worked on a plan to solve the difficulties confronting him as well as other manufacturers and dealers. Direct-mail sales were the order of the day which often necessitated transmission of cash by mail. As early as 1896, Post drafted his first plan to take care of a crying need, a very unique idea, hard fought for, not won, but resulting in nationwide attention and radical changes in the postal system. It is the least known of his inventive ideas, but most assuredly it had the widest of controversial attention. Since the idea was of such intense national interest at the time, the entire story should be told.

Post-Check Currency

The patented and revolutionary idea of C. W. Post

Chapter 7

~

Post-Check Currency

Before the turn of the century the remote areas of the fast-growing country were served by direct-mail sales through the medium of catalogues, newspapers and display-card advertising. In the horse-and-buggy days, farmers and ranchers seldom got to town in bad weather, and many were far removed from good towns. Especially were they handicapped in a diversified selection of goods. It was common practice to order direct from the manufacturers in the larger cities, remitting postage stamps or currency for sums under $5.00, and many times in greater amounts. This was a hazardous business, currency was pilfered from the mails, and postage stamps became stuck together and a total loss to the recipient. The then U. S. postal money order was a highly complicated affair and not accessible to many rural areas, in fact less than half the post offices in the United States sold money orders. Express Money Orders were in existence, for a rather steep fee, out of proportion to small amounts needed, and again not readily available to all areas. Banks issued checks to their depositors, but the fee was high for small amounts. The remote farmer relied on the buried tomato can, sugar jar, or an under-the-mattress repository for cash, with an inborn distrust for those "down-east bankers."

C. W. Post began in 1896 with his drawings and plans to handle this fast-growing need since his own business had its share of stuck postage stamps and small coins lost en route. By 1901 his revolutionary idea was brought to conclusion with a patent of the plan [1] and the matter was introduced to the Congress the following year as the "MacMillan-

---

[1] Letters Patent, Jan. 23, 1901, Serial #44482.

65

Gardner Post-Check Bill."[2] Post proposed that the Government issue $1, $2, and $5 bills (except bank notes); such currency to be designed with blank spaces on the face for "payee and address" and a space for the signature of the sender in the lower right-hand corner of the bill, not unlike present bank checks but issued as U. S. Currency bills. This would pass from hand to hand as ordinary currency until it was filled-in and signed. The moment it was signed it became a draft on the Federal Government for that amount, payable only to the person whose name was written on the face. The issuance of 50¢ and 25¢ currency bills, along with the other amounts, was also proposed. He printed at his own expense, and widely circulated, a pamphlet entitled *Post-Check Currency* which fully explained the purpose and function of the proposed new currency. One excerpt from the pamphlet reflects C. W.'s unselfish interest in the matter:

"The right of the U. S. Government to use the system will be duly assigned by the inventor free of charge. It is estimated that upward of two billion dollars a year are sent through the mails, notwithstanding the difficulties and inconveniences. This amount is largely made up of postage stamps, loose money, coins, money orders and little checks on inland banks."

The National Association of Newspapers, National Association of Manufacturers, Association of American Advertisers, Citizens Association and several hundred prominent business houses proclaimed the wisdom of the plan when the idea reached newspaper headlines. Opposition to it came from special interest groups, such as express companies, the National Retail Grocers, and some banking associations. The bankers took the position that the government would thereby be going into the banking business, when in reality their own facilities were not so far flung as to cope with the needs of the public. The widest coverage in favor of the plan went out over the newspaper wire-service, and the following account appeared on editorial pages of newspapers throughout the country (January 11, 1903):

"Post did not design this system for any profit to himself, he is a philanthropist and wishes to pass it to the people. In order that the public and Congress may fully understand the matter, he has opened offices at 825 Vermont Avenue, Washington, D. C. How does it work? Take the case of farmer Jones who lives

---

[2] H.R. 1350-L, April 10, 1902, Rep. Washington Gardner; Senate #4557, Senate #5201, Senator James McMillan.

miles from a money order station or post office. One day he buys goods from his nearest merchant and presents a $10 bill; he is given change in $1, $2, etc. in Post Currency. These are the same old bills which are now circulated, except that in the lower right hand corner there are two blanks for payee and his address and one line for sender. When farmer Jones returns home he finds his wife has selected merchandise from a distant city for $2.50 and [it] must be ordered by mail. This now means transmission of currency by mail, or postage stamps which are now being refused by many merchants. With the Post Check in his pocket, it is now simple, he has only to write the name of the merchant and his address, place an ordinary 2¢ stamp on the face of the currency as a Revenue Stamp, which protects both parties. The stamp also acts as the Government's fee for retiring the Post Currency after it has been cashed by the merchant, who presents it to his normal banking facilities, such as Post Office or Treasury Station, for which he can accept gold currency or new Post Checks."

A joint committee of Treasury and Post Office officials was appointed to consider the plan of establishing "mail currency" with the Treasurer of the U. S. as Chairman of the Committee. Some members of the opposition set forth their objections on the total cost of re-issuing the currency in these denominations, and much opposition came forward on the fractional issue, which they claimed was reminiscent of the old "shin-plaster" issue of Civil War days. The contention was that it would cost the Government $370,000,000 to retire the old and to issue new "mail currency."

The loudest howl came on the floor of the Senate from Senator Tom Platt of New York, who was President of the U. S. Express Company. Before he took a stand publicly, however, he had been working behind the scenes and had managed to see that Congress adjourned time and again without bringing the bill out of Committee. C. W. began a wide investigation of the practices of Platt and, in time, asked the Congress to unseat the Senator, accusing him of working for vested interests against the good of the common needs. Post's findings were finally justified when, at a later date, a jilted sweetheart of the Senator sued him for breach of promise, setting forth her activities in Platt's behalf while working as his protégé in the Post Office Department against the Post-Check Bill and for the Senator's interest in Express Company matters.

The behind-the-scenes machinations of a few members of Congress aroused Post's curiosity to the point where he instituted a thorough

investigation into the possible reasons why a few men could so ada-
mantly refuse to recognize the hue and cry from the public in general.
The results of the private investigation convinced him of the existence
of many strange conditions in several departments of the government.
Beginning in February, and running through March, 1905, he bought
space in newspapers throughout the country for a semi-weekly column
entitled *Unmasked*. Typical of his courage, C. W. signed each article
and assumed all responsibility for any possible future libel suits.
Through this medium he drew public attention to the then famous Post
Office frauds investigation when Senators were accused of gaining control of the Department for their own private interests. The article gave
facts for the public to digest, and the public, which so cheerfully digested most of Post's offerings, satiated itself upon appearance of the
following lead article:

"At the time of the investigation of the frauds in connection with the Postoffice
Department there was much booming of cannon and noise. A few head clerks
were found guilty of appropriating money that rightly belonged to the people.

"The poor little head of the Money Order Department, and who, by the way,
fought the Post-Check Currency Bill tooth and nail, it seems had some relatives
connected with the concern that was furnishing the paper, and he had to go.

"Then there were others interested in the purchase of some of the supplies, and
they were dismissed and finally indicted, convicted and sentenced to imprison-
ment.

"The house cleaning seemed very thorough, but the job is laughable when the
facts are looked at. These peculations of the people's money were acts of petty
larceny compared with the sums of money taken from the people's purse each
year, and drifted into corporations by some of the same people who distribute
the clerkships.

"I am safe in saying, and it can be demonstrated, that a gift or graft of at
least $34,000,000 a year is paid on an equitable basis for the service rendered.
No legislation can be carried through to save this tremendous loss so long as
the express companies and the railroads have their own representatives in the
United States Senate and House of Representatives. Nor will there be measures
for the relief of the people in other ways, such as needed reforms in postal currency, parcel post, or any reform that will take away from the corporations the
rich fees they now enjoy.

"As an illustration of the boldness with which this work is carried on, I found
that an insurmountable obstacle existed against the adoption of the postal currency, and we put on the trail to find where the trouble lay. This postal our-

rency subject has been discussed by the newspapers and the public for four or five years. Thousands of letters urging its adoption have been received by the Members of Congress from their constituents. Farmers, merchants, workmen, bankers, newspapers and other publishers have continually called for the Post Check, or some measure that would supply the people with convenient money for safe transmission through the mails.

"Now look at the cost to the Government of the present money-order service, ancient and clumsy as it is, devised by a man whose relatives secured profit from the manufacture of the paper, and who was requested to disappear for the 'good of the service' but his terribly expensive methods still obtain. For the fiscal year of 1904 the cost of the money-order service was $5,491,000, as shown by a careful computation made by Capt. H. A. Castle, ex-auditor of the Department, and the domestic money orders issued numbered 50,712,168. Therefore the average cost of making, issuing and redeeming these orders was about 10.8 cents each. Seventy-eight per cent of these money orders were for $5.00 and under, which the Post-Check Currency would replace. This means a net loss, after receipt of fees, to a total of $2,832,980."

Post continued the article with actual cost estimates and showed that the issuance of Post-Check Currency would abolish the money order and its resultant loss, and produce a net gain for the department through the use of the 2¢ stamp on the new proposed currency. While the Post-Check Currency would have to be retired once it was signed, Post was able to show that the cost of retiring the existing currency each year, due to defacing or extreme bad condition, would be a necessary expense at all times. The proposed new currency would keep clean money in circulation, abolish a costly money-order department, and result in a net gain for the Treasury Department of approximately $3,-300,000 per year.

In the second article Post explained to the public that the Post Office Department had not yet been able to produce a paper for money orders that would defy "raising" the amounts. He cited the almost impossible task of "raising" existing currency bills, which paper would likewise be used for the new Post Currency. It was within the second article that Post began his attack on Senator Tom Platt whose interests lay with the Express Money Orders. The third article delved deeply into the patronage granted the U. S. Express Company, as follows:

"In the United States Treasury building a room is devoted to the use of the United States Express Company, of which Uncle Tom Platt is President. Let no one believe for a moment that the U. S. Express Company is owned by Uncle Sam. It is owned by Uncle Tom Platt and some of his associates. Uncle Tom's company has a contract with Uncle Sam to carry money, packages, etc. One of my representatives made request of the Secretary of the Treasury, Leslie M. Shaw, for a copy of the contract between the Government and this Express Company on the grounds that it is a public document, and the people, or any of their representatives, have a right to know its contents, for it provides for an expenditure of public money. Our request was refused, and the statement was made that 'some of these things are not to be given to the public, they wouldn't understand.' I should like to know *why* they would not understand.

"Let the people remember, too, that Ellis H. Roberts, U. S. Treasurer, foe of the Post-Check Bill, is a New York State man, and the New York appointees look to Uncle Platt for life and sustenance. The people will naturally draw their own inferences."

The subsequent articles kept the public abreast of various conflicts of interest evident in the Capitol corridors and on the floor of the House and Senate. Post had a profound regard and respect for a statesman, but he drew-a-bead on any member of the Congress whose interests were in conflict with the common good. In his editorials, with regard to labor disputes, a very fine line was drawn between what he called the "true statesman" and the "burrowing politician." (See labor chapter herein.) Any member of Congress who performed his duties as a statesman was readily recognized by Post with laudatory comment, political affiliations notwithstanding. He crossed party lines most of his life in order to back men whose performances showed that they had the courage to support any measure for the good of the common weal. The last article for his series, *Unmasked*, covered some of the political aspects of the Post-Check Currency situation as follows:

"Some members of the Congress who put politics before statesmanship resented this exposure of a Republican (*Editor:* Tom Platt). I was told that this move would effectually and forever kill the Post-Check Bill, hinting at the sure and hidden wires that would be pulled to punish me for the temerity of telling the public what some of their false representatives were doing with the people's money and interests. Perhaps the prediction may prove true. If so, the Bill will die in a good cause. Certain it is that neither threats nor bribery will prevent these facts being made public. Therefore so long as the Supreme Court has no jurisdiction we were compelled to present our charges to the Senate direct, and the Bill is now before that august body. The charges are supported by affidavits and the Senate is requested to carefully consider them, and if found true, to expel T. C. Platt. Will it earnestly and honestly probe the charges to the bottom and clean its ermine, or will politics and Senatorial courtesy smother the case entirely? We shall soon see.

"Let us take another illustration wherein the people lose about eleven times as much, or an estimated $34,000,000 per year. Let us have a look at our urbane and most popular Senator Chauncey M. Depew, he of the happy countenance, ready story and fine Italian hand. Does anyone suppose that any legislation in favor of the people that would reduce the income of the railroads would meet his approval? Does he not stand in the United States Senate as a representative of the railroads? And when a clash of interest between the railroads and the people arises, is it to be supposed that this gentleman would hesitate, notwithstanding his oath of office?

"We pay the railroads annually $43,926,000 for carrying the mails. The graft is notorious. There are times when the railroads will carry wheat from Chicago to New York for six cents per hundred pounds. A common rate is fifteen cents and that is admitted [in order] to pay the railroads a profit. We pay $32.00 per hundred pounds on letters, $16.00 per hundred on merchandise, $8.00 per hundred on books, and $1.00 per hundred at publishers' rate for newspapers, and yet our Postoffice loss last year was $8,524,912. Suppose we stop the graft of about $34,000,000 a year. The facts are notorious, but the big and sure 'block' is put on every year by the paid corporation representatives acting as members of the House or Senate. It would cost the railroads no more to draw letters, except that the mail matter would occupy more space, therefore requiring either more cars or larger cars to move the same number of tons. I am fully aware that railroad representatives would laugh the statement to scorn. Notwithstanding, the facts are there. Our President [Theodore Roosevelt] has lately been awakened to the need of government supervision of railroads, and it is quite possible the first practical laws may be enacted, for we have an earnest, honest and practical President."

In this manner C. W. Post fearlessly placed the facts before the public. It is interesting to note that he was not sued or damned for strong, personal convictions, but he was not ignored. These inflammatory statements brought hot words from those accused, but no libel suits were filed against Post.

Meanwhile, the newspaper world and leading merchants took up the cudgel. The Association of Railway Employees backed the Post-Check plan, citing their needs for mail-currency to cover small amounts for payments of their insurance premiums by mail. The magazine, *Postmaster* (undated clipping), issued the strongest article after nearly two years had elapsed without any action from Congress:

"Mr. Post is a doer of things, he accomplishes. While he is busy making that which makes 'red blood' for others, every artery in his body is filled with the reddest blood. He is not satisfied with doing for himself, he does for others. In his Post-Check Currency he has devised something for every American citizen at a tremendous cost to himself, without pecuniary rewards."

Samuel Clemens (Mark Twain) wrote Post that the sale of books alone was being hampered by the lack of a system whereby the average citizen could easily purchase a book or periodical by mail. Clemens stated in a letter to Post as follows:

"Therein lies the damage, the prodigious damage, the incalculable damage. If he (the public) could order without trouble or bestirring himself from his chair, the usual 3,000 book run would sell—well, a ton or two."

The National Retail Grocers' Association took a stand in opposition to the Bill based on their conviction that the proposed currency would result in a net loss of business in the retail field. Their trade paper publications maintained that remote farmers could then deal direct with the manufacturers in larger cities, thus by-passing the small local grocer. After a long and unsuccessful campaign for the new currency was ended, the secretary of the National Association of Retail Grocers published the following letter in their trade paper which reflects an interesting analysis of Mr. Post:

"In reading the trade papers of last week I see that you will have no more use for the heading of the article which has been appearing on page one (Anti-Post Currency Bill). Mr. Post, in his reply to my open letter to him of recent date, has made known his determination to cease advocating his Post-Check hobby. He yields most gracefully and his letter shows him to be a man of heart as well as brain, and what he writes will win him hosts of friends, of which the writer will certainly be one. This action on the part of Mr. Post gives us great courage to persevere in antagonizing every measure hostile to the cause of retailing. Keep on letting the public know that the "Retailer Is King"—some day he may feel like acting the part—which we certainly did not do when dealing with Post."

The open letter was signed by William Gray, Secretary, National Association of Retail Grocers, and published in *The Eli*, June 23, 1906. In the same issue, the trade paper published a lengthy letter from C. W. Post in explanation of his stand in behalf of the proposed currency, which set forth the reasons why the currency would have aided the retail grocer rather than harmed him. It was the first instance of the trade paper publishing an article by Post in the six-year debate. His personal explanations of the mechanics of the plan had not been aired previously through that channel of opposition. The Association's abdication, however late, was most rewarding to Post with its acknowledgment of his personal integrity.

The uproar was national, with ninety per cent of the newspapers in the country entering into the fracas over a period of nearly six years. C. W. did not withdraw from the fray until the results of public opinion brought drastic reforms. The Post Office Department stepped-up rural delivery, a wider range of money-order stations came into being, and more post offices were established in rural areas. The newspapers hammered away editorially for better second and third class mail rates, a wider parcel post system, and for a revision in railroad contract rates for carrying the mail. Thus, while Post-Check Currency proposals were withdrawn, the end result accomplished just what Post had sighted as a national need for the good of the common man. The entire program and campaign had cost him a great sum of money, but the publicity earned him vast numbers of new friends for *Postum* products, and the resultant sales reached very gratifying figures.

References:

Leslie's Weekly, Aug. 6, 1903.
Printer's Ink, Feb. 12, 1902.
Fourth Estate, Nov. 13, 1902.
New Yorker, Jan. 25, 1905—"Post and Platt."
Government Printing Office, Bill H.R. 12799; S. 5201, S. 4557.
57th Congress Report #3662, House, Feb. 7, 1903.
House Committee on the Post Office and Post Roads, G.P.O., 1903.
Post-Check Bill, H.R. 7063, G.P.O., 1906.
C. W. Post Before Committee, Jan. 5, 1903, G.P.O.
C. W. Post private files, copies of speeches, news clippings.

Carroll Lathrop Post
(1859-1948)

Brother of C. W. Post and close associate with him in business adventures from young manhood until death.

Mollie (Staley) Post
(1859-1925)

Wife of Carroll Post and devoted "Aunt Mollie" of Marjorie Post.

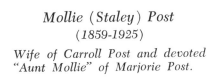

Chapter 8

~

The Hour and The Man

CARROLL L. POST, in a letter preserved in the family files, dated in 1915, after his brother's death, gave impressions of the *Postum Company* and his reasons for joining the firm:

"I paid my brother a visit in 1900 and found that he had built many new buildings, with a plant to make paper containers, called the Battle Creek Paper Company. The business was growing with leaps and bounds, and he asked me to come with him and take charge of the *Postum* sales and to manage the paper plant. I joined him in August 1900, the load was getting heavy, he wanted freedom to travel around the country and abroad in order to keep abreast of the times and the needs of the public. He had also begun another project in downtown Battle Creek, known as Post Tavern, and other plans were projected."

By 1902 the plant had become known as "White City," operating on a twenty-four hour basis, two shifts per day, with 450 employees; and by 1906 the facilities and payroll had more than doubled.[1] Wheat consumption figures for 1900 show fifteen hundred bushels per day, a remarkable appetite for a five-year-old. In a short time this amount was consumed within less than an hour, making it necessary to install railroad sidings for tank car lots of wheat and to erect large elevators for grain storage.

Newspapers had a field day covering the aspects of Food Town, health food, *Postum, Grape-Nuts,* Charlie Post, the Kelloggs and the Battle Creek boom. Not since the days of the Gold Rush had man, woman, and child descended on a locality by every means of transportation, wide-eyed with expectations. The rags-to-riches stories were played to the hilt; this was romance, opportunity, and the pot of gold

[1] *Postum* payroll ledgers, University of Michigan, Ann Arbor.

at the end of the rainbow. All of it was good, free publicity for *Postum* and Battle Creek in general. C. W. was never one to complain about printer's ink when the results rang the cash register, but for all the wary eye on publicity, he could not stand for less than the truth and cold facts concerned with any venture. There were so many stories running in newspapers throughout the country, probing into the wonders of new health foods and the new "king," that Post was entirely used to the idea; however, now and then there would be some ridiculous stories that would need an answer. Post made one such answer in regard to a news account published in the Kalamazoo, Michigan, *Telegraph*, August 16, 1903:

"Gentlemen: I have been handed a clipping from your paper which purports to give the history of C. W. Post in the food business. Inasmuch as I know the man personally and intimately, it occurred to me that the facts and not the fancy might be of further interest.

"Battle Creek has been made famous as a food center by reasons of publicity given by your paper and thousands of others in America, these articles having been furnished and paid for by Post to the extent of several million dollars. It illustrates the power of the press to make conditions.

"This work has *not* grown out of an original preparation by Dr. Kellogg, on the contrary Dr. Kellogg made his food after an article manufactured by a Dansville, N. Y., Sanitarium, as evidenced by a suit brought by the Dansville people against Kellogg. Post did *not* leave the Sanitarium devoid of means; to the contrary the National Bank of Battle Creek can substantiate that they held his securities in a very substantial sum at that time. Your suspender story is amusing and interesting, but quite distorted in facts, which can be verified by anyone interested."

The *Telegraph* story had claimed that Post was destitute when he left the Sanitarium, that his wife made the suspenders and that Post had sold them from door-to-door for a meager living; that he had copied Kellogg's ideas and made a fortune overnight. The distortion of facts had brought on the answer by Post, which he closed as follows:

"Fairy stories about successful business men sometimes lead others into investments that are ruinous to them. It seems to me it is better that the truth be known in order that men can have some tangible basis upon which to form their conclusions.—C. W. Post."

The newspaper in question was doing no more than the balance of such feature stories flooding the country. Many feature writers grabbed at straws in the wind and fed-out fantastic romances of adventure in industry without probing for facts. There were reasons for this sudden interest in the town and in C. W. Post—the whole picture was newsworthy.

The rapid growth in personnel and labor by 1901 had created a housing problem Battle Creek could not accommodate. At this date, Post acquired an eighty-acre tract adjacent to the plant, eventually called Post Addition. The Addition was divided into 579 building lots, and houses were erected at the rate of twenty or more at a time. These were made available to plant workers for the trifling sum of a $4.00 initial payment with an equal sum due monthly, and the project was not closed to any citizen of Battle Creek. No interest was charged on the mortgages, and the houses were sold at actual cost with absolute title passing to the purchaser at the end of his obligation. There were no restrictions as to the number of houses one man might purchase so long as he did not re-sell at a profit. The Addition was beautifully laid off with broad avenues, the chief of which was named for the founder. Marjorie Street led directly toward the plant gate [prophetic], Lathrop Avenue was named in honor of Post's mother. Trees were planted, landscaping included and housekeepers were given an annual award for the best flower gardens. Beautiful gardens and model homes were the chief philanthropy, and a devoted hobby of C. W.'s life.

The Addition was singled out as a revolution in labor-management by providing excellent homes for workers, and C. W. was acclaimed a genius as well as a philanthropist. He somewhat resented the word "philanthropist," it smacked too much of charity to suit him. It would be more accurate to say he was a plain advocate of the "Square Deal." He commented:

"Mix altruism with your business, and business with your altruism. In both cases let it be an altruism that breeds self-reliance in man and makes for individualism."

Thus might be summed up in small compass the philosophy of practical living espoused and followed by Post. He was known to have said that he had never forgotten the words he learned as a schoolboy in his second-reader:

"Help yourself my little man
And then I'll help you all I can."

October 20, 1905.

ADVERTISING DEPARTMENT

Mr. C. W. Post,

        New York, N. Y.

Dear Sir:-

        We are enclosing the Grape-Nuts advertisements omitted from our letter yesterday.
Perhaps any of these advertisements can be reset in a little smaller type, eliminating some
of the white space, to bring them within 3 columns, 8 to 12 inches, and show just as
effectively.

                        Yours very truly,

                        POSTUM CEREAL CO., Ltd.

H

Men and women of cleanliness and intelligence were absolutely essential in the conduct of his manufacturing plant. Such men and women, Post thought, would most likely have the additional qualities of thrift, pride, stability of character, and a zealous care of their health and that of their children. He began to deal with them on that assumption, with the result that his Post Addition (sometimes called Postumville) was a success. It was an altruism that benefited at once the object and subject. The workers in the factory had healthful individual homes. Mr. Post reaped his reward in having labor of the highest possible class. He looked upon the whole happy arrangement, not as a philanthropy, but as a wise investment which was not measured by mere dollars and cents, and yet involved the practical commercial idea. Mr. Post set the pace for the residents by making the immediate environment of his factory as beautiful as possible. The grounds about the several buildings were laid out by landscape gardeners with a view to the highest artistic effect. Broad, rolling stretches of greensward were broken up into a wealth of color by beds of flowers and blooming shrubs, and vines broke the expanse of dead walls, giving suggestion of coolness in the warm summer months. A greenhouse was erected on the plant premises for cultivation and experimentation with plants and shrubs, and still remains standing at the plant. Because of the over-all immaculate appearance, the citizens and visitors to the plant were the first to have applied to the suburbs the title of "The White City."

These were the days of gruesome office buildings and factories with cheerless exteriors, poor working conditions, and dull, barren interiors. Post publicly stated as early as 1901 that the day would come when the business of the country would be transacted in quarters in a style commensurate with the value and proportion of the commerce conducted. He was an absolute pioneer in that endeavor and was acclaimed so by leading newspapers of the day. The plant grounds contained many fine, spotlessly clean manufacturing and processing buildings. Paper cartons were being manufactured for his own cereals and for approximately fifty per cent of the other competitive cereal businesses springing up around Battle Creek. The plant office building alone was a model for the future. This building was a Manor House itself, big, brown Elizabethan, sprawling behind trees on top

C. W. Post

C. W. Post about 1910. The office is as Mr. Post left it in 1914. The fine hand-tooled leather wall covering, original rug, chair, and desk are still in fine condition.

The Elizabethan Office Building on the Plant Grounds, Battle Creek

C. W. Post's private office is in the section over the porte-cochère. The section between the two gables is used as a museum and art gallery.

of a green knoll, an architectural triumph for that day, ivy-clad and set into the best of landscape. The interior was in close harmony with the elegant exterior. The entrance was through a porte-cochère, which was termed "the open door" since the company entertained many thousand visitors per year. In the reception hall were many works of art, notable paintings, portraits, bits of sculpture, rare works in bronze, relics and curios. The room was long and wide, deeply carpeted, beamed ceiling, fine cobbled fireplace with marble mantel, and pewter tankards of Elizabethan days on display. This sort of interior was so unusual for the era that several newspapers undertook to bring it to the attention of industry at large. *The New York World* (Sept. 3, 1903) ran a Sunday feature story, illustrated in color, fully describing many wonders of Battle Creek, but particularly the accomplishments of C. W. Post, saying of the Elizabethan office building on the plant grounds:

"Ascending the staircase, at the top is the private office of C. W. Post, founder of the company, and in all the country, whether Wall Street, or Washington, or wherever one may care to go, there will not be found an office building furnished with equal simplicity and eloquence. The desk of the manufacturer is hidden from the remainder of the capacious office by a hand-carved pearl-set screen from the Orient. A table of simple design, but of rare wood, is the most conspicious bit of furniture in the room. A chair or two from medieval places, appear incongruous in the telling, but nevertheless are wholly harmonious with the old English setting. Passing from Mr. Post's office, the visitor enters a wide corridor which is a museum in itself. There are curious chairs from Venice, a table that once graced the library of Paul the Fifth, Pope of Rome, statuary from Roman ruins, tablets with Latin inscriptions, mosaics from Pompeii, wine jars from the bed of the bay by the Chauteau d'If, the historic gaol of the Count of Monte Cristo, and around this corridor are the private offices of the departmental heads."

In our streamlined, tinted glass and steel era, this sounds ostentatious, but there was nothing sumptuous or ostentatious about C. W. Post, for this was an era to which he and the style belonged. He pioneered in bringing the aesthetic world to the doorstep of labor and industry, since opportunity for the advantages from travel were not then readily afforded labor. The office building in question is now maintained as a museum and gallery and is used as the Post Club House at the Battle Creek plant.

The manufacturing plant, the office building for the plant, and the Post Addition were on the outskirts of the town. When this project rolled along smoothly, Post then turned his attention to downtown Battle Creek with a view to bringing something of a city atmosphere to the town. The first building he erected was the Post Tavern (hotel). The hostelry became the pride of Battle Creek when it was officially opened in 1901. Money was lavished on the hotel with impeccable taste in furnishings and hangings which manifested itself in refinement and elegance. Splendid paintings hung on the walls, acquired in C. W.'s travels to the Old World. Rooms had connecting baths, a telephone was in each room, a luxury then reserved for the more plush establishments of New York, Washington, and the largest cities. To take care of the table for guests, another little business blossomed with the establishment of Battle Creek Creamery, Ltd., which specialized in Pasteurized milk and butter. Public demand pushed this business to a $100,000 yearly profit by 1902. Although the Tavern was given wholly to commercial trade, there was an atmosphere of richness and good taste about it that was, to say the least, very unusual and under the circumstances, almost incomprehensible for a small town in 1901. The dining room, the "parlors," foyer and other public apartments were furnished in a sumptuous manner.

Another notable feature of Post Tavern was the fact that it had no bar—so-called. Let not any bibulous or convivial reader wonder about that. While it had no bar, it had what the owner preferred to call a "tap room" immediately adjoining the office, a retired and quiet corner. Hanging over the door was a wrought-iron sign bearing the alluring legend the "Wee Nippy." After entering the room, the strongest temperance advocate in the world (and C. W. was such) would more than likely be seized with a consuming thirst. The room was fitted in Flemish oak with a dainty buffet at one end, a few tables and chairs, an old-fashioned mantel, some delightful stained glass effects, and a display of appropriate bric-a-brac and objects of art which appealed very strongly to people of discernment, whether bibulously inclined or not.

The main dining room left nothing to be desired. After rather unfortunate experiences with delicately lovely chairs, C. W. designed,

Battle Creek Office Building

A downtown Battle Creek office building built by C. W. Post in 1901. The Post Theatre may be seen in the right background. Both buildings faced the Post Tavern across on the right.

Post Tavern Hotel, 1901

The original building as it appeared until the annex was added in 1913. This original section was recently torn down; the annex remains as a hotel.

The dining room of Post Tavern, as it appeared in 1905, showing the mahogany hand-carved swivel chairs designed by C. W. Post for easier seating and arising from the table.

and had made to order, swivel, tilt-back dining chairs, nicely carved from mahogany. After these were installed at the dining table, the lusty male could rare back in his chair without disastrous results. When the much larger addition was added to the original building in 1913, these same chairs were upholstered in a fine quality tapestry and are still in use in the Post Motel. The original section, built in 1901, was recently torn down for a parking lot, however the 1913 addition has been completely renovated, retaining many of the fine original appointments and panelings. Battle Creek was then, and is now, on the main line of the New York Central Railroad, and Post Tavern became known to travelers from New York to Chicago as a fine accommodation with excellent dining rooms. By the time the hotel was opened in 1901, the old *La Vita Inn* was needed for plant expansion. Accordingly, an apartment was established in the new hotel for C. W. and his family. This continued to be their home as long as they remained in Battle Creek, and was maintained for subsequent visits.

Battle Creek did not have a downtown office building until Post built "Marjorie Block," in 1901, across from the hotel. Another building is still in use as an office building with a large department store occupying the ground floor. In back of that, facing the hotel, was the Post Theatre which was also opened that year. Post had long dreamed of bringing drama and good music to the citizens and workers of Battle Creek. It was with the feeling of great pride that he watched his teen-age daughter march to the stage and present a large bouquet to the then very popular Maxine Elliott who, on opening night, with Nat Goodwin as her co-star, initiated the new theatre.

C. W. made a decision to move his legal residence to Washington, D. C., in 1902. Many factors necessitated the change. His daughter had been enrolled in a very fine private school there (now Mount Vernon Seminary and Junior College) because he wished to have her near the center of his national interests. An office was opened in Washington as a listening post for things political and industrial while Post was actively engaged in labor disputes; also the proposed Post-Check Currency Bill was demanding much time and many appearances before various committees. It was during the time of the hearings on the Bill that he came to know most of the Congressmen. Post was an attentive

age 14   age 15

Student, Mount Vernon Seminary

age 23

Marjorie Merriweather Post

listener in the galleries when not appearing before a Committee; strict attention to matters of common weal were of prime importance to him. C. W. was a forthright foe of any Congressman who placed self-interest above the needs of the average citizen; however, he had a great deal of respect and admiration for most of the members of the Congress and readily supported them.

One of the disadvantages of being a representative of the people at that time was the fact that salaries were not in keeping with the rise in cost of living nor commensurate with the style of living expected. Post was somewhat startled to learn that most Congressmen felt that they could not put through a bill for a raise in salaries. The consensus was that the people in the home areas would not be tolerant of any increase. Post felt that the attitude of the constituents would not be provincial to a point of obviating horse sense. At his own expense, as a spot-check, he created a postal-card ballot circulated throughout congressional districts in various parts of the country. The overwhelming majority of the response indicated indorsement of such a proposition and confidence in their national leaders. It was only after the result of this ballot was published that the salary increase took any sort of tangible form or was regarded with anything like a concentrated support. Many Congressmen, as well as news accounts, gave credit to Post for being the motivating force behind the first proposal for a salary increase.

As the living conditions of Washington gradually became apparent to Mr. Post, he became more and more active in bringing before the public any situation which he felt might be unfair to the average citizen. In January of 1911 he drafted a bill, the purpose of which was to give the residents of territories and the District of Columbia equality in court procedure with residents of other states. The existing law provided that residents of the District of Columbia were rather stray mavericks who could be cited almost anywhere. The draft was placed in the hands of the Hon. Wm. Alden Smith, Hon. J. C. Burroughs, Hon. Washington Gardner, and Hon. Chas. E. Townsend. Original longhand copies of the bill are extant in C. W. Post's files and show very little difference in the proposal as placed before the House by these gentlemen. The ultimate outcome of the proposal has not been researched for the benefit of this story. The incident is cited here merely to show the wide and diversified subjects in which Post would interest himself.

In order to be relieved of many *Postum Company* activities, and to give freedom for travel and outside interests, Post set up a Cabinet of plant management, minimizing departmental contacts. The lineup of functional heads of departments were: F. C. Grandin, Advertising Copy & Space; Carroll Post and S. H. Small, Promotion, Sales & Distribution; E. L. Brandon, Printing & Battle Creek Paper; M. K. Howe, Finance, Accounting, Purchasing, General Over-Sight; H. F. Burt, General Factory Operations; H. C. Hawk, General & Post's Outside Interests. To Hawk fell the supervision of general operations of the Texas ventures, personal stocks and bonds and real estate, with supervision of the Double U Ranch which Post acquired after 1906. Willis Post, a cousin, was general trouble-shooter and eventually was responsible for bringing out *Instant Postum* in 1911. *Canadian Postum Cereal, Ltd.,* was under the supervision of Howe, Burt, Carroll Post, and Grandin. *Grape-Nuts* was under Carroll Post, Hawk, and Willis H. Post. When the standing committee came into being, the various interests of C. W. had grown to include an interest in the Enquirer Publishing Company, *Home & Fireside Magazine,* Young Fuel & Pure Ice Company (which was operated by George and Ed Young with Willis Post), and the labor publication known as the *Square Deal,* the organ for dealing with labor opinions. The Cabinet was set up with excellent salaries, annual leave with full pay, sickness and health benefits and accident insurance, the same as given to plant labor, all of which was unique social reform for the era in question. An example of C. W. Post's close watch on plant matters, showing the type of instructions to his Cabinet, is found among the carbon copies of his letters in the personal file, dated September 4, 1909:

"I have for a long time been under the growing impression that the bread cutting machine in the bake shop department is seriously detrimental to our best interests. We have never been able to avoid making our *Grape-Nuts* loaves of a consistency that would in a way fit the machine instead of making them absolutely right without regard to machine. This tendency may not have been pronounced, but there is no question in my mind but that the tendency has existed, and does exist at the present time. That in itself is a detriment. Then we all know that the wet saws make pasty, slick places which prevent the best results from the secondary ovens. Added to all this there are perhaps 500 or 600 lbs. of lost material in and around that bread cutter every 24 hours, perhaps more, and while some of this goes into the feed, altogether too much of it washes off into the sewer. Everything considering, I am fully of the opinion that it is advisable to instruct, and I am herewith instructing, that the cutting of bread by machine be absolutely discontinued for a period of at least one week, and that the bread be made the very best we can make it and cut by hand in the old way, preferably from the top crust down through the loaf, and not sidewise, for the sidewise cut leaves the crust both on the top and bottom slices. After this method has been continued for a week, I would like to hear the results. I am strongly of the opinion that this would result in better goods and possibly a saving of money. In fact, I feel well satisfied it would be a saving of money. I also wish to instruct that a cold air pipe be established at the proper place in front of the ovens, and a blower heavy enough to furnish plenty of air be fitted thereto. Then we will have gates or doors that can be adjusted so that each baker can have his share of outside air during hot days. This probably will not be needed to be established this Fall for the hot days are practically at an end, but we must absolutely have this device in operation before next summer.

"There have been long and loud complaints about favoritism from Mr. ———— in the Bakery. Information reaches me that whenever we have a shutdown or partial close down, altogether too many of the old hands are laid off and what work there is, given to new men, and frequently to men without families. I will cite as particular instance of this, the ———— boys, and one ———— and one ————. The latter has left. These men, I understand, are single men and comparatively new, but they have been given work, and therefore wages, when some of our old men have been laid off. Little "Shorty" Bristol has always been thrown out when various duties could have been performed by him, probably better than any other man. I am very well satisfied ———— forgets himself at times and makes "pets" and favors them. This is one of his particular failings. He is, as we all know, a valuable man, but he has his failings and this is one of them. I would like to instruct you to . . . explain to him what has been said and warn him against his failing and insist that he correct it. Some two years ago things got rather bad in the Bakery and Mr. ————'s supreme authority was partially withdrawn. I am satisfied that he has ever since that time felt a desire that his full authority be reestablished, and at times has in a very biased and unfortunate manner operated to the detriment of that particular department. In connection with this rebuke . . . please couple it with the statement that we esteem him very highly for his many valuable traits, but that this matter of favoritism must be corrected. The charges have been made repeatedly over and over again for several years, and there is not the slightest doubt in my mind but that some of them are very true, and that policy is entirely contrary to the general policy of the Company. I want to call your attention also to the fact that the night shift for men is a very long one, and never has been satisfactory to me, but I know of no practical manner for eliminating it. One of the best things we can do in mitigation is to pass our night men over to the day shift as fast as possible, and when we take new men in the bakery, let them go on the night turn. This gives them an opportunity to earn extra money until they get a little ahead, and then they in turn may feel a desire to work a little less number of hours and take a little less pay. I trust these instructions will be put in force promptly.—C. W. Post."

From the very earliest days of *Postum,* experiments were constantly undertaken to find new foods of public appeal. One candy item defies all probing for details; evidently it fell by the wayside since no account sheets are in evidence, but a number of pieces of ad-copy remain. *Dextro-Candy* was made from Post Sugar, brought out in 1902 by using a showcard advertising method. The color-cards then popular showed an appeal to children through the use of nursery rhymes with pictures from storybooks and literature. The candy ads displayed Minnehaha, Evangeline and Priscilla in color and were drawn by F. Warde Traver. One copy reads:

"The Mission of *Dextro-Candy* is to supply SWEETS that can be easily digested. *Dextro-Candy* is made from pre-digested sugar, known as Post Sugar, and very similar to grapes and raisins."

What amount of business resulted from the new candy is not shown by extant accounts. Perhaps the public preferred to do a little digesting of its own or remained true to an affinity for *Lowney's* or *Whitman's,* then so popular. A few news clippings from the private scrapbooks would indicate that a new plant for manufacturing sugar was contemplated. *The Peoria Journal,* June 3, 1903, *Detroit News,* April 2, 1903, as well as the *Tribune,* New York City, April 24, 1902, each ran an article concerning the formation of a new company by C. W. Post, organized under the laws of New York, and incorporated in 1902, which called for a new plant to be built at Peoria, Illinois, for the manufacture of sugar from corn, to be known as the *Grape Sugar Company,* or Post Sugar; the matter evidently was not drawn to conclusion. There are no further clippings or comments concerning the proposed plant— nor are there any account sheets or reports which would indicate that any volume of business was garnered, if the matter ever got so far as the manufacturing stage. In view of the great number of ad-copies extant, it would seem that perhaps some manufacturing must have been done. Doubtless the idea was abandoned within a few months.

Original drawing for the packaging of Elijah's Manna, *introduced to the market in January of 1906. Two years later the name was changed to* Post Toasties.

The first packaging under the name Post Toasties *after withdrawal of the use of the Biblical name Elijah. In parentheses may be seen the words "Formerly called* Elijah's Manna" *(see text). Also may be seen on the package is "U. S. 3202, Food & Drug Act, June 30, 1906."*

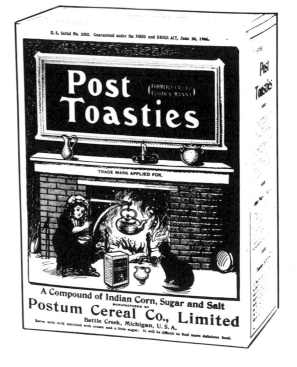

One of the few advertising or business errors ever made by Post was the introduction of *"Elijah's Manna."* This came on the market in January 1906, introduced as a prepared breakfast food made of corn, sugar and salt. The package displayed a picture of the prophet Elijah resting on the rock, staff in hand, with the raven dropping food into the right hand. The wrath of the American pulpit came down on Post; sermons were preached against the advertising, calling it a "sacrilege," and the exploitation of the Bible for commercial purposes. The English had strong enough opinions about the matter to invoke a law against its import. No one who knew C. W. personally would have concluded a sacrilegious intent on the part of the very man who found a way of life and the road to health in the Scriptures. After listening to the railings of many fanatics who deplored the public use of Biblical names, C. W. mused:

"Perhaps no one should eat Angel Food cake, enjoy Adam's Ale, live in St. Paul, nor work for Bethlehem Steel, nor could one have the healing benefits of St. Jacob's oil, one should have his Adam's apple removed and never again name a child for the good people of the Bible."

The unfortunate mistake was corrected in 1908 by recalling the merchandise, instituting new packaging and renaming. *Post Toasties* more quietly emerged, packaged with a picture of Cinderella sitting by the burning fireplace, kettle on the spit, black cat, cream pitcher and the flakes on the floor beside her. In spite of all the bad publicity, little Cinderella did not have to go back to her pumpkin. Between September 1908 and September 1909, she rolled up a net profit of $2,185,820.98, leaving *Postum* lagging at the $1,400,000 mark, and *Grape-Nuts* at $1,700,000, for the same accounting period.

The reader should bear in mind, at the level of 1897, prepared cereal foods for breakfast were almost unknown, with the exception of *Shredded Wheat*, of Niagara Falls, N.Y., the oldest of the pre-cooked foods, but by 1903 millions of words had been written on the subject with much conjecture as to how it all happened. The local grocers, frantic in acquiring more and more space for shelving and window display, hardly knew what had struck. A publication known as *Cereal & Foods* ran a summing-up article on the subject:

"Looking backward, one may see the originality and keen insight that distinguished Mr. Post's methods. They brought him money. They brought him success. He was the pioneer and he had the hard work of the pioneer, and the wonderful yield of virgin soil. He had to educate the people to cereal food and cereal drink. So much is accomplished, thanks to Mr. Post, and now what? We have run the gamut of foods. The grocer wonders where he is going to get shelf room to accommodate more. The grocer thinks the food question is over-done. But there is always room at the top in the cereal world. President Theodore Roosevelt said—'it is the shot that hits the mark that counts.' I'd go after the housewife like Charlie Post did, he did not use a blunderbuss, but an excellent smallest calibre rifle, direct to the mark, for women like dainty suggestive facts." [Scrapbooks of C. W. Post, article dated March 1903.]

Another innovation of C. W. Post, which created some little talk, was a suggestion that newspapers and magazines should print alternate columns of reading and advertising matter throughout the entire publications.[2] The business manager of the *Milwaukee & Wisconsin Sentinel* was so impressed with the suggestion that he proposed to try the plan for one week. Attention was attracted to this "new" idea of ad placement in the publication known as *The Advertising World* in its issue of 1903. This writer has not verified the starting date of breaking news columns with ad-copy, and, judging by daily newspapers today, it is a considered personal opinion the system need not have been instituted.

A well-known weekly "slick" magazine still in wide circulation undertook to give the story of C. W. Post without once mentioning his name, but so thinly disguised that its readers would have no difficulty in identifying the "Breakfast Food Millionaire" to whom they referred. The feature story (May 23, 1903) was intended as a summation of the wonders of advertising, but its lack of factual data on Post's early life was very evident. The story ran under the heading of "Fortunes and Freaks in Advertising":

"In the harbor of New York may be seen a yacht so perfect in construction and so luxurious in appointment that a stranger would probably pick her out at once as the 'floating home of a great prince.' Her decks shine like silver, her brasses glitter like gold. Everything about her is as fresh and clean and spotless as the salt breezes, and altogether she looks like a perfect marine painting set on canvas by a master hand. The name of the yacht does not matter, but the story of her

[2] *Printer's Ink,* June 29, 1903.

being does, for it is as romantic as the beauty herself. She was built by a man, who a few years ago had seldom smelled sea breezes, because he was too poor to make the trip to the coast."

This story continued along the lines of back-tracking the life of Post without mention of his name. It was interesting to note that the article appeared in a certain magazine in which Post would not advertise. This was an era when the average man in the street cast a jaundiced eye on "those rich swells." Perhaps the article was intended to block the flow of business toward the famous cereals of Post, or perhaps it was slanted toward the usual romance of industry. Journalistic practices have long succeeded in projecting into the mind of man the theory that he, too, can become a millionaire overnight, that it is a matter of luck. But few know or realize the vital necessity of basic ingredients—brain, brawn, will power, and a killing pace for him who would succeed.

Post had a profound interest in ships and sailing, but he did not own the yacht to which the article referred. This intense interest was passed on to his daughter, Marjorie, who some years later built the renowned *Sea Cloud*. One event which caught his fancy was the defeat of Sir Thomas Lipton's *Shamrock* by the *Columbia* (1902). C. W. cabled Sir Thomas Lipton, saying the feeling prevailed that the defeat of the *Shamrock*, in the races for the America's Cup, was due to the yachtsmen rather than the yacht. He offered to charter the *Shamrock* for a sum of 2,000 pounds and man her with an American crew against Sir Thomas with a British crew aboard the *Columbia*. Sir Thomas replied that the possibility interested him greatly, that he would not charter the *Shamrock* to Post but would lend her in the interest of sport if Post would outfit her with sail and rigging since she was now without sail. This proposal caught the fancy of sportsmen on both sides of the Atlantic and remained on the front pages of newspapers for many months, with pros and cons from both sides. The *Columbia* was owned by J. P. Morgan, and the event would have entailed his consent and cooperation. After many months of international news items on the subject, Post finally cabled Sir Thomas and thanked him for his splendid sportsmanship, concluding the race must be called off for want of cooperation from the owner of the *Columbia*.

Indeed by now C. W. Post was front-page news; everything he did or said made headlines. No doubt the greatest number of words published would concern his fight for the open shop and the battles with labor leaders, or "labor trusts" as he called them. His convictions and opinions were directed against corrupt leaders of various unions and not against the laboring man's right to join a union. Various labor controversies from his day up to the present have not encompassed such widespread coverage and diversified opinions as concerned the battles from 1902 through 1912 involving C. W. Post.

References:

Original Letter from Sir Thomas Lipton (Marjorie Post May files), Feb. 18, 1902.
Sail & Sweep, April 1902—"Why America Leads the World in Yachting," by C. W. Post.
American Shipbuilder, April 10, 1902.
The Wasp (Pacific Coast Weekly), Feb. 13, 1904—"Post on Advertising."
Success (Detroit magazine), May 1903—"The Industry That Cooks the World's Breakfast."
New Yorker, Nov. 18, 1903—"Notable Business Men" (re: C. W. Post).
Indianapolis Journal, Dec. 27, 1903—"How One Man's Energy Made Him a Millionaire" (re: C. W. Post).
New Yorker, n.d., ca. May 1905—"The Hour and The Man" (re: C. W. Post).

Chapter 9

~

Post vs. "Labor Trusts"

Universal working conditions at the turn of the century were the twelve-hour day at $2.50 per day for unskilled labor. At that time, Battle Creek was paying the highest scale of wage in the State of Michigan. Post had instituted numerous social reforms by his low-cost housing facilities, clean working conditions, and social benefits. He paid the top wage, plus bonus, on the merit system, with the insistence on open shop, and the conviction that man should be his own agent without outside influence.

One labor leader boldly approached Post with the suggestion that White City was paying too high a wage, advising Post labor could be furnished at $1.00 per day if he would agree to closed shop, stating "they're foreigners who *don't know no better.*" Post was so incensed that he promptly showed the caller to the door and informed him that never once had he used "pauper" labor and had no intention of beginning now. Furthermore, he pointed out, the Alms House of Michigan would show that not one inmate there had ever been a worker of Battle Creek and that Battle Creek alone in the country could point to its streets and show the absolute lack of mendicants.

It is significant, in spite of the number of years of bitter exchanges, that not once did White City have any labor problems. The workers were satisfied with working conditions and wages paid and took pride in ownership of their homes. Many of the original workers were still with the plant long after the death of the founder. Time without number labor agitators tried to make inroads on the minds of the *Postum* workers without any appreciable success. Violent strikes were the order of the day, with mayhem and utter destruction rampant at plants throughout the country. One Chicago manufacturer alone endured seventeen strikes that financially wrecked the business.

Among the undated news clippings in the C. W. Post scrapbooks (*ca.* 1904), Post outlined his position in the following words:

"For eleven years Battle Creek has grown prosperous without outside influence, and now we pay our workers the highest wage in the State of Michigan. There is utterly no reason for our workers to join a labor union and keep sending money out of town to maintain union cards and to foment strikes of violent proportions in other areas. Labor unions must be cleansed or stripped of their power by law."

Just as readily, Post turned the guns on industry and management, calling attention to abuses, poor working conditions, or low wages where they existed. He upbraided a meeting of leading manufacturers with the stern warning:

"We should never forget that a natural evolution is in progress—man, both high and low, is restlessly seeking new and better living conditions, the impulses come from God, but the details are carried out by man—hence the errors and mistakes and abuses." [C. W. Post scrapbooks]

Post was several times President of the American Association of Advertisers, later known as the National Association of Advertisers. In 1905 he was elected President of the National Citizens' Industrial Association to succeed D. M. Parry, the prime target of labor leaders. On his acceptance of this position, C. W. issued the following declaration of principles:

"No closed shop—no restrictions as to use of tools, machinery, or material except where unsafe—no limitation of output—no restrictions as to the number of apprentices and helpers when of proper age to work—no boycott—no sympathetic strike—no sacrifice of independent workmen to the labor unions—no compulsory use of the union label. That power through organization be placed in the hands of the people to control the acts of all organizations when such acts relate to the public welfare, thus perpetuate the individual liberty of every citizen and prevent interference with the continuous operations of industries."

Upon publication of these declarations, Charles W. Eliot, President of Harvard, commented: "I find every one of these principles to be in defense of *private and public liberty.*"

It is ironic that Post carried in his pocket, with a great deal of pride, a membership card in the Typographical Union. He believed in the organization of laboring men for purposes of betterment of working conditions and for keeping wages commensurate with the cost of living. He rebelled only at dictatorship from the leaders of the unions when such dictates encompassed unreasonable provinces. This same Typographical Union called a strike against the *New York Sun*, sending word to Post that he must withdraw his advertising from that paper at once, or risk a nationwide boycott of *Postum* products. This so infuriated Post that his answer was in the form of doubled amount of advertising in the *Sun*. *Postum* had long been advertised in that paper, and the relationship had been a cordial one with very satisfactory results. Promptly on the heels of the expanded advertising the Battle Creek plant was flooded with letters from union members all over the country, threatening to back the boycott unless ads were withdrawn from all non-union papers. The man who had instituted social benefits and reforms in working conditions and who paid the highest scale of wage, plus bonus, failed to understand this attitude from the union member public. The workers in White City plants took no such position—their comments were substantially, "you did right, C. W., the *Sun* has been good to *Postum*." They readily realized that what was good for *Postum* and *Grape-Nuts* produced a steady flow of pay envelopes and bonuses, making it possible for each to keep his home. Inspired by their confidence, Post stated in a speech:

"The workman who has no thought or care of whether or not his employer succeeds, I have no use for. Contra-wise I have absolutely no respect for the manufacturer who does not consider the interests and betterment of his employees."

C. W. was never a man of narrow viewpoint and thin skin, his success and fame were great, and being prominently displayed in the news in controversial matters brought forth millions of words from both sides of the various controversies. The private scrapbooks compiled by his staff indicate that a clipping service bureau supplied the national news items. Some clippings are undated, and some are without source information as to the identity of the paper in question, though most of them can be identified. His scrapbooks reflect the broadest of reactions. He did not have the staff delete the adverse opinions on his positions, or any of the mouthings of the "anti-rich" radicals: all sides of published comments are pasted in the books for posterity. A petty man would have ordered the staff to preserve the flattery and destroy the uncomplimentary comments.

Among the leaders of the various labor unions were many sane, thinking men, and Post respected them; only a few extreme radicals created the noise and disturbances. A Peoria, Illinois, labor paper published (1907) a favorable view and reaction concerning C. W.'s latest denunciation of what he termed "labor trusts." Its comments were very much in his favor as follows:

"In our anxiety to learn why C. W. Post is so unalterably opposed to labor organizations, we wrote him early in August requesting him to write an article for this number. To speak reasonably and be blunt about it, nine-tenths of the toilers of Peoria looked upon Mr. Post to be one of the greatest crushers of the poor the world has ever produced. His fiery and hot-shot articles appear at intervals in our daily papers, hot enough to convince the most skeptical that Post, our millionaire manufacturer, is, at best, a 'bad egg.' On the contrary, Mr. Post is known and recognized to be one of the most humane and kind employers in the country at the present time. He treats his employees with utter kindness, consideration, and respect, and has always shown a tendency to follow the teachings of the Golden Rule when dealing with his many employees. We expect to hear some, very few, labor unionists of the many thousands in Peoria, knocking because this letter of Mr. Post's was published in our columns. Yet the rank and file, the conservative men comprising the majority of unionists in Peoria, will freely admit that Mr. Post's article is good, wholesome, nourishing food for sensible thought."

Subsequently, the editor wrote Mr. Post as follows:

"I take pleasure in forwarding you a copy of my journal *The Plain Speaker* containing your article on the labor question. I wish to state that its publication aroused a considerable amount of interest among the laboring element of this city and was made the leading topic of debate in the Trades Assembly Hall last Sunday. *The Plain Speaker* has a circulation of five thousand copies monthly, the subscribers being in the main workingmen, many of them being very radical in their view on labor issues, yet this class warmly endorsed your article." [1]

Perhaps with the idea of answering the labor critics of Post, the workers at the plant gave a testimonial banquet to their founder, in December 1906, one of many such banquets to follow. The press and many "doubting Thomases" were invited, along with staunch friends, to hear just what White City workers had to say. The banquet took

---

[1] The article written by C. W. Post has not been located by this writer.

place in the Post Tavern at a table laden in the style for which the Tavern had become known. There was entertainment for the guests in the form of impersonations, popular in that day, by a Chicago artist, John Ratto, and other performers of the era. The opening address was by George Haines, a worker in the plant:

"This being an opportunity that is afforded us, we wish to express to you the true sentiments of the Postum family. We wish to say, and take pleasure in saying, that the feeling of the Postum family is serene and happy. When we look back over the past and remember the true state of affairs with us, we feel that an intelligent people could not help but appreciate the fact that many advantages have been placed within our reach. When we go back over the past but a little ways and note the few buildings that marked the beginning of one of the greatest advancements of the present day and now look upon the great White City and out over the Post Addition full of comfortable homes and beautiful lawns, we begin to realize the true advantages placed within the reach of the family by their Captain. We bought these homes, have had ample time and opportunity, without any oppression, to pay for them, and when we think of these things the thought naturally comes to us—'Captain, we thank you.' Therefore, we the members of the Postum family, take this opportunity to express to you our thanks for the many acts of kindness that have been shown us by you, and the advantages we have secured through your generosity and consideration of our welfare. We have learned to look upon you as our friend and benefactor and as head of the great Postum works which we look upon as home; we are the happiest and most contented family that we know of."

The answering address by Mr. Post was one of the longest and all-encompassing speeches he had made up to that time. He cited the pitfalls of venture capital, the 'blood, sweat and tears' of management, the long arduous hours expended by ownership on the road up, and the struggle to stay up. He further outlined the gains made by workmen as a whole, showing their status at the level of 1906 against that of a few years prior. Then, a lashed-out denunciation of some labor leaders fairly seared the ears of his audience, with citations from the records, recalling incidents and circumstances of violence he so much abhorred. In part, a few excerpts will highlight C.W.'s views:

"To understand the cause, we must go back a few years. About ten years ago our people saw citizens and good workers chased by mobs of strikers through the streets. There was hate and murder in the air. We saw factories burned to the ground and industry destroyed forever, stopping a flow of wages to good workmen. There were train wrecks, people killed, workmen idle and their families half-starved, merchants ruined forever and the city at a standstill. It took ten years to build back to peace and prosperity. Those were the days of labor-union rule.

"Battle Creek came to be known as the most prominent example of a Free City, free from labor unions, paying highest wages under better conditions. The Quaker Oats Company, Lyon and Healy, the greatest musical instrument company in the country, the Grand Trunk Shops, and various others came and settled here, bringing vast sums of money to our merchants. But a Free Town is a rankling thorn in the side of the grafting leaders of labor trusts, for it pays no toll to support those leaders who want to get power enough to force every working man to pay them fees and to make him quit when they say so.

"Does it surprise you to know there is a worm eating at the root of Battle Creek right now? Well, there is. I learn, with authority, that very recently $50,000 was sent here to worm into our working forces, and just as soon as they can get enough members to do so, their leaders living elsewhere will order a strike, just to show the world that Battle Creek is 'tied-up.' Their method is to *Unionize*, to charge you $1.00 or $100.00, so that they can tell you when and where not to work.

"THESE are the workings of the '*walking* delegate'—he walks into a hardware store and tells the merchant he wants $500 as a contribution to the Union, or all Union members will boycott him; he furnishes the merchant a list and tells him he cannot sell to these concerns, or he must risk boycott. They unionize the police, so that they will not arrest strikers; in Chicago they unionized the Fire Department, which had to stand by and let a non-union plant burn to the ground. Another walking delegate walked into a bookstore and told the owner he could not sell *McClure's, Century,* or *Delineator,* and others, because they were 'unfair' to labor unions. Look at Waterbury, Connecticut, and Wilkes-Barre, Pennsylvania, and a score of other thoroughly unionized towns, where everyone was in fear of everyone else, and the disturbances and oppressions and riots and destroyed businesses that resulted, until the whole conspiracy was overthrown by an enlightened community.

"Beloit, Wisconsin, a city of 14,000 people, prosperous and 'unorganized' from the Union standpoint, had for years been busy attending to its own affairs, attracting industries which located within the corporate limits, filling the coffers of the merchants and townspeople. Labor and management had no difficulties; the people were content and prosperous. In the spring of 1903, two walking delegates, George Mulberry, 5th Vice-President of the International Association of Machinists, and James Hogan, one of the general organizers of the American Federation of Labor, discovered the 'unorganized' town. Under the magical influence of this pair of disturbers, who promised many impossible 'improvements' in the already excellent labor conditions of Beloit industries, the workers became inoculated and intoxicated with the virus of Unionism; they were persuaded their conditions were bad."

Post produced a sheaf of letters from workers of Beloit who had written him of the pitfalls they had endured after having joined the Union in question. Many had supported the called strikes, but in most instances had endured hardships from which they could not recover; after long strikes and payless weeks, many had lost their homes for want of monthly payments. In general, the complete dissatisfaction with their new blight was evident in every letter he passed around the room. Post closed his speech as follows:

"Freedom was guaranteed to us at the end of our Revolutionary War, in which our ancestors fought and died, and its perpetuation was further guaranteed by our Constitution. Don't give that freedom into the keeping of any person, corporation or organization, who will not permit you to be your own agent. Be loyal to the laws of your community of which you are the integral part, and warn off every invader." [2]

This rolling of the war drums and Proclamation of Freedom was answered in labor papers within a very short time. One answer must have amused Post to the point where he had his staff paste the article in the scrapbook alone and bordered for attention—it is interesting:

"The *Grape-Nuts* publicity bureau located at Battle Creek is burning up a few more dollars in getting the asinine views of C. W. Post on the labor question before the public. This call of the wild was recently printed in the principal dailies of the country at a cost, says Comrade Post, of $20,000. We have often thought we would like to see just how much of an ass this man would make of himself, and we are now entirely satisfied. He has out-parried Parry. For deliberate falsehood and misrepresentation we don't believe this latest effort of Post has ever been equaled. At the same time we are convinced that the continued publication of these articles of the Battle Creek Don Quixote has proved and will continue to prove of great benefit to the Union cause. They are such a tone as will make the Union man a better Union man, and will cause the fair-minded man outside the Unions to be filled with disgust at the deliberate misrepresentations indulged. More power to you, Mr. Post. While your manifestoes of freedom in the advertising columns of the daily papers do not prove that *Grape-Nuts* is very much of a brain food, yet we feel that if we had a few more like you the organization of all workmen into labor Unions would only be a matter of a short time. We're hoping that your money lasts for many more Freedoms." [3]

[2] Reported in full by the *Battle Creek Enquirer*, December 11, 1906.
[3] Publication and author unknown, clipping not identified.

Apparently no answers with point by point arguments appeared in the labor publications, though Post had made the challenge by citing case histories of acts of violence and destruction by the radical elements within the unions. Most of the answers took form in the theme of attempted degradation and the "hate the rich" song. They poked a finger at his world travels, art collection, and general affluence, calling him a nabob who no longer knew the workingman. These accusations were from the radicals, and not once from any man who knew him or his plant workers.

In the spring of 1907, Post was a member of the Commission appointed to look into child-labor problems, composed of representatives of the National Association of Manufacturers, American Federation of Labor, General Federation of Women's Clubs and the National Civic Foundation. The meeting was held in the (old) Shoreham Hotel in Washington, D. C., and called to order by President Theodore Roosevelt. Samuel Gompers of the American Federation of Labor was at the head of the group, with each organization represented by an impressive list of members. The Commission conferred with Oscar S. Strauss, Secretary of Commerce and Labor (Labor was not raised to separate Cabinet status until 1913), Charles P. Neil, Commissioner of Labor, and S. D. North, Commissioner of Census. The child-labor problems of that era have been extensively dealt with over the years and need not be repeated here, except to set forth the view of Post, who was intensely opposed to the use of child labor unless said "child" was old enough to work and the only means of support for a family; even so, C. W.'s views were adamant on the question of age limit.

In the midst of the labor quarrels, Post was drawn from the fray long enough to step deep into the mire of another fight. This one cost him a pretty penny. The trouble started over an editorial appearing in *Collier's Weekly,* which flayed the products of Battle Creek, many manufacturers, and Post in particular, under the heading "The Great American Frauds." Its wording was ill-advised, vituperative and ugly. *Collier's* stated that Post's advertising made impossible claims of curative powers for *Grape-Nuts,* that it could not cure appendicitis, that this was "lying and potentially deadly lying, and furthermore the endorsements from leading medics of the day are purely fictional." C. W.

dipped a pen in a little vitriol and answered with half-column ads, which admittedly cost him $150,000 to publish. He accused the magazine of using blackjack tactics to force him to advertise in the publication—"when a journal wilfully prostitutes its columns to try and harm a reputable manufacturer to force him to advertise, it is time the public knew the facts." This little paragraph so wounded the feelings of Peter F. Collier, Robert Collier, and Norman Hapgood, the editor, that no balm short of $750,000 ($250,000 each) could soothe them.[4] Other publications took up the fight with sharp words and no restraint. One editor of a publication in which Post had no financial interest, nor was its text from Post's pen, lashed out:

"*Collier's*, the Great American Yellow Roorback, has taken up the despicable task of trying to browbeat and bulldoze several thousand manufacturers and professional gentlemen who are in licensed businesses, under the hypocritical cloak of 'protecting the public from being victimized by swindlers.' *Collier's* is decrying these men for no other reason than they won't buy advertising space they offer for sale."[5]

In spite of the fact that the Colliers first unsheathed the sword and drew blood, they sued for libel. Post filed a countersuit for libel, and the whole thing flowed from court to court, up through the Appellate Court to the Supreme Court, until 1913. Judgments were rendered only to be reversed. Post won the final round, but it cost him a great deal of money. However, while the paid advertising in answering *Collier's* ran into considerable sums of money, this again explains the success of Post in marketing his products by keeping his name before the public. The consumer was constantly aware of the man as a crusader for good causes, with the courage of his convictions. He knew the value of argumentative aspects in advertising and was one of the first to use that approach long before the *Collier's* incident. Each time *Collier's* issued an editorial about Post or his products, C. W. bought space in leading newspapers and magazines for the sole purpose of answering the challenge; the public fell into the habit of looking forward to the next round. Actually the year of 1907, when all this began, was the largest single year of total volume of sales since the founding

[4] *Colliers*, July 27, Sept. 21, 1907; Dec. 14, 17, 31, 1910; Jan. 7, 14, 21, 28, 1911.
[5] The publication and author will remain unidentified for best of reasons; clipping in Post's scrapbook.

of the Company. Post, who knew his Bible well, must have felt that the Babylonians had a point for publicity when they said: "Go to, let us build a city and a tower whose top may reach unto Heaven, and *let us make a name lest we be scattered.*"

The *Square Deal* was Post's medium for delivering red-hot opinions and findings on all labor questions; however, extensive paid advertising in newspapers carried most of the inflammatory words from his pen. The magazine came into being about 1906, and was put together by E. L. Brandon at the Battle Creek Paper Company. The printing was farmed out, but the composition, folding, stitching and mailing were done at the paper company. By 1912 the magazine had grown to a wide circulation, necessitating a separate company known as *The Square Deal Press, Ltd.,* Jos. W. Bryce, Editor. By that date, the publication carried a great deal of paid advertising by such corporations and organizations as Buick Motor Company, Shredded Wheat Company, American Steam Pump, on through many widely-known names. Surprisingly, the Battle Creek Sanitarium subscribed for a large advertisement to explain the cures offered, such as "hydrotherapy, phototherapy, electrotherapy, mechanotherapy, radium, rational diets and rest." Articles and open letters from leaders of industry, labor, the advertising world, and private citizens were published over the individual signatures of the authors. Most of the articles emanating from Post's pen defended the individual laborer, but castigated the closed shop. His denunciatory comments were directed only at the so-called "labor trusts." Labor leaders chose to ignore the fact that Post defended the rights of the individual union member, but deplored corrupt leadership and their methods of violence and destruction.

Hundreds of articles on the subject of Post, from 1900 through 1912, reveal that there were far more favorable comments than criticism, and that a great many original enemies did an about-face and defended him. Labor papers lifted words from context and suited them to their own purpose, while the pro-Post newspapers dealt heavily in favorable word coverage, only to be accused of bias in favor of a million-dollar advertising program. Somewhere between the two lies the answer. It is apparent that the man never fell short in benevolence to his workers. C. W. just as freely expressed himself against a fellow manufacturer who made it necessary for workers to organize for self-protection, and championed the workman's right to do so. Post had long been an advocate of the adoption of the Canadian law for settling labor disputes. The law was written into the Canadian statutes with the good will of both the employers and trade unions. It provided for the arbitration of all trade disputes, in which national utilities were affected, before a strike or lockout could be declared.

Based on the principles of arbitration and nonviolence, the National Trades and Workers Association was formed in Battle Creek in 1910. The Association was organized by Joseph W. Bryce, one-time president of the State Association of Railroad Men, who disapproved of the methods of the heads of the Federation and conceived the new organization. C. W. at once applauded Bryce's organization and made headlines (*New York Tribune*, June 10, 1910) when he offered Ex-President Theodore Roosevelt a salary of $100,000 per year, to be paid out of his own pocket, if the former President would head the newly formed Association. He stated:

"I have long known the President, for many years, and know that he favors labor organizations but deplores the method of strike violence advocated by the leaders, the same as I do. We both believe in the benevolent aspects of the Association, but we know that conciliatory methods are the only answer."

Roosevelt felt he could not accept the offer though he gratefully acknowledged Post's confidence. Within the next two years (1912) Post gave the National Trades and Workers Association a building located at Battle Creek (Phelps Sanatorium property), valued at approximately $450,000, to be used as a Benevolent Home for Workers. Upon taking up the obligations of the Association, July 19, 1910, C. W. made a lengthy statement concerning the mission of the Association. He recalled how, when a boy in Springfield, he lived not far from the old Globe Tavern where Abraham Lincoln had boarded. This was previous to the outbreak of the Civil War, and the atmosphere was surcharged with the spirit of independence and freedom. These circumstances had a powerful influence on the boy, and Charlie grew up imbued with the spirit that was rife at that time. His statement was:

"You do not originate many ideas yourself, you are often the wireless instrument that only spells out the message that has been sent by someone else. It seems reasonably plain that the good Lord and Ruler of this world has it as part of this plan that human beings join in societies or organizations. It is evidently an inherited motive. Therefore, we have had societies under one name or another since the days of Babylon. There are church organizations of various kinds. There are clans of Scotland, the Tongs of China, and fraternal organizations. . . . I have heard of people who objected to organizations of labor on the grounds that some members used violence and committed crimes. Many times in past history there were crimes committed by zealots of the church, but that fact should not be considered a sufficient reason for annihilating the church. Trade organizations are necessary to equitably balance the scales of industrial life. . . ."

Post was especially sensitive to a two-faced position or *double-entendre* on the part of any labor leader or political figure. Senator Robert M. La Follette had Presidential aspirations in the coming election of 1912, and, in the late fall of 1911, his campaign manager petitioned the leaders of Battle Creek to invite La Follette to speak in that city. Naturally the matter was handed to C. W. for his opinion or leadership in a civic matter touching that city. La Follette was running on a platform of "Warrior Upon Special Interests Groups." Post could not reconcile the platform publicity for La Follette with the facts as seen in the campaign posters; therefore, his answer to the campaign manager was the usual straightforward approach:

"I am struck with the incongruities in your announcement. The printed slips make strong claims for Mr. La Follette as a champion for the overthrow of political bosses and the trusts and the combinations and recites that he has for many years been the leader in the war against special interest groups and in favor of the establishment and vindication of the rights of the individual citizen. "In strong contrast your letterhead is confronted with the label of the Typographical Union and the most marked example of special interest in the labor trusts, with its deadly hatred for the common citizen who dares to do business without first paying tribute to the trust. I am in favor of the organization of workingmen, but deadly opposed to the trust method of the American Federation of Labor, or the Typographical, or any such trust. It is apparent your label is placed there to placate the union, but it is a deadly warning to those of us who abhor the trusts."

The letter was released to the newspapers by the campaign headquarters for La Follette, and again Post made headlines: "Postum Cereal Millionaire Breaks With La Follette." [6]

[6] Post's scrapbooks contain some twenty to thirty news clippings from various sources covering the subject of La Follette.

Unless one studied the newspapers, trade publications and various periodicals of the era from the 1880's through 1912, it would not be possible to realize the vast amount of violence and destruction by labor that wreaked havoc upon industry within that period. Complete awareness of the condition somewhat explains Post's adamant position with regard to the absolute power of any one leader of a labor organization; and why he hammered away for the power to be vested in the individual laborer, collectively represented by vote through democratic principles, not dictation and tyranny of leadership through fear.

The destruction of the Los Angeles *Times* Building in October of 1910, and the resultant trials and exposures, finally awakened the public to many facts long claimed by Post. J. J. McNamara, Secretary of the International Association of Bridge & Structural Iron Workers, together with his brother, J. B. McNamara, was brought to trial for the crime, both of whom confessed to long years of dynamiting construction work when contractors would not "listen to reason." Their chief dynamiter of nationwide building construction was one Ortie McManigal. While McManigal was not directly involved in the destruction of the *Times* Building, he confessed to six years of destruction, first by dynamite, then by nitro compounds. While languishing in jail in Los Angeles, he wrote a book outlining every detail of every destruction for which he was personally responsible. His book, *Ortie McManigal's Own Story of the National Dynamite Plot*, went into minute details with exact dates of when and where he had met J. J. McNamara, as well as other labor leaders, for instructions and supplies. He pointed the finger of accusation, with proof, at the Machiavellian machinations of many radical leaders. He went so far as to state that Samuel Gompers was thoroughly aware of the plots while offering rewards for information or conviction of any such dynamiters. The McNamara brothers made the statement that Gompers and his associates on the executive committee of the National Federation of Labor had knowledge, not only of the original dynamiting campaign, but acquiesced, approved and encouraged the effort to bribe and intimidate witnesses, and as a last desperate effort, to corrupt the jury before whom any such case should be brought to trial.

When the *Times* case came to trial, Clarence Darrow, the nationally known defense lawyer, with an impressive array of legal aids in his corner, was retained by Gompers to defend the accused. The Los Angeles County Prosecutor was without ample funds for investigative work of the various dynamiting incidents. The National Association of Manufacturers banded together and formed the National Industrial Council to give moral support and financial aid to the prosecutor. Before the trials were ended, and as damaging evidence was presented against the plotters, Clarence Darrow walked off the case. The trials brought out the facts in detailed account of the strike of the Industrial Brotherhood of Teamsters in Chicago (1910), which resulted in the murder of 21 nonunion men, 1,011 court cases of criminal assault and 803 convictions; fines amounted to nearly $12,000 for assault, and the estimated loss in wages was something near $5,000,000. Over twenty people were killed in the *Times* explosion, and there was no hesitancy on the part of the public to call it "murder." McManigal was able to lead the investigators to hidden caches of dynamite and nitro compounds, and to prove his various connections with the apprehended criminals. In closing the book, he made complete acknowledgment of ignorance in accepting propaganda from the corrupt leaders, with the following statements:

"I was convinced that C. W. Post was an enemy to labor, I had been taught that he wished to strangle the workingman. I did not investigate these facts, I accepted them. No man in America has recognized the truth of what I have said so thoroughly, nor labored to overcome existing conditions within the unions by remedying their defects and creating virtues for them, more effectively than C. W. Post.

"More than 500 witnesses and thousands of pieces of documentary and other physical evidence corroborated my story. Such are the facts of the greatest plot to destroy that this country has ever seen. It has been called a 'frame up' and I have been called a lying spy and traitor. When the arrests were made, labor throughout the country was told that the McNamaras were not guilty and that they were the victims of an ambitious Burns Detective Agency. On the strength of this they collected hundreds of thousands of dollars from the workingmen all over the country for the defense. And then they [the MacNamaras] stood in court and pleaded guilty. Even then labor was not convinced. Some said Darrow sold out. Darrow was tried for bribery. Some said this was part of his agreement with the district attorney. The public is indeed hard to convince."

Within a few days after the *Times* explosion, and before the criminals were apprehended, Post invited Samuel Gompers to come to Battle Creek and express his views in the public auditorium. Gompers' speech on that occasion was devoted to snide and scathing denunciations of Post. The auditorium was filled with men invited by Gompers from the ranks of Union men, and a goodly sprinkling of pro-Post men. There was loud applause, laughter and stomping of feet when Gompers made his snide remarks, and boos from Post supporters at the same time. Gompers became quite emotional when discussing the Los Angeles dynamiting, and vowed by his Holy Redeemer that he felt the plot was not a plot, that the explosions had been caused by chemicals stored in the *Times* Building. He called attention to the fact that the American Federation of Labor had offered a handsome reward if proof could be presented to show that labor had been responsible. This was in the face of evidence of an unexploded bomb found under a window of the private residence of General Harrison Gray Otis, owner of the *Times*.

Shortly after the apprehension of the dynamiters, Post made a test-run of the Sherman Anti-Trust Law, by suing Gompers for $750,000 for being in violation of the Law. He quoted freely from speeches by President Taft and Governor Woodrow Wilson who had cited the real meaning of a trust. Post compared any trust in existence with the operations and machinations of the labor leaders, stating:

"A combination [the Unions] organized to control labor, extract fees from each member, force up the price of their product, which is labor, and restrict its supply. Every dollar extracted comes from the pocket of the citizen, and not from the leader. The sand-crab politician burrows deep in fright of the threat against him at the polls by the so-called 'labor vote.' What they do not realize is that the average worker is an honest, law-abiding citizen, even if he has been forced to join the trust to keep his job. Every law-abiding citizen should write his Congressman and demand that he defend the common good. The country does not need, nor want, a power to control workmen, close industries, tie-up railways and shipping, dictate the conduct of human beings, and wreck the economy of the country as a whole. Nor should the workman be forced out on a strike, sacrificing pay envelopes, and losing his home, wrecking other people's property, falling into financial distress from which he (or industry) may never recover. Don't forget—a few pennies pay-raise may result in added dollars in cost of many commodities, with the result that the worker has less money left in his pocket after the raise than before."

During this battle and jockeying for position, Post kept on the heels of the Congress for action against violations of the Anti-Trust laws by labor "trusts." While it will be shown herein that Post was quite adept at the drawing board, no mention has been made of his skill with cartoons. During the "trusts" battle, he issued many editorials through paid newspaper columns which were headed by his very pointed cartoons. One such illustration was directed at the members of the Congress who were "ducking" their responsibility to the people. Post drew the following cartoon for heading the editorial: Uncle Sam in the Speaker's Chair in the House; Sergeant-at-Arms bringing down the aisle two resisting members; the seats contain only four or five members, with six rising to leave; doors jammed with members trying to get out; clerk starting the rollcall; caption "Congress Playing Hide-Out." Uncle Sam speaks: "Come on back, boys, and let your Uncle give out the lessons." Question: "What is a sand-crab politician?" Answer: "One who burrows in the sand at the sound of footsteps and reports 'absent on important committee business' when asked by his constituents why he did not vote to protect citizens and property." Post went on to ask his usual question: "How does this type differ from a Statesman? The answer is—in many ways. One way in particular—the sand-crab variety spends his time planning for re-election, and he will lick the dust from the boots of any one who will vote for him. The Statesman? He stands up bravely for freedom, liberty and equal opportunity for all of his constituents, rebuking the few who seek control over the many."

One of the great landmarks in the field of labor litigation is the famous Buck Stove Case. [*Samuel Gompers vs. Buck Stove and Range Co.* 221, U. S. 429.] C. W. Post was drawn into this controversy by a great admiration for James Van Cleave, then President of both the stove company and the National Association of Manufacturers. Mr. Post was a man of strong convictions. What he believed he was prepared to support. The more important the convictions the more aggressive the endeavors. His interest in this case was no less influenced by an extreme disapproval of the boycott and secondary boycott, the implements of destruction used by the A. F. of L. Not only did the labor leaders demand a boycott of their victim's product, they engaged in the secondary boycott. The *secondary* meant that their business was withdrawn from anyone who patronized the subject of their attack. The Buck Stove Company had never had a strike until 1907 when a dispute with a small number of employees led the A. F. of L. to place it on the boycott list. This was a trifling matter until Mr. Van Cleave was named President of the N. A. M., whereupon the Federation indulged in an all-out attack on the stove company. Mr. Van Cleave was forced to turn to the courts for redress from "improper attack." The United States Supreme Court issued a temporary restraining order against the boycott in December 1907, which became permanent in March of 1908. In December of 1908, after the trial, Gompers, Mitchell, and Morrison, respectively President, Vice President and Secretary of the A. F. of L., were found guilty of contempt for continuing the boycott in face of the restraining order. The defendants appealed. After four years of litigation, a large stockholder of the Buck Stove Company undertook to compel Van Cleave to surrender to attack. At this point, C. W. Post stepped in and purchased $100,000 of stock in the company in order to assure Mr. Van Cleave control of his company and to continue the litigation upon principles involved. The Supreme Court ultimately held that when power developed was used to restrain trade or commerce by conspiracy it was the duty of the government to protect one against the other. The decision was of immense importance because it prohibited a continuing use of the boycott. It established permanently a vital principle of law. The near capitulation of the stockholder, prevented by the intervention of Post's moral and financial assistance, probably changed the course of this vital question.

One would think that C. W. Post had enough to handle with labor activities, advertising and manufacturing, a constant search for the betterment of working conditions, and the Post City projects. In spite of the many involvements, he constantly sought ways to help the individual worker. An especially interesting aspect was his financial support and groundwork for an entirely new idea in our country. At the level of 1910, workmen's compensation was unknown. Post prodded the National Association of Manufacturers into an examination of such a program then existing in Germany. A committee was sent to Germany to learn all ramifications of such plans and compensation, resulting in the National Association of Manufacturers backing a proposal to Congress for Industrial Indemnity Insurance. The program was outlined to include the introduction of scientific devices for accident prevention, to institute lectures on prevention, and to provide first-aid facilities. The following is from a speech by Post before the Manufacturers' Association (October 7, 1910):

"I am very strongly inclined to the belief that the industry should protect and provide for those who conduct it. That means employees as well as employers. Now, as it stands today, the employer, who is supposed to have a little longer head than the employee—which is perhaps the reason he has passed from an employee to an employer—generally provides profit enough from the industry to put something on the shelf and take care of himself in sickness, accident or old age. Of course some do not do this, but it is reasonable to suppose that most of them do.

"Now then, the workmen live on too narrow a margin of safety. So when sickness or an accident intervenes, their reserve is generally too small to care for them.

"I am inclined to believe that industry should be so conducted that a reasonable amount each year should be set aside to cover the unexpected which may, and will, happen to some of our employees. I think the employees should have wages raised enough to warrant their contributions to this fund in addition to the contributions of the employer. . . ."

Post continued to speak before many groups of manufacturers and industry at large on the proposal, with strong emphasis on accident prevention, coupled with first-aid, or in-plant clinics. The Manufacturers' Association took up the fight with full conviction after listening to Post's wise and pointed arguments. The plan did not come to fruition until after Post's death, but most assuredly workmen's compensation today can look back to the groundwork laid by a very great humanitarian. The radical labor leaders chose to ignore these proposed benefits, and all other revolutionary ideas of Post's; they preferred to have the laborers believe that any benefits accruing to them would come only through a "war" upon "Capitalists." The expression and feeling were in too wide use to ignore, hence C. W. made his answer in another public address:

"In our country today stand many of the feared so-called 'Capitalists.' Who are they? You will find by looking back into their histories that most were once

'Workers' too. How did they become 'Capitalists?' There are thousands of manual workers who have the saving habit. Money saved represents the work, manual or mental, of the earner and is therefore stored energy which can be released at the proper time. Saved money is Capital, whether it be 50¢ or $50,000. Frequently these savers release this energy and invest it in some industry and thus pass out of the class of manual workers and pass into the class of manual and mental working Capitalists. Let me illustrate a particular case where I know all the details. Let me call them George and Jake.

"George and Jake worked side by side as moulders on wages. The machines on which they worked made faulty castings. George believed that he could improve the machine and perfect the castings. Jake said 'Why bother, it's not our money or machine, we get our wages.' Nonetheless, George worked overtime and in spare time perfected a new machine and sold it to his employer for a very nice sum of money. He put that profit into a little business of his own, it grew, he prospered, creating a whole new circle of workers and wages. This means a better prosperity for the merchants, school teachers, doctors and a variety of other workmen.

"Do I have to tell you that Jake is still working as a moulder? Do I have to add that he ceased to speak to George? George was a traitor to labor, he became a Capitalist. There will always be Jakes with us, but, alas, too few like George."

When the cudgel was finally laid down in January 1912, Post stated it was not his intention to retire entirely from labor issues, but to devote his time to the National Trades and Workers Association. In his sign-off editorial, captioned "The Round Up," he took the position that all previous public denunciations on "Unionism" had now been justified and vindicated by recent developments, federal investigations of the dynamite plots, revulsion of sentiment, and the McNamara confessions. The "Round Up" was released to a press-wire and appeared as headlines in all member papers, as well as in European papers. Ex-President Theodore Roosevelt had clashed openly with Samuel Gompers over the McNamara case (1911) stating: "Murder is Murder—in the instance of the dynamite outrages perpetrated against the *Los Angeles Times*—an outrage of dastardly iniquity whereby he [the striker] not only wrecks individual's property, but with callous indifference takes the lives of scores of innocent people." Gompers answered Roosevelt in a speech delivered at St. Louis, where he disclaimed any knowledge of the identity of the perpetrators. The labor leader called attention to Roosevelt's article (*Outlook*, April 15, 1911) lauding *Collier's Weekly* for its stand against patent medicine frauds and C. W. Post's *Grape-Nuts*. He accused Roosevelt of carrying water on both shoulders, by patting the back of *Collier's* one time and grasping the hand of Post at other times.

The "Round Up" was met with comments from most papers in this country and in Europe. They applauded the results of Post's long battle for sane labor conditions based on the principles of mediation. American foreign language newspapers, which issued long editorials in defense of Post's various tirades against the "trusts," were largely circulated among the working class. A Duluth, Minnesota, paper printed a summarizing editorial, knowing full well they would be accused of bias in favor of *Postum* advertising, and perhaps be accused of being bought. In an effort to forestall that very attitude, the editorial began with the recognition of such conditions. The summary stands up very well when placed against the actual facts concerned with labor-management at Battle Creek in general, and Post in particular:

"We believe every working man, union or non-union, will say *Amen* to Post's most recent address where he stated: 'I am not a warm advocate of a lot of foolish maudlin sympathy that has paraded under the name of public welfare. We do not provide any marble baths, lecture rooms, reading rooms, or books. Those who understand workmen at all realize that first and foremost they do not want to be subjected to a lot of gifts and charities that would place them under servile obligation to their employer. The American workman wants an honest first-class price for his labor and then he wants to be left alone to follow his own individual ideas as to his way of life and the use of his money. If he wants a bath or a book, he wants his own way of getting it. I believe in the welfare work which makes it possible for the man to help himself, but it does not include holding a milk bottle to his lips until he is weaned. I do not hesitate to say that if I were a competent workman, employed by one of the industries that operates on the *grind* principle, then I should be a member of a labor organization for the purpose of defending my own rights and those of my fellows against insuperable tyranny.'

"Mr. Post's battle with Unionism is as to his own industries, he will not have the employees of his plants organized—they are not organized and he has never had a strike. He won this battle by the only method possible, by making working conditions better for his employees than organization would make them, by leaving no material gain to be secured through unionism. Every employee who remains two years finds five per cent of his two-year wage deposited in the bank in his name. Each year thereafter he gets a ten per cent bonus on top of highest wages paid each week. He also builds houses for them and sells them at cost, conveying full title, and in case of injury the employee is cared for and his wage paid during disability. These features, with ideal working conditions, sanitation and safety devices, have kept unions out of his plants. They are the only devices yet to have a permanent effect against unionism." [7]

More than half a century has passed since C. W. Post took up his position against labor leaders; this summary and its conclusions are evident. There is no question but that Post instituted social reforms which are taken for granted in this last half of the century. When it all began before 1890 the working conditions for the laboring man were fraught with unsanitary conditions, poor wage scales, and complete lack of social benefits. That Post was instrumental in bringing about better wages, excellent factory buildings, and social reforms, there is no doubt. These intervening years of labor-management disputes might be carefully reviewed in the light of events so long ago. It would appear that Post has been vindicated for an adamant stand— also, that he knew abuses would come from man—that not all employers would be benevolent, nor would every workman carry his load.

[7] Scrapbooks of C. W. Post; *Duluth Times,* Nov. 12, 1911.

Chapter 10

~

There's A Reason

FROM THE INCEPTION of Post's first advertising instituted for *Scientific Suspenders,* back in 1889, *Postum* in 1895, *Grape-Nuts* in 1898, and on up through a vast advertising program, the slogan remained *There's A Reason.* The very phrase became a part of the speech and written word of its father, or "there is utterly *NO* reason" when there *WAS* no reason. To C. W. Post, logic was a way of life. There was a reason why he had to get well, a reason why *Postum* was better for mankind than coffee, a reason why *Grape-Nuts* replaced starches, a reason why *Post Toasties* tasted better. The slogan was fed out through all possible advertising media covering any *Postum* food products. Regardless of where Post might have been traveling, the final draft of any proposed advertising was sent to him for personal approval or corrections. Though the plant could boast of its own extensive advertising building and staff, C. W. constantly took a hand in the layouts and created most of them. Some of the original rough drafts, sketched out on brown paper, are now in the personal files of his daughter.

The unfortunate "Elijah's Manna" shows many drafts. There is one marked #1 where he had blocked off the top section for the sketch and thereunder had written the copy. The sketch calls for a raven on the back of a chair near a man at a desk, one foot raised in gesture, saying, "Say, honest boy, you would like a dish of Elijah's Manna with cream —it needs no cooking, 10¢ at your grocer's." Sketch #2 shows the raven sitting on top of a door, with copy to read, "Quote [quoth?] the Raven, never more will my tribe carry food for Prophets, modern day saints and sinners and citizens buy Elijah's Manna." There are a great many more of the crude drawings and roughed-out copy covering the

117

proposed program for Elijah's Manna, including the one previously mentioned herein. At the bottom of each of the drafts the phrase *"There's A Reason"* was to be included. The final draft for the new food, which caused the ultimate explosion from the pulpit, is shown also in fully roughed-out detail with instructions to the staff: "Show Elijah sitting on rock in foreground, give him long beard and medium length hair to the shoulders, staff in hand, skins over shoulder and leg, right hand receiving—palm up—food being dropped from raven's claws, just above hand—make Elijah and raven large, show flock of ravens flying toward Elijah, show some trees in background—copy to be—Elijah's Manna is made from selected maize, or Indian Corn, softened, rolled thin, treated with Maltose sugar, and carefully cooked, ready for instant service with milk or cream and sugar." When the matter had finally been resolved and the tumult and shouting had died, *Post Toasties* emerged, but C. W. never once laid the blame for the ill-advised ad on any of the staff; he accepted the verdict and realized the error in judgment. If some of the ad copy sounds ridiculous today, there is no reason to assume that advertising has surpassed the infantile stage—not when one considers the present-day singing-commercials.

The plant submitted a layout to Post for a new three-grain cereal planned for the market, with obvious difficulty in naming the proposed product. Apparently the advertising department felt the need to flatter him by naming the new item for one of his hobbies, the Double U Ranch in Garza County, Texas. C. W. promptly sent a brief note and a few sketches off to the plant, to the point and clearly defined:

"The question of naming the new food seems to have caused more difficulty and exhaustion of grey matter than would have supplied fetching names for all the babies in a country. Double U would kill it with the fat folk as sure as 'Trinity' would with the sky pilots and their passengers. Don't like 'Porre' either, sounds like 'sorry'—try Porre-Jero, or use Tri-Pod in favor of the three ingredients (wheat, rice, corn)."

Among the many fields of advertising used by the company, C. W. had a special affinity for Elbert Hubbard and the Roycrofters of East Aurora, New York. [Elbert Hubbard, Editor of *The Philistine;* author of *A Message To Garcia*] Post was the author of a long, analytical article on Hubbard, whom he had known in the early days of *La Vita Inn,* where Hubbard had once been a guest. One Roycrofters' series was known as *Little Journeys—To Homes of Reformers.* The first inside page was bought by Post for advertising *Grape-Nuts,* and it seems likely this ad could have been the beginning of the "endorsement of champions." In 1902 Elbert Hubbard's son, Sanford Hubbard, age 15 years, posed for a *Grape-Nuts* ad: "Diet principally *Grape-Nuts,* Never ill a day." A 1907 copy of *Little Journeys* includes another of the "champion" endorsements: "While I was training for a track team, my daily jogs became a task until I was put on *Grape-Nuts* twice a day. *Grape-Nuts* gave me my ginger—There's A Reason." Post's article on Hubbard appeared in *Human Life* for March 1910 and reflects a devotion to the principles of the Roycrofters, with this final characterization of Hubbard: "Elbert Hubbard is holding the candle close to the page where tired humanity may read words of peace, and the light shows both ways." Post frequently stopped at the *Roycroft Inn,* drinking in what he called "the rich mental cream which rose from the Fra's mental milk pail."

There is no question but that Post pioneered present day advertising and was the originator of the championship endorsements, testimonials, and the prize-contest idea. *New York Magazine of Mysteries,* November 1904, ran an early cash prize contest for Postum:

"More boxes of gold and many greenbacks—325 boxes of gold and greenbacks will be sent to persons who write the most interesting and truthful letters on the following topics:

1. How have you been affected by coffee drinking, and by changing from coffee to Postum? 2. Give name and account of one or more coffee drinkers who have been hurt by it and who have been induced to quit and use Postum."

The great Albert Lasker admits that in his early advertising days he was strongly influenced by Post's advertising copy.[1] Lasker referred to Post as a "hypnotic advertiser." The tremendous success of Post and the *Postum* products is a study in marketing that well needs extensive scrutiny. He was an innovator in every sense of the word. *Printer's Ink* for May 31, 1905, gave a partial answer to the sudden rise of Charlie Post and his products:

[1] "The Personal Reminiscences of Albert Lasker," *American Heritage* (1954).

"Everywhere among manufacturers today there is a widespread interest in advertising to reach the consumer. This could not have been said *a year ago*. Then the manufacturing world had an indifference to advertising, if it knew anything about it at all, or a profound ignorance of the whole subject.

"But suddenly this manufacturing world has developed an intense, anxious interest in both advertising and the consumer. It is glad to talk plans of advertising and discuss trade-marks with solicitors, where a year ago the latter would have had no hearing."

The little pamphlet for which Post was best known was *The Road to Wellville*, which was copyrighted in 1903. It was an eleven-page booklet, about three by five inches, with a miniature edition made up for inclusion in packages for overseas shipments when foreign markets became a heavy export business. The booklet recommended mild exercise, the necessity for drinking water regularly, proper breathing, and gave outlines for menus. Breakfast, of course, included *Grape-Nuts*, lunch found a spot for *Grape-Nuts*, and with the night meal one could have a salad topped by *Grape-Nuts*. Mental suggestion and the power of positive thinking were thoroughly explained, with admonition to obtain the proper amount of sleep and rest. These were the things which had helped Post to "Wellville" and the principles upon which a business was built, though it is doubtful the father of it all ever got the proper amount of rest.

In 1909, the *Postum Company* issued another booklet which could be obtained by direct mail request to the Company. This was written and edited by R. M. Sterrett, M. D., under the title *Elements of Dietetics and Nutrition*, published and printed within the plant's own facilities, and copyrighted by *Postum Cereal, Ltd.* Post had originally written such material himself, based on his own knowledge after exploring the subjects as deeply as possible without medical training but with a better grasp than was had by the average layman. Most of the material in the doctor's booklet reflected substantially the same information set forth in the very earliest of Post's own words, though the approach by Dr. Sterrett reflected his medical training.

C. W. Post seems to have found the greatest response to the type of advertising which employed the provocative approach—the challenge to the reader—which, for some unexplained reason, did not

Instant Postum *introduced to the market in 1911.*

Willis H. Post
(1854-1930)

Cousin of C. W. Post and member of the firm who evolved Instant Postum.

irritate nor alienate the consumer—who was either amused or arrested in his purchasing power. One of the early ads (1904) for *Postum* placed in newspapers throughout the country had captions in three separate paragraphs with bold, black letters of CRIME—TRIAL—VERDICT: "A CRIME—to put a drug in your stomach—a TRIAL—10 days is all you need in coffee's place—the VERDICT is always in favor of *Postum* —put aside the drug drink, the reward is big—There's A Reason." This particular ad brought forth paid advertising from coffee importers, who employed hot words and a direct challenge to "prove." The war between the two factions raged on for many years, advertising reaped a harvest, *Postum* reaped great profits, coffee business increased, and the public looked forward to the next round of challenges and answers.

Grape-Nuts, being the outstanding leader at the time, seems to have warranted the greatest amount of attention and advertising expense. There was a constant changing and improving in ad copy, always with attention focused on a challenge or a reason. One ad showed a large fish, captioned—"Only a LIVE fish can swim upstream —which are you? *There's A Reason.*" One might ponder the merits of advertising copy half a century ago against ad copy today—there would be little difference in the over-all approach and copy.

The first three *Postum* products continued to jam the grocers' shelves and to roll up startling profits until *Instant Postum* came on the market the latter part of 1911. This product was evolved through the efforts of Willis H. Post, a cousin of the founder, and long-time member of the firm as well as an associate in the old Fort Worth days. No one had dreamed of the potential of the new drink, but startling enough, C. W. shortly wrote to a friend: "This is the most amazing of our products; it is positively a race horse leading three thoroughbreds." The assault ads displayed a picture of the package and explained in simple words: "No cooking or boiling is necessary—just place a spoonful in the cup, pour hot water over it—it is ready to drink." The rush for the new time-saving product jammed the mails at the plant, and housewives seemed to love finding the morning drink all but ready to consume. It is more amazing that the coffee people took many years to popularize their own present instant product, notwithstanding the old G. Washington instant coffee many years ahead of the present brands.

When C. W. died in 1914, *Postum, Grape-Nuts, Post Toasties* and *Instant Postum* were the only products for which *Postum Cereal, Ltd.* was generally known. The fifth prepared food item did not come out until shortly after the death of the founder. *Post Bran Flakes* was in the process of experiments when he died but was not announced to the public for another year. It then took a heavy lead in the field and quickly rose to the top.

There most certainly *WAS* a reason for many things that made this man an international figure and a millionaire in a few short years. There was a reason for everything he did, including his private philanthropies and his beloved Post City project. Post City was closest to his heart and a devoted experiment.

Chapter 11

~

Post City, Texas

COMPARED to other millionaires of his day, C. W. Post's ideas of relaxation took far different directions. True, he travelled widely, acquired excellent objects of art, such as fine marine paintings, Roman curios and the like, maintained several homes and owned a startling automobile. But real pleasure invariably meant an involvement in some project calling for hard physical labor and intense energy. From the early days of the Fort Worth subdivision, which ended with a break in health, the dream remained steadfast that there should be a community of model homes where families could acquire a home on low down payment, easy monthly payments, and where the bread-winner would be placed in juxtaposition to means of livelihood. He had remarked time without number that he did not believe in philanthropies to glorify the donor. The only sane helping hand offered one's fellow man should be the opportunity to help himself, not charity without self-respect, not doles, not libraries and museums, but a chance to earn that which was coveted. The State of Texas with its wide and seemingly endless space, agricultural potential, cattle raising, and the sparse population at the turn of the century, became a colonization dream.

As success grew, C. W. began to think of turning his fortune toward helping his fellow man to help himself. With this dream in mind, sometime during 1905, Post contacted Tom Stevens of Fort Worth, a known authority on ranch lands, with a wide knowledge of the western part of the state, and made him the agent to locate the desired Texas lands. Stevens was to scout the western section, seeking the proper site for the dream community. In the following spring, Stevens advised Post that he had found what seemed to be right for location and availability.

In February of 1906, C. W., with his wife, daughter Marjorie, and son-in-law Ed Close, together with Tom Stevens, made the trip to the western plains to inspect the proposed purchase. The trip was made by rail as far west as fifty miles southwest of Wichita Falls, and from there the balance of the journey was made by hired hacks and springboard wagons, with mule teams and outriders, a long, rough journey. His daughter recalls her first experience with a blue norther on that trip. The overland caravan had a rough enough time, but to encounter a "blue" was near disaster. Somehow they found a two-room roundup shack, which in reality was a corn storage bin, but it saved the day by possessing a stove. They spent the night in the tiny shack and thanked their stars for the pitiful little stove with its greedy appetite for corn cobs. The next day Post insisted on looking up the owner of the shack and reimbursed him for the corn and comfort. A few weeks later, Post made the contract to purchase the famed Curry Comb Ranch and other lands. From the *Houston Chronicle*, February 16, 1906:

"C. W. Post, the Battle Creek multi-millionaire, may turn his energies toward developing the wonders of Texas. He is keeping his own counsel however. In company with his family he left Fort Worth yesterday with Tom Stevens for Colorado City, and from there he will see a ranch several miles northwest of that city. Mr. Post formerly lived in Fort Worth, and he says he would rather spend his spare time there than in any city or place he knows. His father and mother still live there. Should the trade be closed, Mr. Post, who is a strong advocate of printer's ink, will undoubtedly do more advertising of Texas than has yet been done by any other single individual."

The Fort Worth Star (March 9, 1906) covered the return trip as follows:

"C. W. Post returned Thursday from West Texas where he completed negotiations for the purchase of Llano, or Curry Comb Ranch, of 112,000 acres. Mr. Post made no final announcement of his intentions, but it is rumored his son-in-law and daughter will spend part of each year there. J. F. Lofton of this city was secretary of the Curry Comb, and E. T. Ambler of Dallas was the president of the company owning it. It is situated in Garza, Llano and Crosby Counties and is considered one of the finest of West Texas ranches. There are about 8,000 head of cattle on the ranch at the present time, but they were not bought by Mr. Post. He has leased the ranch back to the former owners for the time being."

When the news reached Michigan, *The Kalamazoo Enquirer* (March 15, 1906) covered the story by an interview with Mr. Post, as follows:

"Interview with C. W. Post regarding rumor of purchase of large Texas ranch and his plans for the future—on the matter of the future, he said very little, however confirmed the purchase as follows: 'We spent about six weeks in Texas to give time to inspect several ranch properties. We ran into a bad norther, a rough experience while traveling with our own overland outfit, but the folks were not hurt any by it. While my representatives were inspecting some properties, we went down to Chihuahua, Mexico, and joined Mr. Stillwell, President of the Kansas City, Mexico & Orient Ry. This road from Kansas City to Topolobampo, Mexico, is about 500 (*sic*) miles, the shortest line to the Pacific. I have been interested with Mr. Stillwell and others in building the line which is now in operation in Oklahoma, Texas, and Mexico. We traveled east and west over the road with Mr. Stillwell in his private car. When we returned to Fort Worth, Ed Close and I went out and inspected my agent's report and bought the well-known Curry Comb Ranch of 112,000 acres and another adjoining it of 50,000 acres. It is beautifully covered with grass and a fine herd of cattle and range. There are about 12,000 head of cattle on it now. It is 75 miles from the nearest railway station to the headquarters, but we are going to push the railway through that property. There are some farms on it where corn, cotton, sorghum, and other things are raised. Watermelons get to be over 50 pounds, wild plums grow by the wagon-load, as well as wild grapes. It cost me $600,000, and we expect to spend a few months each year there for the outdoor life. The altitude is about 2,000 feet, and neither very hot in summer, nor cold in winter."

It was evident that Mr. Post was not ready to tell the public of his plans for the model community. Before the year was out, Post had acquired between 225,000 and 250,000 acres of land on the dividing line of the Panhandle and Staked Plains region, where the Cap Rock escarpment falls into the canyon and mesa country, around the headwaters of the Brazos. The acreage encompassed a great part of Garza County, spreading across the Lynn County line. To the Curry Comb Ranch was added the John B. Slaughter ranch of over 47,000 acres. The T. G. Oxshear Ranch, of better than 24,000 acres in Hoxley County, was purchased somewhat later. Other lands in Garza brought the total well over the estimated 225,000 acres. Here was built Post City, which was named the county seat of Garza County in 1907. *Post City, Texas*, by Chas. Dudley Eaves and C. A. Hutchinson,[1] is an excellent account

---

[1] Published by the Texas State Historical Association, Austin, Texas, 1952.

of C. W. Post and the complete story of the colonization of Garza County toward the fulfilment of Post's dream.

By 1907, a seething tent city was set up, activities buzzed forward in every direction, streets were laid out, and street lighting and landscaping set in. Homes were built ranging in price from $1,500 on up to more costly dwellings. The $1,500 homes could be had for a down payment of $30.00 with $15.00 due monthly. The rules laid down were that no man could contract for an indebtedness greater than his indicated ability to pay. No interest was charged, and absolute title passed to the purchaser when final payment was made. The underlying principles were that it would be a model community of individual home owners, self-sustaining, where a man could own a home cheaper than he could pay rent. Every bit of it was for sale below cost, all built and paid for by C. W.; no profit was taken from the venture. A machine shop, stone quarry, hotel, fine school, churches, department store and shops were constructed. No buyer appeared to purchase the department store for some time, hence Post promptly managed it himself until the right man came along. Post helped every man willing to settle there; however, none could be a public charge to the community but had to be industrious and intelligent, showing a willingness to work. Doctors and ministers were induced to settle there, and the first hard rule laid down was that no spirituous liquors would be sold within the community, a ruling not too well received nor obeyed.

On the outskirts of the town, the farming community was platted. Farms were laid out in 160-acre tracts, homes built, outbuildings erected, water piped in, and each was equipped with proper farm implements. The ground was particularly suited to long-staple cotton though it had not been grown in Texas. Kaffir corn, peanuts, Indian corn, and farm vegetables were excellent growers though this was semi-arid country.

When setting up the farm plats, Post had the happy thought that if the farmhouses were placed on the corners of the cross-roads, four neighbors could be adjacent, thus giving them a friendly nearness for neighborly visiting in those days of few telephones and fewer automobiles. This bright idea caused him more trouble than the entire town project. The "friendly" neighbors complained of the dogs biting the children, the chickens got mixed up, and bedlam resulted. In desperation, Post became so exasperated by complaints and constant harangue that he went to the expense of moving each house square to the middle of its tract, neighbor away from neighbor. After that, peace seemed to reign.

In the book *Post City, Texas* (op. cit.), this venture is so completely and well recounted that there is no necessity of including countless and detailed facts here; however, highlights and additional incidents are of interest. By the end of 1907, Post City had passed the tent-town stage, 50 houses were up, the hotel under construction, and a stone store building almost completed. Supplies and materials for this entire project had to be hauled by mule train. Tom Stevens was sent to Kansas City to purchase mules for the train. The mule train had to make the hazardous turns around the Cap Rock area. Supply trains pulled up day after day, unloading equipment, along with canned foods, staples and hard-to-get merchandise; perhaps *Postum* and *Grape-Nuts* were included though not a matter of record. Huge and elaborate barbecues were prepared over open-pit fires in the best Texas style; when the news went out far and wide about the new opportunity, nearly 2,000 people poured in for the first barbecue.

The project was incorporated as the Double U Company and chartered March 23, 1907, with Battle Creek as headquarters under the management of H. C. Hawk. When the story reached the newspapers, Hawk's mail was flooded with applications and inquiries regarding the new low-cost model community. The first year, Post employed a general manager at Post City to supervise construction and all details of the new town; however, one year later he made drastic changes and dispensed with the services of one-man rule. A board of managers was then installed, made up from the most energetic of Post City citizens. It would not be possible for C. W. to remain on the scene; in fact only several trips per year would be likely. He had a small, modest home constructed for himself in the beginning. Somewhat later, a very substantial home was built embodying many comforts and beautiful interiors, and though it was ready for occupancy before his death, he never had the opportunity to live in it.

Water for the town site was one of the grave problems of the venture. There was known to be a sheet of water, held in porous sand formation, under the Great Plains. In line with Post's plans to tap this sheet, an engineer was brought out from the East, who advised Post that drilling for water would possibly result in failure, aside from the fact that it would be tremendously expensive. The plan was abandoned in favor of drilling a well in the break lands. Two hundred feet down, the driller struck salt water, and below that was pure red clay. While the experiment did not produce fresh water for the town, "Pacific Coast Salt Water Bathhouse" was created to make use of the site. Fresh water, which had to be hauled down to the town in wagons, was finally located at the springs under the Cap Rock by W. E. Alexander (the one-year local manager). The springs could not supply the quantity needed, and wells were later drilled on the plains and water piped down into the town, a temporary solution of the water supply problem. The outlying farms and cattle grazing areas suffered greatly for want of rain, which was certainly an uncommon visitor to the Great Plains. Post decided, however, that he could do something about rain.

C. W. had lived in Texas in the 80's when rain-making was in its heyday. Conjurers made trips up and down the dry lands where luckless homesteaders had selected dry parched lands of the Southwest. A great deal of conjecture about the success of rain-making had come to Post's attention in those earlier days. The more he pondered the possibilities, the more likely seemed the tales of rain resulting after great battles, such as Napoleon's battle days, the talk of the Civil War veterans and their stories of heavy rainfall following intense cannonading. Experiments had been made with some success, but whether by scientific device or nature's peculiar tricks remained unknown. Post remained convinced that it could be done. The first preliminary experiment at Post City came in 1910, and the following is quoted from Post's letter to the board of managers of the town:

"I want to have you at once and without further delay perfect a suitable kite to carry up the two pounds of dynamite I want to use. Get this kite perfected and make fifteen or twenty of them and order 150 pieces of dynamite containing two pounds each with five-minute fuses. Get all of this matter necessary with cords, etc., ready for me to make some experiments when I get there in May."

The experiments were made in May, but Post found them entirely too dangerous for the community with the method used, and there had been no success with rain. No further efforts were made in 1910, and early in 1911 improved operations reported no rain. To this he replied that the methods used by the men were not in accordance with his instructions. Throughout the summer of 1911, various trial methods were used but netted no rain. More elaborate plans and a complete change in ideas extended into 1912.[2] Finally, newspapers all over the country reported that C. W. Post seemed able to control the very elements of heaven—heavy rain fell on Post City at a time when no rain was reported elsewhere in the general area. Out of 22 of the dynamite battles, rain fell eight times, and it was still in experimentation at his death in 1914, but the project was called off thereafter. It was a tremendously expensive proposition.

The outskirts of the town comprised the 160-acre farm tracts. The sites did not sell as readily as was hoped. There was extreme pessimism among farmers as to the potential of the growing season owing to the lack of moisture. Post, in his customary way of personally tackling problems which defeated others, set out with experiments to find the likely profitable crops. By 1908 an extensive experimental station was set out on a number of the farm sites which had not been sold. Grain sorghum (not sweet or corn sorghum) had proved highly successful on the dry western plains of Kansas. Post decided this could be the answer as an admirable drought resistant grain. The experiments proved highly successful and a life-saving crop. Vegetables, with the exception of potatoes, did extremely well, watermelons were prize winners for size and taste. Fruit trees had been a hobby of Post's at the Battle Creek Post Addition, but the hazards of damage to fruit trees by jack rabbits, drought, sandstorms and high winds of the Texas plains, were limitless. This difficulty was met head on by construction of rabbit-proof fences encircling the orchards, with chicken wire around each tree. Swamp cypress trees were planted on the north and west side of each farm orchard, in order to take care of the sandstorm dangers. Water? Well, one could always haul it in wagons and water each tree—and it was done. Eventually these

[2] *Harper's Weekly*, Feb. 24, 1912, "Rain-Making" by C. W. Post.

experiments proved to the doubting Thomases that obstacles and hardships could be overcome with a little brain and brawn plus obstinate pioneer courage.

Tree planting was as important within the town limits as fruit trees for farmers. Shade trees on the wide streets of the barren, shadeless areas, were set out in the very beginning. A wide variety was selected from areas where similar conditions existed; catalpas, black locusts, chinaberry, and Carolina poplars were imported in seedling stage. One hundred thousand imported seedlings were set out in the experimental stations. Trees had been planted approximately thirty feet apart on many of the town's streets in 1907. By 1909 almost every street was tree-lined, with other trees started on the roads leading out of town.

Everything needed to be done to make the town a thriving community was done by the pull on Post's purse strings. A laundry was set up in the town, and a telephone company, which was sold to Southwestern Bell in 1919, was put into operation. Primarily, C. W. felt that cotton would one day be *King* in West Texas, and it was toward that goal that he worked enthusiastically. The Postex Cotton Mill was planned in 1911, under H. W. Fairbanks, and opened for operation in May 1913, for the manufacture of sheets and pillow cases. *Garza* and *Postex* were the trade names made widely known by the mill; at one time the production of sheets and pillow cases reached 23,500 per week, not an inconsiderable amount in view of the area and era concerned. The mill remained in the hands of Post heirs until 1943, when it was sold. It accomplished what Post wished, it gave employment and payroll to the community. Lubbock was little more than a name when this cotton kingdom was planned, but before Postex Mill was ready for operation, the railroad had reached the town of Lubbock; today it has become a cotton center, leaving Post City far behind the goal.

Post kept his promise to the community and to himself that the railroad would soon reach Post City. By early 1908, the Roscoe & Northwestern had reached Snyder, Texas, and by 1909 was completed into Fluvanna, but by then the Santa Fe had completed its line into Lubbock, approximately 50 miles northwest of Post City. At once a good, passable road was hewn out of the Cap Rock area for easier access from Post City into Lubbock. The first passenger train reached Post City on January 15, 1911, by backing down into the town from Lubbock. (*Post City, op. cit.*) C. W. had enjoyed a close and intimate friendship with the president of the Santa Fe, and letters from Carroll Post indicate that this friendship had a great deal to do with bringing the tracks into Post City.

An early experiment in socialized medicine was instituted in Post City about 1910 when Dr. A. R. Ponton, late of the Sante Fe Railroad, came to town. Ponton made a canvass of the residents to see how they felt about paying a fee per month into a fund which would insure medical care when needed. The idea met general approval. Post was highly in favor of the plan and assisted the doctor by suitably equipping a two-story building to be used as a clinic, or sanitarium, which was ready to be used for surgical operations in the spring of 1913.

The community was thriving by 1909 when a strong petition was made to Post to create banking facilities for the town. By May the bank was organized as First National Bank of Post City. H. B. Herd was made President; his son, John Herd, was teller; W. O. Stevens, half-brother of Tom Stevens, was named assistant cashier. C. W. held $26,000 in capital stock of the $50,000 issue.

The ups and downs of operating a community, the constant headaches of keeping everything on an even keel was a wearing and tiring ordeal for one man. More than anything else, C. W. wished the community to stand on its own feet and not to lean too heavily on one man. Financial help was poured into the venture and the more he helped, the more the people expected help. The manager of the hotel proved completely inadequate in his operations; he was constantly at odds with the commercial travelers coming to the hotel and this resulted in the venture being a money loser. When Post learned that the wife of the hotel manager had put up her diamond ring as security for her husband's debts, he ordered the ring immediately returned to the woman, and in addition sent funds for her use.

The pace had begun to slow somewhat in Post City when C. W. started unloading the farms as rapidly as possible at extremely attractive rates. He withdrew to his Santa Barbara home, feeling once again exhausted and in distress of pain. The unloading of the acreage continued for a number of years after his death, and by 1917, 612 farms had been sold. The community remained in the hands of the Post heirs for a few more years. Marjorie Post came to the rescue of the distressed farmers in 1919 after a long drought had pushed them to the wall. Her loans to the drought-ridden farmers totaled many thousands of dollars during those trying times, but they resulted in saving the economy of the area.

Post had a strong feeling about the possibilities of oil under the Great Plains region. When the Gulf Refinery was built at Fort Worth, a pipeline was constructed from there to Saltillo, Texas (near Sulphur Springs, Oklahoma), to connect with the pipeline there, in order to pipe oil *into* Texas from the Oklahoma field.[3] Post then brought a geologist out from the East to ascertain the possibilities of a great pool lying under the western plains of Texas. The geologist confirmed Post's suspicions, but illness prevented further pursuit of the matter; however, C. W. gave stern advice to his family that one day a good oil producing area would lie nearby. Today, Standolind Refinery is located on property originally belonging to Post, roughly two miles west of Levelland. Within the Lubbock trading area, approximately 30,000 producing wells, gasoline plants, carbon black plants, and refineries stand within sight of Post's original property.

C. W. Post's era and fortune developed after the days of the railroad barons and before the advent of the automobile magnates. He emerged between the two as a great captain of industry. Had he lived, there seems little doubt that Texas oil would have been on the agenda as another project worthy of his endless imagination and energy.

[3] *Fort Worth Record*, Feb. 25, 1911.

Chapter 12

~

Front-Page News

RETIREMENT never came to C. W. Post though the attempt was made as early as 1900 and up through 1905, at which time Post City activities began to absorb much of his time and energy. It would have been impossible to withdraw from a scene where every labor, political, merchandising and manufacturing problem called for comments or active participation. It mattered not whether comments were made upon any issue, he was front-page news. The private family automobile caused more news coverage (however distorted) than perhaps a national incident might have caused.

Post purchased a car seen on display in one of the automobile shows of 1908, When the first long tour was taken with his wife and Mr. and Mrs. H. B. Herd, newsmen throughout the country were alerted to "cover it" and wire back a description of this "palatial touring car." Obviously no two reporters arrived at the same conclusions or descriptions. Several papers carried headlines with varying ideas of what the car did contain; some called it a veritable Pullman car with hidden beds, costing $25,000. Fortunately, the original bill remains in the private files. There is no doubt that it would have caused comment in the year 1908, but specifications do not indicate all that was accredited to it. The car was a Pierce Arrow, "66 H.P., 12 feet between wheels, heavy leather upholstery, 2 trunks on top, 4 trunks on the rear, hot and cold water in the tonneau, compartment for food storage and service hampers, a 'convenience' in the tonneau, telephone connection, whole thing to be painted old coach yellow and black, total cost $8,250." For the era, a telephone connection alone would have caused considerable gawking of the populace, and the "convenience" brought forth many snide remarks, hence there is no doubt that it was news. At that date the American highways of hard surface were few and far between, most roads were gravel at best, and most assuredly there was little to be had in the way of conveniences between towns. The overland tourist went prepared for any emergency, with equipment to include pick and shovel, tow chains and extra gasoline, fully prepared to pay the local farmer to bring the horse and pull the car out of deep mire. Oldtimers can tell stories of many holes purposely dug by the local farmer, since a tow fee was not picked up every day—the horse was still the master of the road in 1908.

Testimonial dinners to Post were given from the Eastern Seaboard to the far West. Banquets were so frequent on the agenda that one wonders how he survived the fare. When he arose to make acknowledgment to the gatherings, every word was taken down by the press and full coverage appeared in newspapers at once. Other speakers at such functions were lost to posterity while C. W.'s words were quoted throughout the country. One clipping in the scrapbooks covering a banquet brings to mind a very colorful political figure, perhaps still remembered by the oldsters as "Uncle Joe Cannon." Post's opening remarks, as quoted in the *Adcrafter* (1911), referred slyly to the sumptuous repast before him, as follows:

"This reminds me of a little session I had with Uncle Joe Cannon in Washington last week. Uncle Joe had a friend from Danville district come down to Washington to see him. The fellow was an old-fashioned farmer, and Uncle Joe put him up at the Raleigh where he lived. Uncle Joe is a sucker for sweet corn, as am I. The old farmer watched Uncle Joe gnaw away after six or seven ears of corn, stacking the cobs up on the side plate. Finally the old farmer looked at him and said: 'Joe, what do you pay for board at this tavern?' Uncle Joe said: 'I pay six dollars a day, Uncle Billy.' The old farmer thought on it a moment, then exploded: 'Good God, Joe, don't you reckon you could get a better rate down at the livery stable?' So—I suppose I better talk plenty to pay for this repast tonight."

Post's name was frequently bantered about as a possible Presidential candidate, a position to which he in no way aspired, and on one occasion avoided a gathering likely to have inspired a push to place his name in nomination. News coverage shows that campaign buttons did appear at the Chicago Convention of 1912, with his name and picture thereon, but these were quickly withdrawn when Post learned of the possible draft. An article published in the *Battle Creek Enquirer* (Jan. 21, 1912) covers one phase of this movement:

"Mr. Post was invited to attend the Jackson Day banquet by Norman E. Mack, Chairman of the Democratic National Committee. Mr. Post's attendance caused much comment in political circles in Washington. As a matter of fact, his acceptance of the seat of honor at the speaker's table was with the understanding that he might do so only as a casual observer. Woodrow Wilson was the principal speaker, along with Senator Robert Taylor of Tennessee. Senator O'Gorman of New York was toastmaster."

Additional substantiation of this movement is found in a news clipping dated June 12, 1912, from the *Marshall* (Michigan) *News*, as follows:

"Friends of C. W. Post of Battle Creek, circulating 'Dark Horse' buttons in Chicago! Some of Post's ardent admirers have been circulating his photograph buttons among the delegates at Chicago the past week bearing the slogan 'There's A Reason' and labeled 'A Winner' with the idea of starting a boom for him as the 'Business Man's Dark Horse.' Mr. Post treats the matter lightly and comments that he has NO political aspirations.

The reason for the sudden spurt was outlined in the *Battle Creek Enquirer*, June 16, 1912:

". . . the delegates who launched the boom insist it was based upon a serious need of the present time for a capable and forceful business man to head governmental affairs. It was found that the expression reflected a very general sentiment among the delegation who have wearied of the noise and factionalism, and are representing the desires of the folks at home for something more substantial in politics. With Taft and Roosevelt at each other's throats and with the party hobbled and tied by the fear of a deadlock, it is a ripe time to spring a compromise 'dark horse.' Inasmuch as the country hasn't had a business administration in a long time, it's about time we had a President who would know how to organize the government departments on a practical basis, who has no fear of any political entanglements and who would run the government strictly for and in the interest of the people themselves."

The history-making convention of 1912 needs no comments here, and to the most casual observer the ultimate outcome is known. It remains, however, a very great compliment to Post that his name came up. His interest in national politics had long been intense. Beginning with the great "third term" controversy in 1907, his comments and opinions were sought by political figures as well as political writers. The *New York Herald*, March 3, 1907, devoted a full-page story to "Shall President Roosevelt Be Re-Elected?" Prominent politicians and businessmen were quoted for pro and con opinions. Post's comments were included with those of leading men of the time, such as Governor John S. Wise of Virginia, Representative Warren Kiefer of Ohio, Senator Stephen Elkins of West Virginia, John Wanamaker, Henry Watterson, Thomas Patterson, and a great many other eminent men. C. W. was quoted as follows:

"I am a strong advocate of continuing a capable Executive in the Presidential office so long as he may live or can be induced to serve. In successful commercial operations we do not shelve first-class executives because we think it would be pleasant for some of our friends to see how it feels to occupy the chair. . . ."

One very touching tribute was paid to C. W. Post through a poem dedicated to him by Edgar A. Guest, a popular poet, on the opening of Post Tavern Annex in October 1913. At that time, Guest was with the *Detroit Free Press* and a special speaker at the banquet; on that occasion the humorist read his poem to the assemblage. Newspapers considered the tribute to be news-worthy and quoted it in its entirety:

"Some envy you your millions, some envy you your fame,
Some envy you the building great on which is carved your name;
Some envy you your luxuries and some your great success,
And some the force for doing things which you today possess.
But I—I saw a young man gaze at you as you passed by
And O, I envy you that look that lit that youthful eye.
I do not envy you your chance to give in large amounts
When all is done it's not the size of the gift that counts;
I do not envy you because you own this building fine,
I might not be a better man today if this were mine,
But did a young man look at me in such a grateful way
As I have seen one look at you, I'd be happier today.
I do not envy you your wealth, I might gain that and more
And still not have one single friend come smiling at my door.
A man might climb the topmost heights of fame and stand apart
The cleverest one of all the age—and be a cad at heart.
I envy no man's skill, but, O, I'll say to you tonight
I envy you the grateful look that made that boy's eyes light.

I envy you his smiling face, his kindly thoughts of you.
I envy you the splendid deeds that some day he will do;
For in his eyes, I read of you, not sordid gifts of gold
For which, so oft, the taker finds his manhood he has sold,
But kindness in a larger sense, above all place and pelf,
I envy you the chance you gave that youth to help himself.
I have no wish to leave behind great monuments of stone,
I'd rather leave my finger prints on living flesh and bone.
I'd rather leave behind one, who when I've gone, shall say:
'He helped me up to better things, he smoothed my troubled way.'
If only one speak this of me, I shall not fear to die
And so tonight I envy you that look as you passed by."

All such tributes and acclaim were received by Post with very great humility. No recognition, however lavish, changed the man one iota. He remained humble, quiet spoken, and withdrawn in personal demeanor. For all the firebrands issued from his mighty pen there was nothing personal intended. He was the hard, exacting taskmaster of the business to be done. Bitter words were never directed to individuals, they were used to defend the principles and causes he believed in, reflecting absolute courage in the matter of his convictions. Because he did not become personal in his quarrels, he could make and keep warm friends, and frequently the enemy came over to his camp. The warmth and kindness of his personality on direct contact invariably surprised those who had heard about him; not until a personal meeting would they realize the greatness of the man.

Honors, tributes, accolades and success fell as a mantle lightly worn upon the shoulders of a great Christian spirit. Life was intense within the body of this quiet, soft-spoken gentleman in whom the fire of accomplishment burned brightly and intensely hot for fifty-nine years. But, as fires react, the heat diminishes, the flame dies down, the embers soon become simple cold ashes when the bellows of ambition are not supplied. The tired mind and body of C. W. were beginning to weary of pumping draft upon the coals, of feeding fuel onto the flame. The old ills were once again plaguing him; so much had been done, so much accomplished, that no new causes seemed worthwhile challenges to his depleted nerves and energy. Toward the end of 1913, the time had come to withdraw from the scene.

Judge

GRANT E. HAMILTON

A Merry Christmas to Judge's Friends and All Their Hobbies (C. W. Post encircled).

C. W. Post.

Chapter 13

~

The Mansion *Was Ready*

THE FIFTY-NINE years and seven months of C. W. Post's earth tenure covered a period in American history which encompassed the maximum of startling events for a like period of time. Those years would compare favorably with developments in the second half of the 20th Century. Discoveries in electronics and nuclear physics in our time are no more amazing to the populace than many developments in Post's era; many of the present wonders were made possible by inventions and ideas projected in his lifetime. There was no shortage of wars and rumors of wars from 1854 to 1914. The conflicts of that era alone took more American lives than all wars since that time. In actual cost of American lives on the battlefield, the Civil War, Indian Wars, massacres, Spanish American War and Mexican border disturbances totaled more fatalities than World Wars I and II and the Korean War. It was the great era in every field concerned with the emergence of the United States as a world power.

As a lad, Charlie Post stood on the streets of Springfield and watched the return of Civil War veterans. He saw his father act as a member of the honor guard to bury the Great Emancipator. The golden spike, linking the first transcontinental railroad, was driven when Charlie was 14, and he was just five years of age when Drake drilled the first oil well in Pennsylvania. Edison's phonograph and incandescent lamp were forerunners of singular significance. The Wizard of Menlo Park excited the populace again in 1893 with the Kinetoscope (the beginning of moving pictures). The Curies made announcement of their discovery of radium in 1898. The Wright brothers got their flying machine off the ground while Henry Ford was endeavoring to

Charles Rollin Post
(1826-1919)

Caroline (Lathrop) Post
(1824-1914)

take the world off its feet. The tunnel under the East River in New York, 1908, was an engineering feat of great significance. The first ship-to-shore wireless, the Panama Canal Act, Alexander Graham Bell's inventions, discoveries of the North and South Poles, the dedications of the Bartholdi Statue of Liberty, and Washington Monument, were events well remembered by C. W. These were not insignificant accomplishments when we recall the ultimate outgrowth of some of the discoveries. America was looming large as an economic power.

Many of the distressing railroad riots, mob control of Pittsburgh by coal strikers in 1877, the great labor disturbances in England in 1890, and the Haymarket riot, taught Post many answers to labor's demands, a problem attendant on the country's growing pains, its transition from an agrarian to an industrial power. He was almost the first, if not actually the first, to pay top wages to labor with social benefits thrown in. He stood tall in the middle of a great era. Those were the days of "moving forward" in America, the era that founded the great fortunes which have established the economic possibilities for the new frontiers. Just one month after Charlie Post's death an Archduke would be shot in a town whose name most Americans could not even pronounce, an incident that would involve America in a "War to end Wars." A new phase would begin in America, change the mode of living, step-up the immense industrial potential and evolve a whole new pattern. A great era and a great man would end their cycles almost simultaneously.

The first indication that C. W. Post was not in robust health came in the late fall of 1913 when he seemed to show signs of strain and depression. In December, he was prepared to deliver a strong speech against President Woodrow Wilson and the new Income Tax Law at a banquet to be held at the Bellevue-Stratford Hotel in Philadelphia. Word arrived at the last minute that Post had been taken ill in New York and that the speech would be read by Charles W. Dunn, a New York lawyer. Post's speech, as read by Dunn, set forth violent opposition to the President and the constitutionality of the tax law, and made the announcement that he had hired ex-Senator Joe Bailey to test the law. The banquet drew newspaper attention through a general run of ill omens and misfortune. Another speaker died en route to the meeting, one Arthur N. Wilson, president of the New England Wholesale Grocers. In general, Post's speech was one of the very few ever given where his viewpoint and prognostications were utter gloom for the future. The announcement of his illness in New York was the first news the public was given that his health was of concern. Nothing further was mentioned on the subject until January when the Chicago newspapers put headlines on page one that C. W. Post had broken down from overwork and mental strain, and that he had gone to his winter home in Santa Barbara for an indefinite stay.

From January to March, C. W.'s days at Santa Barbara alternated between the old zip and drive and moods deeply immersed in pain and despair. Finally, in March, newspapers all over the country ran banners across page one, "Michigan Millionaire Races With Death Across the West." This was called a $5,000 train ride in a private car, non-stop from Santa Barbara to Rochester, Minnesota, where the Mayo Brothers would operate for appendicitis. Mrs. Post, the family physician Dr. J. C. Bainbridge, a nurse and chauffeur accompanied him. The private car of the president of the Santa Fe was attached to the Santa Fe at Los Angeles, a pilot car was sent ahead to side-track through-trains onto spurs in order to speed the special train on its journey. It resulted in the fastest crossing ever made up to that time. This was not something for which the family had asked, but an accommodation offered out of utmost regard and affection for a prominent man. C. W.'s daughter, Marjorie, dashed from Palm Beach in her light summer clothes to a cold and snowy Rochester. His parents were living at Fort Worth, and due to the frailties of Carrie Post they could not make the trip to be with him. However, daily messages were sent to them by their granddaughter and Carroll Post.

The extant diary of Carrie Post shows a day-by-day account of the news of the operation and the progress of her son. On March 10, 1914, she entered: "Telegram today, C. W. operated for appendicitis, thank dear God for success." A few days later she recorded: "Carroll and Willis are now with C. W.—good telegram from Carroll, C. W. sitting up and eating." And by April 15th, the little diary shows: "C. W. and Lelia gone to Santa Barbara, recuperation excellent." For the balance of April and the first week in May at Santa Barbara, recuperation progressed well enough, with days alternating between excellent spirits or utter depression of spirit and will power, and with some return of pain. The family and nurses kept close attendance upon C. W. to bolster his spirits. Then an entry in Carrie's diary, in a faltering and shaky hand, is recorded on May 9, 1914: "Telegram of our dear son's sudden passing away, we leave him with his Maker, he is safe, dear blessed boy."

While the entry in Carrie's diary is simple and in accordance with her religious ordinances, the national news coverage was far from a quiet announcement of the death of Charles William Post. There was an effect of stunned disbelief among the many friends and business associates. Most of the larger newspapers in the country placed the news on the front page, in bold, black headlines with mourning-border around his pictures. The body lay in state aboard the private car, the *Lecompton,* which was attached to the Santa Fe once more for the trip back to Battle Creek. The train was met at Albuquerque by Carroll Post and H. C. Hawk, among others, who had immediately left Battle Creek to accompany Mrs. Post and party on the final journey. Marjorie and Ed Close immediately left their Connecticut home for the last rites.

Seldom has the death of any private citizen had such impact upon the general public, nor more glowing tribute, both in unanimity of expression and the depth of sentiment expressed. Battle Creek came to a standstill in all its industry to pay tribute to the man to whom the town owed so much. The façades of the buildings were draped in black crape when the entourage arrived, but it was removed on request of the family. The day of the funeral found the streets stilled of all traffic, lined by thousands who came to pay their respects. News pictures of the funeral procession show lines of people on the sidewalks and curbstones wiping tears from their eyes, quite reminiscent of such pictures published on the death of Franklin Roosevelt, though Post was a private citizen rather than a world figure. Long before the church doors opened at 3:30, the crowds gathered on its lawn and formed lines down the streets. Many of the people had been waiting since early morning in order to be assured of admission. The services were conducted by Reverend T. A. Mills, assisted by Reverend Roswell

C. Post, a cousin, and were held at the Independent Congregational
Church. On either side of the church walk, 1,000 *Postum* employees
formed a guard of honor. The procession from the church to the cemetery was a solemn march and included all employees of the *Postum
Company*, together with honor guard, *Postum* cabinet and manufacturing representatives from throughout the country at large. This was
the day of community tribute to one whose genius had wrought great
transformations in their lives.

Simultaneously, memorial services were held at Fort Worth and
Post City in tribute to the man whose hand and heart had likewise
touched their communities. Reverend Roswell Post epitomized the
humanitarian in his sermon that day when he said: "Charlie Post, we
love you, because you first loved us." Carrie Post expressed her mother
love and deep abiding faith with the little verse she penned upon her
son's death:

> Dead! do they think and say?
> Thy mother's love says—nay!
> Through eyes beholden, that I can not see
> I feel thine arms encircle me,
> O'er the strange mystic Border Land
> There seems outstretched an Angel hand;
> And when thy spirit free had flown
> There came soft whispers, all thine own—
> 'God is my life, I am not dead,
> The *Mansion* is ready.'
> —*Caroline Lathrop Post*

The private family files contain several thousand telegrams, letters,
poems and tributes which came from throughout America and abroad.
Organizations in which Post had an active interest passed resolutions
of respect and memorials to him. It was indeed a vast and singular
tribute to a well-beloved man. This was the man who had come to
Battle Creek, ill and despondent, just twenty-three years previously,
who, in a short span of years, created a vast industry, taught the public
new eating habits, and startled his contemporaries with many innova-
tions and by building a fortune and a cereal empire in less than five
years. This was the final tribute to the one who belongs to that band
of men whose iron will enables them to face every obstacle, overcome

every discouragement, survive every hardship, but never lose faith in the future generations, the greatness of a city or country, or faith in themselves. C. W. Post left behind him many monuments in the hearts of men, and to the future he left a daughter carved in his own image who would carry on in benevolence and love of humanity. A twenty-seven-year-old young woman was to inherit a fortune and to become the owner of a thriving business and, unlike many such beneficiaries, she was to increase and expand her inheritance and to do good with it. No story about C. W. Post would be complete without a searching look into the life of his daughter, Marjorie Merriweather Post.

C. W. Post Mausoleum at Battle Creek

1916

J. Gelert, Sculptor.

C. W. Post Monument in Downtown Battle Creek

1944

Marjorie Merriweather Post

Chapter 14

~

Marjorie Merriweather Post

Choosing a life of involvement, Marjorie Merriweather Post has brought the stimulus of challenge, the warmth of compassion, and the touch of charm to the execution of all her enterprises. Beneficiary of three hundred years of American ancestry, of which she is justifiably proud, she also inherited the talents of her inventor-businessman-humanitarian father. She has given of her time, talents, taste and treasures to multitudes of people in many parts of the world who have benefited by health, beauty and enrichment. Marjorie Post has been the recipient of decorations by five foreign governments, honorary degrees from three American universities and countless citations.

Should this country have the desire to claim a storybook lady bountiful, there would be no need to look beyond the splendid graciousness, personality, and generosity of this delightfully charming woman. Her vast charities and philanthropies alone indicate "giving with a heart." She believes, as did her father, that man needs a helping hand first to help himself; and following Post's belief, she strongly advocates extending a bountiful hand to the youth of America. What she has done for old friends and worthy causes cannot be told since she has long forgotten the magnitude of it and would not permit publication of the facts if they could be learned. Countless people have been helped in unbelievable and touching ways, aside from the publicly known philanthropies. (The career details of Marjorie Post are given under Curriculum Vitae [q.v.].)

Whether one sits before Marjorie Post at the conference table or dinner table, the charm, grace, ability to put one at ease, the sense of humor, all come across to the listener who might well find himself entirely entranced. In the field of adornment, raiment and jewel might be there, but this writer has left her presence more than once without the slightest recollection of, and the complete inability to describe, the superficial. One departs with a picture of beauty through serenity, peace of soul and goodness of heart, topped by a very excellent business mind and sense of humor. The ready wit and total awareness of modern expressions usually greatly surprise the younger generation. As one college lad expressed it, "she sure isn't yesterday—she is tomorrow." Living in the past, or with the past, is one of the things which bores her, she lives for and with tomorrow's world—there has been no stoppage of mental growth. Business executives of all ages have been impressed by her awareness and searching knowledge of almost any type business under discussion. She is *of the earth, earthy.* There is not now, and never has been, a time in her life when, if financial fortunes had deserted her, Marjorie Post could not have emulated her father.

The writer has been asked by those who have not had the privilege of personal contact: "Is she really as lovely as her pictures?" The answer is—"lovelier!" "But," comes the next question, "isn't this due to clothes, access to excellent beauty care, all that money can buy?" "No"—this kind of beauty comes from within, it is not veneer, she would be just as pretty and charming in calico. The delicate features, lovely hair, and bodily structure were born there, and she has learned how to make the most of a good heritage.

The private guest lists of Marjorie Post are comprised of people who are amusing, good company, or of common interests; guests are not invited because it seems socially expedient to entertain them. The most rewarding of the social functions, to her, are the enormous affairs for young people, such as ballet groups, aspiring young musicians, college groups, Boy Scouts, and the like. As a hostess she is particularly happy moving among these young people, watching them enjoy the beautiful home and grounds, the finest of appointments and collections, knowing full well that this is a rare and singular treat for most of them. The ability to present perfect programs of entertainment was born in the early days; it has been nurtured through the years by experiences around the world. There has been a lifetime of orienting, establishing and managing homes as a setting for the required social activities.

If one should assume that charm, social graces, beauty and gayety are the sole attributes of this lovely lady, how fooled he would be. The blood and training of C. W. Post have produced in Marjorie one of the keenest minds of her sex. The work-load stacked up before her each day would founder many a businessman. She has the tasks down to a system whereby she wades in and finishes them off without missing the smallest memo. There are endless decisions to be made covering philanthropies, social calendar, extensive property and business management, each supervised and checked in detail. These are not passive chores, chairmanships and committees, they are active participations. In Post's day, it was said that he could hit the bull's-eye of a bargain with every shot, and he taught his daughter all the trade secrets. When this writer complimented her for the deft handling of complicated business, financial and personal matters, a soft but amused laugh escaped and, with twinkling eyes, she commented: "You should know some of the utterly ridiculous and costly mistakes I have made!" In financial activities, astute and profitable decisions have emanated from this disarmingly feminine woman.

The essentials that Marjorie Post had to learn from earliest childhood were grooming, good manners, the value of a dollar, and that "beauty is as beauty does." The first years at Battle Creek encompassed her early childhood. Those were not easy times for a small child whose mother was in constant attendance upon an ill father. When health returned to C. W. Post, his business activities were rapidly developing into a vast industry and time was a precious element, but he made the time available for all the little things a child expects. The following days of success, sudden fame, and rise in fortune covered the formative years of the little girl. Such a transition could be expected to spoil or turn the head of any youngster, but this was the daugher of a practical, far-seeing man. Though Marjorie was adored and worshipped by her parents, there was no thought of allowing her to mature without a practical approach to life's daily problems. Ella Post guided her daughter's footsteps through the feminine aspects of life, the delicate, dainty facets of a growing girl; nevertheless Dad had his innings with more emphasis on the practical necessities. He taught her all the things usually reserved for boys in a family, though none of the femininity for which she is known was erased.

While attending public school in Battle Creek, Marjorie had to cross a section of the town not especially genteel and to pass the lumberyard of an agricultural implement factory. Lumberyards in those days were fair game for all the rough boys of any community. C. W. was well aware of the conditions, consequently he prepared his daughter for any possible emergency. Marjorie was taught boxing technique, with her father as sparring partner; he felt the exercise was excellent for both of them as well as good defensive knowledge. This training stood her in good stead more than once in her life. The first time a useful occasion arose resulted from one of the boys walking backward in front of Marjorie and her chum, taunting them with ugly remarks. Suddenly the boy found himself flat on the ground and, upon arising, he gave off the 1898 equivalent of "wow!" After that, the girls were permitted to pass the lumberyard without much interference from the toughies. The next time such a drastic measure was necessary Marjorie was Mrs. Edward B. Close. Walking along at the Vanderbilt Cup Races with her brother-in-law she noticed a rough-looking lad approaching with his eyes glued to her purse, the jeweled top of which was protruding from her coat pocket. She did not have time to say one word to her escort before the boy reached to snatch the purse. She let go with the well-taught right to the solar plexus, and doubled up the would-be snatcher to the amazement of her escort. Throughout life Marjorie Post has been able to rely on her own resourcefulness without reverting to feminine guile. Drastic measures have not been necessary since those early days, but she remains physically fit by extensive walking, dancing and, believe it or not, bicycling.

After C. W. had returned to "Wellville," a great deal of time was devoted to Marjorie's training. The family's many trips to Europe had a twofold purpose: while C. W. carefully examined dietary matters, educational tours designed for Marjorie were of utmost importance. Upon one occasion the entire family, including Aunt Mollie, Cousin Willis Post and his family, made a tour of the English countryside by "coach-and-four"—246 miles in a fortnight. The coach-and-four had long been relegated to a by-gone era, but C. W. felt that this would be a special kind of education for his daughter, one of atmosphere and leisure to explore the points of interest. A stop was made at Reading so that they could examine the Roman curios recently excavated from the ancient city of Silchester a few miles away. The next stop was at Silchester itself; here they explored the actual ruins where the excavating was still in progress. The tour continued on through the lovely Marlborough hills, to a view of the Salisbury Cathedral, whose spire was probably the highest in the country at that time. The itinerary included the Counties of Middlesex, Bucks, Berks, Wilts, Somerset and Devon, where all places of interest were carefully examined. This kind of unique planning had been carried out on previous journeys for the benefits to Marjorie's cultural background. There were similar trips to Switzerland and France.

Ella Post was a tiny, erect little figure, with lovely white hair worn high on her head. Marjorie cannot recall her mother with other than white hair, possessed of clear, almost transparent skin, and deep-set, large grey eyes. Mrs. Post's manner was quiet and serious. Her very nice singing voice put her in demand for church choirs, and for little social groups among friends. Her interests lay in world travel, art, literature, and music. She loved to dance and was very adept and graceful. A set pattern of social life in Battle Creek did not interest her very greatly; she preferred to remain quietly in the background while her husband rapidly became an internationally known figure. As her health faltered, Ella Post found that the Battle Creek climate did not help the situation; consequently she traveled to various parts of this country and abroad. Marjorie remained in Battle Creek because it was not always possible for her to leave school for such protracted trips. During these times, Marjorie became quite close to, and devoted to, her beloved Aunt Mollie, the wife of Carroll Post. Mollie Post was humorous, full of grace and extremely hospitable; she loved to entertain with originality and a flourish. Marjorie Post gives full credit to Aunt Mollie for lessons learned in the art of entertaining.

When C. W. Post traveled throughout the country in the early days of *Postum* to examine factories of other manufacturers, Marjorie was frequently taken along. As a result, father and daughter built up an unequaled companionship and understanding. It was thoroughly understood that Marjorie could not make the trips with her father unless school grades were up to par; even so, the schoolbooks were taken along and Dad heard the lessons each day. The only *grave* problem on those trips was the braiding of Marjorie's long hair, one chore that completely defeated her father, but somehow he always managed to find a kind soul who could and would accomplish the trick. The purpose of the trips was to acquaint his daughter with conditions existing in the field of manufacturing and plant management of many kinds of businesses. She recently recalled for this writer:

"I think I saw the manufacturing of every kind of product imaginable in those days, and every kind of machinery and equipment was explained to me by Dad. Some were very interesting, others dull and boring, some establishments were very decent places of manufacturing, but others had far from pleasant working conditions for the laboring man. This always distressed my father who believed so strongly in excellent working conditions. But I loved every minute of the trips with Dad, and I know now that he had a purpose for everything he did— and I am sure I did learn a great deal."

Indeed, C. W. had a firm grasp of what he was doing for his growing daughter; his plans included the eventualities of the far-distant future when she would become the sole owner of his business. One of his prime targets was to have her understand everything associated with the *Postum* products. While still little more than a child, she was called to sit in on business conferences of the cereal company, unobserved but observing all that transpired between her father and the department heads. When the meeting was over, she was expected to relate exactly what took place, the meaning of the conference and plans for the future. After her own conclusions were recited to her father, he methodically explained all steps of the conference and briefed her on the reasons for future plans. In line with this same idea, she was made thoroughly acquainted with the plant machinery, the operations, and the working conditions as well as the workmen. This knowledge paid good dividends when ownership, at age 27, unexpectedly fell upon her.

The little-girl-days were much the same as surround any growing child. On the grounds around *La Vita Inn*, where the family lived until 1901 when they moved to the in-town *Post Tavern,* were moles, rabbits, raccoons, stray cats and dogs. Moleskin coats for dolls were ultra in those days, and Marjorie was taught how to trap moles. She was expected to skin the mole, tack the hide to a shingle, salt it down every day or so, then have the skins dressed when there were enough for a doll coat. This seemed like fun to a little girl, and she learned the technique very well. Just how well she learned it did not dawn on her until one day many years later. After Marjorie married Ed Close, she and her father and husband were on a hunting trip in West Texas, where they killed fair-sized game. With a sly grin, her father teasingly informed her that she should dress-out her own game; she had long ago been taught how. With a grin to match his, she proved she had not forgotten the lesson learned.

The meticulously groomed Mr. Post was just as attentive to details for others as for himself. He could not tolerate carelessness in fit of clothes, nor bad combinations of colors. Copies of old letters from his files show that many of daughter Marjorie's clothes were ordered by C. W. direct from New York and Chicago. In each instance not only were her exact measurements given, but very definite instructions were outlined for quality of fabric, certain color trims, with kind and quality of lace specified. He constantly admonished his daughter about erect carriage, grooming, and personal charm. With her mother a lovely, very gracious lady, and the constant reminders from her father, it should surprise no one that Marjorie Post became known for her grooming over and above style or "au couturière," which to her trained thinking must begin at the top of the head and end with the feet. Appearance of nails, hair, skin and bodily carriage are her first concern; after that the garment well might be something that has suited her fancy for several seasons.

C. W. changed his legal residence to Washington, D. C., about 1902, so that he could be near the center of many of his outside interests in labor and political affairs. His daughter was placed in a fine private school in the District of Columbia. It was about this time that C. W. and Ella found their worlds growing far apart. He had become an international figure with great demands upon his time, a situation not compatible with Ella's quiet, retiring way of life. Her main interest

Marjorie Merriweather Post—Her First Ball Gown

in Washington was to be near Marjorie while she attended school and to act as hostess and chaperon for her. During those Washington school days, the widening breach between C. W. and Ella Post resulted in a divorce. In many ways the divorce made life easier for Ella; freed from the responsibilities of the wife of a prominent executive, she could now live as quietly as her inclinations indicated. Marjorie remained in close contact with both parents, never growing apart or favoring one over the other. Her parents were sensible people, and adjustments were made so that Marjorie would not be too greatly handicapped by the separation. On November 7, 1904, C. W. married Lelia Young, a former secretary in the Battle Creek plant. This was just one year before Marjorie married Edward B. Close.

During her first years in Washington, Marjorie was a beautiful and popular school girl at Mount Vernon Seminary (then located at 1100 M Street). She was in demand for Naval Academy Hops and the normal gay life of late teens. Her mother, who accompanied her to all weekends in Annapolis, found herself popular with the midshipmen when they learned that Ella Post was an excellent dancer. Her "card" was filled by the boys almost as soon as her daughter's program. But history repeats itself. Marjorie found herself in the same position many years later when her own daughters were of an age to attend the dances at West Point. The graceful dancing of Marjorie Post is widely known and discussed today; it is her favorite pastime. Her "round and square" dance invitations are highly prized by the fortunate guests. The dances are unique in that she has devised a plan whereby the most stumble-footed can dance. A crew of professionals is engaged —there are male and female dancing partners for the guests. Anyone who thinks he means to be a wallflower suddenly finds that he not only can dance, but he is having the time of his life. By this unique plan, the excellent dancer is not tied to someone who cannot dance— no wonder guests report they have never had so much fun. As recently as her seventy-fifth year Marjorie Post May danced a beautiful and intricate exhibition tango with a professional partner for a charity benefit performance and was widely acclaimed for her gracefulness. It is easy to imagine that her mother was likewise adept.

On December 5, 1905, Marjorie Merriweather Post married Edward

Marjorie Merriweather Post
(*Mrs. Edward B. Close*)

Ella Letitia (Merriweather) Post—Wedding of Daughter Marjorie, 1905

Bennett Close in New York City at Grace Episcopal Church. Mr. Close was of an old New York family.[1] Marjorie's wedding was not an elaborate one, but the wedding gown was exquisite and the talk of the guests; it has been preserved for future generations. Her mother was beautifully dressed, and pictures of her for that occasion are included herein. When the bride started on her honeymoon, a letter was delivered to her on the train; a letter characteristic of her father. The contents gave notice to her that a very substantial sum of money had been deposited with her securities as a special wedding gift. With the permission of the owner, the letter is quoted here since it gives an insight into C. W. Post's closeness to his daughter:

"Dear Little Sweetheart: Well, the small toddler, who has been over the road so long with Daddy, is now a grown woman and a small toddler no more. It naturally brings a tinge of sadness to realize that the *little* girl of the past, with whom I had so many good times, has faded into the past, but I am more than comforted with the splendid young woman grown from my small pal of years ago. Daddy feels well repaid for every effort he has made for you, my sweet daughter, and now I feel very sure you are going to be happily married, and I find myself liking Ed as I would a boy of my own. Always remember that Daddy is somewhere around on call and that he loves you always, my sweet daughter. Yours, Daddy."

Only those who knew C. W. well and intimately would have attributed such sentiment and expression to the hard-driving businessman of Battle Creek. He was a man capable of very deep and abiding sentiment, while at the same time not tolerant of a dereliction of duty in others. He began separate funds for Marjorie while she was a very small child, and devotedly increased her holdings throughout his life. She was already financially independent when the wedding gift was made.

In addition to the securities, Marjorie's father gave her the deed to The Boulders. C. W. had started this house at Greenwich, Connecticut, for Marjorie when she was sixteen years old. The Boulders lay on a beautiful piece of land, a brook flowed through it and entrance to the grounds was over a bridge, up a winding drive to a porte-cochère. It was a rather ambitious undertaking on the part of Mr. Post to establish such a home for his daughter long before a wedding was antici-

---

[1] The land, upon which Grace Church stood, had been given to the original parish by the great-great-grandfather of Ed Close.

pated. His idea was that, if she was ever to learn, she was old enough at sixteen to select furnishings, supervise and handle a piece of property. The immense house and the landscaping of the extensive grounds had been designed to C. W.'s highest standards. Marjorie had great fun helping with the planning, furnishing and decorating. When she went to The Boulders as a bride, her father assigned her a housekeeper for just six months; after that she was completely on her own to manage the household and grounds. There was a fair-sized staff in the house and a number of hands for the grounds; she had to manage the staff, pay all bills, keep strict accounts and surrender the books to her father at the end of the first year. Her first accounting showed the books to be six cents off—much to her consternation, he made her check for the error until she balanced the accounts. It would have been so simple to supply the six cents.

The Boulders was the birthplace of the two Close girls, and the home of Ed and Marjorie Close until it caught fire in 1917 and was severely damaged. It was sold later that year to the Montesorri system of schools.

C. W. kept a watchful eye upon his daughter and her new responsibilities. Though he in no way interfered with her marital affairs, he continued to admonish her strongly in matters of expenses and finances. A suite of rooms was maintained at The Boulders for his use at any time. But wherever he was, letters flowed back and forth with good fatherly advice or suggestions on phases of private and financial matters. On one occasion he wrote his daughter sharply about "waste," the letter reads as follows: "Do not have the men haul away those extra rocks until you make up your mind where to put them, hauling them around more than once can be an expensive proposition and a complete waste of money." At another time he expressed a definite opinion about Marjorie's attempt to ride her favorite horse side-saddle. This caused him to blow off a little steam, as follows:

". . . fashionable or not, no daughter of mine can ride side-saddle and endanger her neck, there is only one way to ride a horse, and that is astride in the western fashion where you can be in command of your position and your horse, and that is the final word I intend to say on that subject."

The bride's gift from her father

"The Boulders"

Greenwich, Conn.

Ella (Merriweather) Post and Granddaughters

Adelaide Close   *Eleanor Close*

1915

Marjorie Merriweather Post
(*Mrs. Edward B. Close*)

The strong father-daughter devotion is more understandable when one realizes the sensitive nature of C. W. Post. He found it extremely difficult to watch or endure pain in others; though his strength of will was sufficient to overcome most obstacles, he was quite squeamish about the sight of blood. Marjorie's first child, Adelaide Close, was born at The Boulders. Her mother had been with her through much of the pregnancy, but at the last moment Marjorie asked that her father come sit by her bed. During the ordeal, she held so fast to his hand that, unknowingly, her grip caused his heavy gold ring to bury deep into the flesh until blood flowed from his finger. When the birth was over, C. W., who was an absolute teetotaler all his life, walked over to a chest, poured a stiff drink and downed it in a gulp. The thrill of having his first grandchild soon overcame his shakes, but he was quite certain that there need not be any more grandchildren. When a second child, Eleanor Close, was born seventeen months later, Marjorie did not call for her father. The Boulders afforded a heavenly shelter for the Closes and the visiting grandparents and great-grandparents of the two little Close girls. The first sorrow to strike the home was the death of Ella Post in 1912 while visiting friends in Washington, D. C. This was followed two years later by the death of C. W. Post.

Upon the death of C. W., Marjorie Close found herself absolute owner of *Postum Cereal Company*, manufacturers of four cereal items of tremendously popular appeal—*Postum, Grape-Nuts, Post Toasties* and *Instant Postum. Post Bran Flakes* was introduced to the market the year following Mr. Post's death. The business was under the management of the "Cabinet" trained by her father, with Carroll Post and Willis Post actively associated in the Company. Before his death, C. W. had outlined to his daughter several general ideas of expanding the business by merging or buying other existing products on the market. The rumbles of World War I prevented the immediate pursuit of this program. During the balance of 1914, 1915 and 1916, Marjorie and Ed Close commuted from New York to Battle Creek for active participation in the business; for a short time Ed Close was a member of the Company and temporary living quarters were engaged in Battle Creek.

When the United States entered the war, Ed Close enlisted and

By—P. Tartoué

Eleanor Post Close and Adelaide Brevoort Close

served with distinction. Marjorie immediately became active in all phases of war work. She equipped No. 8 Base Hospital at Savenay, France (2,000 beds), which grew to be the largest base hospital in the war. She entered Red Cross work with enthusiasm, rolled bandages, knitted and formed groups to participate wherever she was, whether New York, Palm Beach or elsewhere. With these duties there was the first necessity of being a devoted mother to two growing girls. However, Marjorie found time to join the delegation to Washington in 1917 to meet with Woodrow Wilson in behalf of Women's Suffrage, a cause in which she believed.

In addition to all the other responsibilities and interests, the cereal company needed part of her time for advice and consultation; she knew every piece of machinery and most of the old employees by name. War contingencies presented many problems in the manufacture of the cereal products. The Government had taken over corn flour as a substitute for wheat; this meant that *Postum Company* would have to find many substitutes in order to manufacture its products. All such obstacles were met and surmounted by building a corn mill on the plant grounds and finding proper use of Kaffir corn, Milo maize and other substitutes in order to ride out the war and stay in business. This was done with very satisfactory results.

During the days of residence at The Boulders at Greenwich, and shortly after the death of her father, Marjorie found it necessary to maintain an apartment at 375 Park in New York City for easy commuting to Battle Creek and the New York office of the plant. This soon proved inadequate accommodations, necessitating a larger place so the Closes could have their daughters with them, rather than commuting to Greenwich. Accordingly, the Closes bought the Burden house at 2 East 92nd Street in New York, a very large and fine mansion which they acquired in 1915.

After the war, the marriage of Marjorie and Ed Close did not return to normal, and they were divorced in 1919. One year later she married Edward F. Hutton of the brokerage firm of E. F. Hutton & Company of New York. (His brother, Frank L. Hutton, married Edna [5 & 10] Woolworth, whose daughter is Barbara Hutton.) With a new partner in marriage, Marjorie also had a new and able hand with the *Postum*

Frank Salisbury portrait

Marjorie Merriweather Post
(Mrs. Edward F. Hutton)

Company. Hutton became associated with the Company in that year and by 1923 was Chairman of the Board. Prior to this, Marjorie had installed her friend Colby Chester, Jr., as Assistant Treasurer; he became successively Vice President and, by 1924, President, to succeed Sam Small who had risen from the ranks to President. Chester ultimately became Chairman of the Board, and Chairman of the Executive Committee. He was made Director Emeritus at the same time Marjorie Post May was made Director Emeritus of *General Foods Corporation* (1958).

Marjorie Close was living in the Burden house when she married Ed Hutton, and it was there daughter Nedenia was born to them in December of 1923. Ed and Marjorie Hutton enjoyed world travel combined with an intensely interesting and busy social schedule. They had as their guests, and were guests of, the internationally known figures from many walks of life. For their own enjoyment and that of their guests there was a successive ownership of beautiful yachts, a shooting preserve on the Combahee River in South Carolina, a country place at Roslyn, Long Island, a camp in the Adirondacks, a winter home in Palm Beach, and of course the Burden house on 92nd Street (which ceased to be a house in 1924).

Ed Hutton was wealthy in his own right, a yachting enthusiast, sportsman and popular New Yorker. Activities began to roll along rapidly for Marjorie and Ed in private life as well as in business. These were the "roaring 20's" and developments roared in all phases of American industry as well as private life. It was at this time that *Postum Cereal Company, Limited,* began the merging of various other well-established products.

The first merger with the *Postum Company* was in 1925 by the addition of *Jell-O*, of LeRoy, New York, which had been in the hands of the Woodward family since its creation in 1896. The merger was followed in 1926 by including Inglehart Brothers' *Swan's Down Cake Flour* and *Minute Tapioca*. In 1927 *Walter Baker's Chocolate, Franklin Baker & Company Coconut* products, and *Log Cabin Syrup* were added to the fold.

Walter Baker's Chocolate had been on the American market since Revolutionary War years when Walter Baker built his chocolate mill on the banks of the Neponet River between Dorchester and Milton, Massachusetts, sometime before the war began. There is a romantic tale associated with the familiar picture of the chocolate girl who has always appeared on Baker's chocolate. The story goes that a dashing Austrian prince went one day to a chocolate shop in gay, 18th-Century Vienna. There his eye and fancy were caught by one of the waitresses. He wooed and won her, and as a gift to his bride, commissioned the Swiss artist Liotard to paint her portrait—just as he found her in the chocolate shop. The original *La Belle Chocolatière* hangs in the Dresden Gallery. For many years its facsimile has appeared on the familiar flat, blue package of Walter Baker's product. *Postum* acquired the trade-mark with the merger.

In 1928, Cheek-Neal Company's *Maxwell House Coffee, La France* and *Satina* laundry aids, and *Calumet Baking Powder* were acquired; and in 1929 *Certo Pectin* was added. Several perishables, such as *Hellmann's Mayonnaise,* and canned and bulk oysters, were part of the chain, but these were sold to other companies when *Postum Company* decided to withdraw from the perishables field. *Diamond Crystal Salt* was part of the business for a time, but it, too, was sold. Also, in 1928, the company began the manufacturing of *Sanka* under contract with the European originators of de-caffeinated coffee. This arrangement was continued until *General Foods* took over the assets of Sanka Coffee Company in 1932. The manufacturing of *Atlantic Gelatin* in bulk, for photographic uses, ice creams and varied products, was started in 1930.

When the *Maxwell House Coffee* transactions were in negotiation, for the first time Marjorie Post Hutton had great qualms and reservations—her father had built a fortune and an empire opposing coffee! Fears were assuaged when the merits of a sound business investment were apparent.

Mergers continued until *Postum Cereal Co., Inc.,* took over *Frosted Foods* in July, 1929, and acquired the patents and equipment originated by Clarence Birdseye of Gloucester, Massachusetts. His patents were held under the name of General Foods *Company;* with this merger the result was a new corporation to be known as General Foods *Corporation.*

A side-light to Birdseye products is interesting. About 1925 or 1926,

Marjorie and Ed Hutton were aboard their ship in the harbor of Gloucester, being provisioned for a trip to sea. A frozen goose was brought aboard with the supplies. When the goose was served for dinner that night, Marjorie was so delighted with the tenderness and flavor that she immediately sent to the galley to learn more about it. She was informed that it had been bought in the town from some plant where the owner was convinced that quick-frozen foods were the answer to long preservation of perishables, and that the particular goose served had been frozen for many, many months. Marjorie immediately insisted that she and Ed Hutton investigate the plant, talk to the owner and learn all the facts. She was so entranced with the general idea, she insisted that Hutton explore the possibilities of buying the company. At that time, Birdseye was in extreme financial difficulties, standing on the brink of bankruptcy. Ed Hutton was not then convinced that the whole idea was a very practical one, due to the enormous expense to the retail grocer for installation of proper equipment for maintaining storage of frozen foods, notwithstanding the problems of transportation from processor to retailer. The plant could have been bought at that time for around two million dollars, including the invaluable patents; but the temptation to buy it was dismissed until 1929; by that time, Birdseye was on a strong financial footing and in a position to demand ten times the 1926 price.

In acquiring the above products, the guiding spirits had eyes trained upon well-established, solid, profitable products already popular with the consumer. With the exception of *Frosted Foods,* the public was thoroughly familiar with each product, but frozen foods were slow to catch the housewife's fancy. It was an up-hill pull to convince the public that frozen food was not the old "cold storage."

Amusing stories could be told concerning the advertising of some of the new products. *Maxwell House Coffee's* slogan was "Good To The Last Drop." So many letters poured into the plant asking "What's the matter with the last drop?" that *General Foods* printed a folder quoting Shakespeare and the Bible to prove the inclusion and grammatical correctness of its slogan. With the acquisition of *Maxwell House* the plant introduced a new idea to the market with the "Vita Fresh Packing" slogan, guaranteeing absolutely fresh coffee when the housewife opened the can, a new sales appeal through a vacuum packing process. This proved a highly effective program against Standard Brands' earlier practice of "dating" its *Chase & Sanborn Coffee*. *Maxwell House* was the parent coffee for individual packing slanted toward geographical tastes; Eastern and Midwestern states got a medium blend; the Pacific coast required a milder blend, and the South was furnished a walloping big proportion of Santos coffee—which made it stronger as preferred in the South.

Another peculiar incident in acquiring the new products was the addition of *Jell-O* as the first product outside the original *Postum* line. *Jell-O* grew out of a cereal coffee, an early and unsuccessful rival of *Postum*, called *Grain-O*, concocted in 1896 by Orator Francis Woodward at LeRoy, New York. At the same time, P. B. Wait, also of LeRoy, made a cough balsam and laxative herb tea. Neither Woodward nor Wait made any money out of their products. They combined forces and Wait began to experiment with powdered gelatin, granulated sugar and fruit flavoring. They called it *Jell-O*. The combination tasted fairly good, but Wait's sales tactics were inadequate and the public remained unconvinced. Mr. Wait sold out to Mr. Woodward in 1899, and within the next 26 years Mr. Woodward built *Jell-O* from a local product to a national commodity—with an excellent profit to himself—thus being able to demand a substantial consideration when *Jell-O* was acquired by *Postum Cereal Company*.

Minute Tapioca has been a strong profit item from the beginning; however, amusing incidents have emerged as regards it. The plant has politely rejected some of the very solid and serious suggestions from the public such as: 1) to promote the use of tapioca at weddings instead of rice; 2) to use tapioca in pea-shooters instead of peas; 3) to soak tapioca in fish-oil and sell it for caviar. In spite of all advertising to the contrary, the *Pearl* style tapioca still remains known to the trade in popular slang as "fish-eye dessert."

Mr. Post, in his early days of manufacturing, did not escape consumer suggestions for slogans and ad-copy. There was one received by Mr. Post that long amused him and all who saw the seriously suggested copy. This was a post card, mailed from the tropics, which pictured a native woman dressed in far less than a sarong, the exposure from the waist up showed sadly drooping appendages, and lettered thereunder was: "Grape-Nuts Made A Lady Of Me!" The card was treasured for years until it fell apart from age.

Marjorie and Ed Hutton thoroughly enjoyed all and sundry incidents which came forth from the new business. They spent much time at the plants, but their private lives were of intense social interest and involvements. The management of one residential establishment is enough for most women, but C.W.'s daughter has maintained several beautiful homes. The decor, the furnishings, the decisions about every item placed in each room are carefully thought out by Marjorie. Emphasis is on charm and comfort with exquisite taste manifested throughout. Beauty of individual objects surrounding the guest is the first requirement, and the hostess knows and loves rare and fine antiques. For the comfort of family or guest not one item is overlooked; everything within the house is for ease of movement and convenience. The aides and assistants are numerous and exceptionally well trained— many have been in her employ for years and have served with selfless devotion and loyalty.

Marjorie's collecting of rare objects of art is a long and interesting story in itself. In the beginning of the collecting days, Sir Joseph Duveen (later Lord Duveen) played an important part in laying the foundation of her art education. During World War I, he suggested various courses in art appreciation and tours to be made of fine museums and collections in Europe and America. This guidance resulted in her extraordinary ability to make knowledgeable selections.

The Burden property was sold for the erection of a large apartment building in which was built magnificent quarters for the Huttons. Mollie and Carroll Post owned an adjacent house at #4 East 92nd with a joint garden to #2. Their property was sold at the same time, and an apartment for Aunt Mollie and Uncle Carroll, adjoining the Huttons,' was included in the new building. The fine paneling and mantels were removed from the Burden house and installed in the new apartment for the Huttons. There was a private entrance for the family with a separate elevator and doorman; the elevator whisked the visitor straight to the Hutton quarters. The first floor of this private apartment (actually 14th floor up) was entered from the elevator

Burden House   1915-1924

#2 East 92 Street, New York City

Nedenia Marjorie Hutton

directly into a foyer hall which could be converted for dancing. The Close girls were at an age when space was needed for their debut parties and social activities. The apartment was almost unbelievable in size and accommodation and it included a garden and playroom on the roof for Adelaide and Eleanor.

The first Palm Beach home, called Hogarcito, was located on Gulf View Road connected with the Everglades Golf Course. This house proved entirely inadequate for growing girls who had an endless number of house guests, and for their mother, a very popular and generous hostess. Marjorie Hutton therefore started a quest for a piece of property between the ocean and Lake Worth, which had to be on a coral reef for steel anchorage thereto in defense against hurricanes. Together with Lytle Hull, the agent, she crawled through jungle masses seeking the ground upon which to build the beautiful Mar-A-Lago. Construction had required four years when the house was formally opened on January 1, 1927. This is perhaps one of the loveliest residences to be found in America today; it is doubtful that it could be duplicated in these days for want of the expert handcraftsmanship that went into the building of it. Marjorie Post has recently announced her desire and intention to will Mar-A-Lago to the State of Florida for a scientific and educational research center.

Marion Wyeth, a very well-known architect, was employed to carry out Marjorie's designs and ideas. Joseph Urban, a recognized Viennese architect, was engaged for the interiors, decorative stone motifs and other rare decorations. Urban sent to Vienna for Franz Barwig, the Viennese sculptor, who executed the magnificent stone carvings, truly one of the finest façades, as well as beautiful interiors, in this country. The general design of Mar-A-Lago is an adaptation of Hispano-Moresque, crescent shaped, with an upper and lower cloister along the full length of the concave side of the crescent facing Lake Worth. The interiors are outstanding and unique in the use of extraordinary stone sculpture.

Each suite in this wide, crescent-shaped house is carefully and beautifully appointed. The periods and styles of the rooms are Dutch delft, Adam, Venetian, Portuguese and so on to the owner's Louis XVI suite. The suite set-off for daughter Deenie, then just three years old,

"Mar-A-Lago"

Palm Beach, Florida

To be willed as a Science and Research Center

was done in fairy-tale background. There are two rooms in the tower section which were planned at that time for the visiting beaux of the older girls. The rooms were done in a thoroughly modernistic design, one room on each level as one climbs the winding stair to the tower. The stair well to the tower is circular around a central pole of metal, with a rail of heavy chains; the stairs are open on the risers and a little difficult to navigate. They open onto a terrace at the top of the tower which commands a panorama of the ocean, Lake Worth, and a view into the distance for a number of miles.

The upper cloister of the second level of the house is well equipped with wicker furniture and unbelievable comforts where one can enjoy refreshments or lazy lounging. The Dutch suite off this cloister should be partially described since Mrs. Hutton designed it in honor of her mother, who was particularly devoted to delft. The head and foot of the beds are done in very old delft tiles, as are the mantel and lighting fixtures. This theme has been carried out in the entire suite, including the design of the rug, the linens and appointments, with delft tiled bath and dressing room adjoining.

The ground floor patio of Mar-A-Lago is very unusual in that it is round, paved with startling stones in black, white and yellow in a fascinating design copied from one in the Alhambra. These particular stones were discovered by Marjorie Hutton while walking on the beach at the shooting preserve at Great South Bay on Long Island. The stones are round and worn to a smooth, high polish, indicating countless years of lying on a beach. They were gathered for the Huttons and shipped by the ton-lots down to Palm Beach and laid to form the patio on the inside curve of the crescent-shaped structure, surrounded by the loggia. The plants and flowers are in profusion, mostly in pots for easy removal in case of storms, and for exchanging with others as they come into seasonal bloom. Mar-A-Lago is a dream residence; it gives one the feeling of having stepped into the Arabian Nights. The grounds surrounding this perfect home are thoroughly in keeping with everything else, beautifully landscaped, extending from Ocean Boulevard back to Lake Worth. Posterity will once again be benefited in a very generous and foresighted way by the gift of Mar-A-Lago to the public.

Marjorie Post first acquired an interest in ships and sailing from her

The Sea Cloud

father when he became interested in pitting the *Shamrock* against the *Columbia*. Her marriage to Ed Hutton intensified this enthusiasm—yachting and sailing were his favorite pastime and sport. It began with the *Lady Baltimore*, a beautiful little powerboat which looked like a baby destroyer with two funnels. This was succeeded by a very much larger boat called *Huzzar III*. Then came the schooner *Huzzar IV* of three masts and almost ideal. Soon Marjorie Hutton was laying plans for a fabulous square-rigger; the project required five years for completion. The ship was brought forth in 1931 to maintain the traditions of the sea; built at Kiel, Germany, the barque was one of the largest and most powerful auxiliaries ever in private use. Her sails alone did not carry her; there were four diesel engines aboard. From the comfort and beauty of the furnishings in the shelter deck, through the salons, from state rooms right to the foc'sle head, it was almost inconceivable that any ship could be so perfectly outfitted. The figurehead of carved wood, a golden eagle whose wings extended back along the bow with talons and beak on the forepeak, was awarded a prize for design at Milan. In all, there were six staterooms for guests, each equipped with electric fireplace and every convenience.

The water-tight bulkheads could be operated from the bridge, a feature which no passenger steamer had at that time. There was equipment for showing the latest movies, a barber shop, a complete laundry service, and a fine hospital well equipped with operating table, operating lamps, and all the instruments needed for any doctor to care for family, guest or crew. The galleys were important when one considers that as high as 400 guests could be entertained, and of course always a crew to be fed. She carried every piece of modern equipment known then to the maritime world, including ship-to-shore telephone, radar and Gyro, and on through the necessities. She was christened *Huzzar* (actually the 5th of the *Huzzars*), but upon the divorce of Marjorie and Ed Hutton (1935), she was renamed the *Sea Cloud* since the name *Huzzar* was closely associated with Ed Hutton. Many a visitor to Palm Beach might remember the famous ship lying at anchor in the harbor at Christmas, sails furled, and her riggings strung with Christmas lights. In World War II, the *Sea Cloud* was generously turned over to our Government for the sum of one dollar per year. She lost her rigging when she was converted to a fighting lady. A complete metamorphosis took place. She was returned to her patriotic owner at the War's end, and once again the re-rigging and refurnishing took place. But she sails no more for the owner who built her. She was sold a few years ago, the last of the great Clipper ships.[1]

During the depression years from 1929 through 1935, Marjorie Hutton found many ways to cut-back personal expenditures in order to divert funds to the aid of the depression-ridden people. She maintained food kitchens in the slums of New York (operated by the Salvation Army), where thousands of men, women and children were fed throughout six years of the distress period. She was Vice Chairman of the Emergency Unemployment Relief in addition to her private charities, which amounted to untold sums. She had long collected gems and laces of historic significance to bring to America for future museum display. The gems were stored in a bank vault in order to save insurance premiums; the premiums alone served to feed additional needy people. The yacht was kept in commission during the depression in order to avoid putting additional people out of work. No persons employed in her private enterprises were needlessly discharged because of the national economic conditions. Marjorie Hutton was convinced that normalcy could not return by retrenching and cutting back employment, though her own net income was as drastically reduced as that of any other person caught in the depression. How much of her reserve was spent for public good during those trying times is not known, nor ever will be. In these efforts Marjorie was reminiscent of her father.

After the divorce of the Huttons, Marjorie married the Hon. Joseph E. Davies [*Mission to Moscow*], a prominent Washington attorney and adviser to President Roosevelt. Shortly thereafter, Joseph Davies was named Ambassador to Russia and Marjorie Davies became the first Ambassadress to serve that post after resumption of diplomatic relations with the Soviet Union. At the particular time the Davies were assigned to Russia the policy of the State Department was one of wooing the Soviet Union; Communism was not then considered a particular threat to the American way of life. When Marjorie Davies took over as Chatelaine of the Embassy at Moscow, a transformation took place

[1] *Seafarer Magazine*, April 1952, by Cmdr. Clyde B. Ault.

Marjorie Merriweather Post
(Mrs. Joseph E. Davies)

which resulted in a thoroughly modern, and perfectly appointed American Embassy. The Embassy was supposed to be completely furnished, but the Davies found grave gaps in equipment and furnishings. While the residence itself had all the possibilities of being a magnificent embassy building, it was sadly lacking in modern conveniences. Marjorie Davies went to work on it with her usual perfect taste and many of her own furnishings. Much of the food for entertaining had to be sent in from Warsaw and Helsinki, for there was little available in Moscow in the way of fresh, green vegetables or fruit. This was a grave problem for all the embassies. When lettuce and endive were shipped in from Belgium, the guests were so happy to see something green that they almost ate the plates.

It was during the Russian assignment that Marjorie Davies intensified her collecting of very rare Imperial Russian objects of art. The Soviets had large government warehouses (Commission Shops) where they held confiscated property. On the 20th anniversary of Soviet rule these stores were thrown open to the public. Various objects had been taken from them for placement in Soviet museums and for creating new museums, the balance was opened to public sale. The merchandise was piled in heaps upon the floor, no arrangement of any kind was made to identify anything. Under dust and dirt and an accumulation of trash were found very rare Russian icons, silvergilt chalices, porcelains, enamels and valuable objects of art. The chalices were sold at five cents per gram weight of silver content. It was from this heap that Mrs. Davies uncovered many of her rare and important pieces. A very fine and unique lapis lazuli chest was found in a Commission Shop. These remarkable discoveries in Russia are now part of Mrs. May's outstanding collection of antiques housed in "Hillwood." This is the property willed to the Smithsonian for a public museum.

After three years' duty in Moscow, the Davies were assigned to Belgium. Originally they had been advised that the assignment would be in Germany, but Adolf Hitler was creating grave disturbances at that time and the assignment was switched to Brussels. Marjorie still feels quite lucky that she was not sent to Germany; the American government had bought an enormous building near the Brandenburg Gate which she would have been required to furnish entirely.

Upon arrival in Belgium, the first chore necessary was a thorough house cleaning of the Embassy; structural changes had to be made to accommodate modern conveniences. It had been a fine, historic house, but neglect had resulted in unfortunate conditions. It was built in the early 1880's, in the style of an Italian townhouse, for the Marquise D'Assche, a Russian Princess. Albert was living in this house when he became King of Belgium, and his son Leopold III was born there. The house was supposed to have been furnished, but there was a complete lack of the necessary appointments to make it worthy of an embassy. As part of her early training, Deenie Hutton, then fourteen years of age, was permitted to furnish her own quarters. This she managed with good taste and judgment, with a few necessary suggestions from her mother.

World War II soon necessitated the dismantling of the whole Embassy. Mrs. Davies was on vacation in the States at the time the State Department issued the order that no embassy family was to return to European assignments. All of her personal and cherished possessions had to be returned to the States under trying conditions. No linens, silver, glassware or china were furnished by the Embassy; therefore, Mrs. Davies had supplied these from her private furnishings. This was an embassy where the U. S. Government expected an ambassador to entertain on a very lavish scale, consequently fine appointments were considered more necessary than whimsical. Getting everything all properly packed and back to the States in wartime was a grave problem. The furnishings were sent back on several different ships in event of attack in transit. The private packer told her that en route back with one load he saw two torpedoes, but fortunately both missed the ship. In spite of all the pleasure and glamour surrounding an ambassadorial appointment, many ambassadors could relate tales of private and personal expense incurred beyond the realm of common sense, and almost insurmountable problems that are expected to be resolved promptly.

When the Davies returned to Washington to *Tregaron*, Marjorie Davies went into war and relief work in her usual well-planned ways. Using her time and energy for challenging charitable and philanthropic projects and war efforts is one of the things that does not faze her— this is her stride—she has had a lifetime of such experiences. There always has been, and there always will be, so much to do; she will never stop so long as there is a worthy cause to be accomplished.

There have been many homes in Mrs. May's life, each of which has had the attention and touch of her deft hand. The camp in the Adirondacks has been a family joy since 1921 when it was acquired. This property is on the St. Regis chain of lakes at the far end of Upper St. Regis Lake. The whole camp is built on a hogback of land between two lakes. The approach is by motorboat, for there are no roads, just a trail where one could hike in if he wished. The back lake is one of a pair; they are called the Spectacles and are twelve feet higher than St. Regis, draining into it. After landing at the private dock and boathouse, one steps a few feet away into a quaint bird-cage type elevator which carries the visitor, as an escalator, eighty feet up the heavily wooded slope. Here begins the main body of the camp. The principal building houses the enormous living room, main dining room, pantries and kitchens. The living room boasts an extraordinary collection of American Indian craftsmanship and lore. There are stuffed animals, cigar-store Indians, llama rugs, bear skins, and many fine examples of Indian bead work. The room has a tremendous fireplace at either end; heating is augmented by a central heating system when needed. The entire theme of the main building is carried out in accordance with the rustic mountain camp decor, though on a far more elaborate scale than could be found in any such surroundings.

The side walls of the dining room are covered with peeled birch bark, giving a silvery shimmer to the room. When Marjorie Post suggested the use of peeled bark for these walls, the builder advised her that it was impractical and would not withstand time. Her judgment has been vindicated these forty years later by the perfect condition of the walls. There are polished handhewn beams across the ceiling, large cobblestones in the enormous fireplaces, combining to give the atmosphere of a mountain lodge. Adjacent to the main building, on either side of it and across the top of the ridge about thirty feet apart, are the guest cabins. Each cabin is complete with bedroom, bath and sitting room, and many have screened porches. They are decorated to conform to their names—Mexican, Black Room, Blue Room, Green Room, Dacha, Mocba, Honeymoon, and so on up and down the ridges. Guests seem to enjoy the hospitality of the hostess at this particular location more than at any other home. There are all sorts of amusements available, such as water-skiing and boating, swimming, golf, fishing, first-run movies two nights a week, and of course the round and square dances that are held regularly. The camp is enjoyed by guests from far and wide and from many walks of life. It is a place of refuge for the family and friends away from jangling telephones and pressures of everyday life, yet with many forms of amusement if one so desires. It gives complete relaxation and enjoyment amid fresh mountain air.

In 1955 Marjorie Merriweather Post bought a very fine piece of land, approximately twenty-four acres atop a rolling hillside facing Rock Creek Park in the District of Columbia. Here was built "Hillwood," the museum created for future generations when it becomes the property of the Smithsonian Institution. The home was started when Marjorie and Mr. Davies were separated and divorced, and was finished for her occupancy in 1957. In June of 1958, Marjorie Post married Herbert A. May, Pittsburgh industrialist. Though Hillwood will not become a museum in her lifetime, she is so overly generous in sharing it with organizations, schools, and the public that one sees more strangers about than the family. While the house is already planned for museum display, it has maintained its warm, homey atmosphere.[2] The view from the entrance hall extends through the library doors beyond the south portico unto a view of the Washington Monument far in the distance. It is in the foyer hall where one begins to appreciate just what Marjorie May is giving to the public, the very rare and valuable collection which has resulted from the wisdom of her selectivity.

Hillwood is a breathtaking place. The grounds are perfectly landscaped with a formal French garden, a rose garden, and the Japanese garden with several bubbling pools and waterfalls. Here, too, is the beautiful Friendship Walk. The Walk was the gift of 150 friends and

[2] At the Fifteenth Annual Williamsburg Forum (1963), Mrs. May gave an illustrated lecture on her "Hillwood" collection. She recounted incidents of how and where rare items were collected and why they have been collected. Mr. Marvin Ross, Curator at Hillwood, gave the factual history of articles shown. The lecture has been repeated at the Sulgrave Club, Washington, D. C., and will be repeated at the Henry Clay Frick Department of Fine Arts at the University of Pittsburgh.

especially dedicated to the popular hostess of Hillwood; it contains a number of dedicatory plaques expressing admiration, esteem, appreciation and love for Marjorie May.

The first "Hillwood" owned by Mrs. May was on Long Island near Roslyn. This has been left until last to describe for the reason that Mrs. May sold the property to Long Island University for the creation of the C. W. Post College of Liberal Arts, to which institute of learning she is a devoted benefactress. The residence, long and rambling, with approximately 200 acres of ground, was formerly the home of Marjorie and Ed Hutton and acquired in 1921 as a country place. Ceremonies held on November 29, 1954, brought to fruition the long-projected establishment of a strong new college centrally located to serve the rapidly expanding Nassau and Suffolk County areas of Long Island. Moreover, the college is admirably equipped to attract students from throughout the United States and abroad and has splendid resident facilities on the campus. The first applicants for admission to the college were accepted in March 1955, and the first class began its instruction in September 1955. The initial faculty numbered 11 and the initial class 121. At the beginning of the 1961-62 academic year, the faculty had grown to 220 and the total enrollment was 3,800, including 1,600 full-time day students. The remainder were enrolled in graduate courses and in evening courses at Post College and its extension in Hauppauge, Long Island. The rapid growth and acceptance of the college has exceeded fondest dreams and expectations. The college offers a general education as fine as that available anywhere. Its classrooms and laboratory facilities are completely modern. The basic structure of knowledge and understanding, the foundation of later specialization, is carefully built at Post. Specialized studies are provided for those who want to prepare themselves for a specific field of endeavor.

The campus, one of the most attractive in the Nation, is enhanced by 126 acres of beautifully landscaped grounds, flowering gardens, stately trees. The buildings are of Colonial, Federal and Tudor design. The college is only one hour by train or car from mid-town Manhattan with its limitless opportunities for cultural enrichment. The majestic Gothic fireplace, the magnificent wood carvings, the leaded glass windows, and beautiful interiors of the original house have been main-

Unfinished portrait by Douglas Chandor, 1953

Marjorie Merriweather Post
(Mrs. Herbert A. May)

Japanese Garden   South portico

Hillwood, Washington, D. C.

Drawing Room
"Hillwood," Washington, D.C.

~

The Smithsonian Institution one day will inherit Hillwood,
*including the contents of the drawing room, as a museum.
This Louis XVI room encompasses outstanding examples of
porcelains and furniture of that period. On the background wall
may be seen the important portrait of Empress Eugenie, by
Winterhalter. The frame is one which was made for hanging
the painting in the Tuileries. The vitrines on either side of
the portrait display fine Rose de Pompadour Sèvres on the left,
and the beautiful turquoise Sèvres on the right. Two sofas, with
twelve chairs, are upholstered in tapestry from the Gobelins looms
in flower design from Tessier. The suite was made for Louis XVI
and Marie Antoinette as a gift for Prince Henry of Prussia.
The tapestries on the wall are Beauvais after the cartoons of
Francois Boucher. The round table on the extreme left has
a border of jewel lapis lazuli, the center is of lapis and
tiger-eye. The rug is an outstanding Savonnerie.*

The first "Hillwood" at Roslyn, Long Island
Now the C. W. Post College, Long Island University.

tained. The setting, the accomplishments and the rapid growth and acceptance of the college would warm the heart and please the man for whom it is named.

The private homes of Marjorie Post in no way indicate lavishness for the sake of personal aggrandizement; if these were the sole contributions to philanthropic endeavors, this might be true, but her enterprises in the field of philanthropy are far reaching. The homes have been her way of life, her way of sharing untold beauty with friends and deserving groups from the youth of America. These accomplishments alone afforded vast payrolls—the employment of countless numbers of laboring men and skilled craftsmen, gardners, domestic staff, seamen, artists and laymen. It is one of her ways of helping man to help himself. If we may paraphrase the lines of Edgar A. Guest (1907) in tribute to her father: "*She* helped me up to better things, *She* smoothed my troubled way."

Mrs. May was the recipient of a very singular honor when she was read into the Congressional Record (April 20, 1960), by Hon. James G. Fulton, citing her great selflessness. She was the first woman to be "pinned" by the Boy Scouts of America and was largely responsible for the establishment of their Service Center in Washington. She helped to establish and equip a 400-acre tract Scout Council Camp in Post City, Texas. The National Capital Area Council, on the Boy Scouts' Golden Anniversary year, presented her a plaque in appreciation which now stands by Friendship Walk.

"Music for Young America" is one of Mrs. May's favorite projects. This is held in conjunction with the National Symphony Orchestra, the cost of which is underwritten every year by Mrs. May. The concerts are free to all visiting youngsters to the Nation's Capital and are held for a five-week period during spring vacation when Washington bursts at the seams with visiting school children. The concerts total over thirty free performances for these visitors. Director Howard Mitchell estimates that well over 100,000 students have taken advantage of this offering since its inception in 1956; for better than eighty percent of them, this has been the only opportunity to hear live symphonic music. The concerts are kept on a very high level and are not played-down to their particular age brackets. In tribute to Mrs. May, the National Symphony Orchestra conducts the "Merriweather Post" contest for young aspiring musicians, none can have reached his nineteenth birthday. Prizes range from $1,500 first prize, $750 and $350 for winners of the finals, and include violin, cello, and piano divisions. The contestants must have first won regional, or elimination, contests in local or home areas. "Music for Young America" was the long-time dream of Director Mitchell, who felt that the tourist buses swarming into the Capital with school children every spring were an untapped source for disseminating symphonic music. At a Symphony Board Meeting, he wistfully commented: "We're muffing a priceless opportunity by not introducing these students to good music." Mrs. May quietly answered: "I think I would like to do that." She then excused herself from the room while she called her investment counselor. Since that time "Music for Young America" has been a reality. The greatest satisfaction that she has received is from expressions of gratitude contained in thousands of letters from these fortunate children.

The C. W. Post Field, Battle Creek, was dedicated there in November of 1961. This met a long-felt need for an adequate athletic field for the city of Battle Creek. Since 1907 various attempts had been made to fulfill the athletic needs of the high school on the old "knitting mill site." Not until 1921, with contributions from the Chamber of Commerce, the high school class of '21, and a $300 donation by the Boy's Athletic Association, did much of a field survive on which the boys could hold their school games. In the year 1929 the high school yearbook again made a plea for a satisfactory field, but the cost was so enormous it remained only a dream. The final answer to those needs is found in the dedication program, November 3, 1961: "Yes, Students of 1929, thanks to present and former School Trustees for their careful planning, to the citizens of Battle Creek for their solid support, and to Mrs. Marjorie Post May and the Post Division of *General Foods, your dream has come true.* Battle Creek is proud to have had an important role in the life of Marjorie Post May. It was here that she spent her childhood and attended our public schools." The facilities include a well-lighted football field, modern stadium seating 7,000, seven all-weather tennis courts, quarter-mile all-weather track, three softball diamonds, jumping and pole vault pits and runways; a total of 25 acres of play space for junior and senior high school physical fitness classes. During the summer months, the entire area, with the exception of the football field, is used by the City Recreation Department. Here again, forty-seven years later, is the manifestation of C. W. Post's helping hand to the youth of America.

Marjorie Post May has long been regarded as the lady bountiful of Mount Vernon Seminary and Junior College. Since those school days of long ago, when she was a student in the old building on M Street, thence the great hall on Nebraska Avenue, and now the beautiful installation on Foxhall Road, Mount Vernon has been one of Marjorie Post's great loves. She has watched the school's progress carefully, and her efforts to make it grow have not been inconsiderable. She has been the beloved godmother of each succeeding class for many years.

An example of Marjorie Post May's "generosity with a heart" occurred just as this book was ready for the press. This is an exemplification of the kind of special treat that only she can plan from start to finish. Twenty-four teenagers were selected on the basis of merit at Central High School in Battle Creek for a special three-day visit to Washington. Since Mrs. May's private plane could not accommodate the children and chaperons, a DC 7 was chartered for the round-trip flight. When the plane landed at the National Airport, Mrs. May was on hand to greet each guest. Standing by was a chartered air-conditioned bus, complete with a knowledgeable guide, for use during the three-day visit. To the utmost amazement of the students, Mrs. May dismissed her car and chauffeur and boarded the bus with them for the trip to their hotel. One youngster was so startled he was heard to whisper: "Gee, you mean she is going to ride with us when she could ride in *that!*" When they arrived at their hotel rooms there were gifts of a pound box of chocolates, an air-travel bag, and a White House Guidebook for each.

The following three days were a whirl of activity for one dazed group of young people. A complete sight-seeing tour was arranged to include Mount Vernon, a specially conducted tour of the White House, the National Gallery of Art, Music for Young America concert, and all points of interest in the Nation's Capital. The first evening was started off with a dinner at "Hillwood," followed by a trip to the theatre to enjoy a popular musical; for many of the students it was the first opportunity to see a live show, highlighted by a visit backstage to meet the cast. The finale on Sunday was a luncheon in the main dining room at "Hillwood" with the finest of appointments on the table, a menu to delight the appetite of each, and the companionship of a happy hostess who personally conducted the tour of "Hillwood" gardens and museum. During the luncheon, the grateful students presented Mrs. May with a gold, oval tray which had been gold plated by the art teacher at the high school and etched with scenes from Marjorie's childhood in Battle Creek. It showed the old *Postum* barn, the apple tree beside it and her childhood swing. When the afternoon came to a close, Mrs. May again boarded the bus for the trip to the airport and stood waving her handkerchief as the plane taxied off to return a group of exhausted but thrilled youngsters to Battle Creek.

This was the same kind of special planning executed by Marjorie May three years ago when she entertained a group of thirty students from C. W. Post College, in which instance the planning was scaled to their more mature age bracket. The thank-you letters which have come to the hostess from these young people and their families have proved the merit of her unique ideas; the experiences are heart-warming for donor and recipients.

These are a few of the things Mrs. May permits the public to know. What she does not wish published are the facts concerning her private philanthropies, the great number of individuals helped in confidence. In this area are countless young people whom she has educated. When schooling is furnished, it is without the stigma of charity. The boy or girl will be sent off to college with the necessary clothes and financial help to place the student on an equal footing with all other students of the chosen school, but the arrangements remain in confidence. If the student is worthy and shows proper aptitude, higher education is made available. No one will ever know the approximate number of such cases. In the strictest secrecy the less fortunate friends of long ago have been maintained in beautifully delicate ways. The purity of heart shows itself in the touching "little things" thought out by one so heavily burdened for time, the delightful non-essentials, as well as necessities, that often surprise the recipient. These are people who have been found worthy and concluded to be proper for assistance. Hundreds of begging letters pour into the offices of Mrs. May, but unless investigation proves a need exists, nothing will be done. She is a wise, careful business woman, thoroughly aware of sucker-lists, and she cannot alone shoulder many additional financial burdens.

Aside from private funds directed to philanthropic endeavors, Mrs. May has given of her time and talent to "causes" for many years. Charitable organizations consider it a coup when she is persuaded to head a fund drive—it is well known that her drives are unique and produce results. As an example, in the present season she permitted the Salvation Army to use "Hillwood" for its annual fund-raising bazaar. The results reached far above best expectations, and this has been the past history of all endeavors in many fields.

The lovely lady has had a wonderful array of experiences, a unique childhood, fulfillment in maturity and her share of heartaches along with much happiness. She has spanned the age of transportation from horse and buggy, bicycles, through all types of automobiles, private sailing vessels, a private railroad car, and on up to her own private airplane, *The Merriweather*—a cycle accomplished by very few. A great personal satisfaction comes to her in bringing Old World objects of art and rare historic gems to America for Americans, where she feels they should be for the future. The historic diamond necklace given by Napoleon to Marie-Louise upon the birth of the King of Rome has been given by Mrs. May to the Smithsonian Institution, and now rests beside the famous Hope Diamond in the Museum.

Marjorie Post May is the exemplification of the "all-American woman," witty, charming and talented. She is proud of her three delightful daughters, grandchildren and great-grandchildren. Daughter Adelaide (Mrs. Augustus Riggs) loves outdoor life, horses, dogs, and field sports. Daughter Eleanor (Mrs. Leon Barzin) is a dainty Dresden-doll type of beauty who is devoted to her Paris home, and has an intense interest in music, art, and antiques. Daughter Nedenia (Mrs. Stanley Rumbough) has her field in television, radio and motion pictures as Dina Merrill. The girls are talented, beautiful, and each an individualist. They have not attained an age when they can escape a strong admonition from their mother if she thinks they need it.

Many amusing incidents, showing the humor and straightforward-
ness of Mrs. May, have come into the situation since this manuscript
has been in work. She has that sly-wink in personality not unlike her
grandfather Rollin Post, and the same twinkling grey-blue eyes of her
father. While this writer was at Hillwood for an early morning conference, Mrs. May was hurriedly dressing for the next appointment;
her physical appearance without make-up was amazing. Her nails,
skin and hair, and the lack of age-lines of any significance are a
marvel. (She fools no one about the years, her age is not a secret.)
When this writer noticed Mrs. May removing a layer of oil from her
face before applying make-up, the woman-like question popped out:
"Is that a very special Swiss or French lubricant?" Handing over the
bottle, she said: "Smell it,"—the odor was very familiar, strangely
reminiscent. With an impish smile, she resolved the question: " You
can buy it in any drug store—it is castor oil and I have used it for
years." When we asked permission to use certain recent photographs
of her in this book, she hurriedly flipped through the selection and
threw out the "best" one with the comment: "Don't use that one, the
photographer got carried away with himself and touched out all the
wrinkles and lines—here, this one is better, the proper lines and
wrinkles are still there." The lady does not need flattery, for it has come
from all walks of life in every language, but it has not thrown her off
balance. After many years of extreme flattery (yes, even from a King),
she still blushes and becomes self-conscious in the face of it.

Many glowing words have been written about Marjorie May, in all
types of news media, describing her minutely. With head held high,
she walks as though facing into a welcome breeze. No one has mentioned her lovely mouth; it is the mouth where one finds the "mirror
of the soul," the up-turned corners indicate her serenity of spirit, and
goodness of heart. Her whole being reflects a complete dependence
on God. There is much about her that can be better described in the
words of Samuel Ullman [Reader's Digest, Dec. 1945] when he wrote:
"You are as young as your faith . . . So long as your heart receives messages of
beauty, cheer, courage, grandeur and power from the earth, from man and from
the Infinite, so long are you young . . . Nobody grows old by merely living a
number of years. People grow old only by deserting their ideals. Years wrinkle
the skin, but to give up enthusiasm wrinkles the soul."

C. W. Post once told his daughter that if she were shipwrecked on a deserted island, she would organize the grains of sand. A special piece of advice she best remembers from her father was: "Never let money possess you, never worship it. Do good with it, make it work for you, keep it busy." She has the same drive, the like appreciation for the beautiful, the awareness of the needs of the youth of America, and her father's kind of love for fellow man. She had to choose a life of involvement, the daughter of C. W. could not have done otherwise; all the essentials learned in early childhood are still well remembered. C. W. Post gave unto the next generations a fond daughter produced in his own image.

Marjorie Merriweather (Post) May and Great-Grandchildren

Marjorie Post Waller   Ronald Timothy Waller   Post Stevens Waller

Yousuf Karsh photograph
Board of Directors' Room

Director Emeritus
General Foods Corp.

Marjorie Merriweather Post
(Mrs. Herbert A. May)

Curriculum Vitae
of
Marjorie Merriweather Post May

Scholastic:

Elementary—Battle Creek, Michigan, public school.
Mount Vernon Seminary and Junior College, 1904.

Honorary Degrees:

Litt.D., Long Island University, 1955.
LL.D., Hobart & William Smith College, 1958.
L.H.D., Bucknell University, 1962.

Executive:

Owner and Operator, *Postum Cereal Co., Ltd.,* (1914-1922).
Mem. Bd. of Dir., *General Foods Corp.,* (1936-1958).
Director Emeritus, *General Foods Corp.,* (1958–).
1st Alumna Trustee; 1st Life Trustee of Bd., Mount Vernon Seminary.
Mem. Bd. of Exec. Comm. and Mem. of Bd. Dir., National Symphony, Washington, D. C.
Mem. Bd. of Exec. Comm., Washington Chapter, American Red Cross.
Mem. Bd., National War Funds, Inc., World War II (1943-46).
Chmn., National Women's Council, U. S. Flag Assn., 1933.
Mem. Bd. Dir., National Savings & Trust, Washington, D. C. 1959.
Mem. Advisory Comm., National Cultural Center, Washington, D. C.

Member:

Mem. Delegation to Washington, to consult with Woodrow Wilson in 1917 to gain Women's Suffrage.
Mem. Council, Corcoran Art Gallery, Washington, D. C.
Mem. Fellows of Virginia Museum of Fine Arts, Richmond, Va.
Mem. Board of Dir., Good Samaritan Hospital, Palm Beach.
Fellow, American University.
Mem. Bd. of Dir., Washington National Ballet Foundation, Inc.

Philanthropies:

Equipped No. 8 Base Hospital (2,000 beds), Savenay, France, World War I.
Maintained Food Kitchens in slums of N.Y.C., operated by Salvation Army, 1929-1935.
Vice Chmn. Emergency Unemployment Drive, N.Y.C., 1929-1935.
Hon. Chmn. Parcels for Belgian Prisoners & Parcels for Belgium, 1940-44.
Sponsorship "Music for Young America," since 1956.
Co-Participant with *Post Division* of *General Foods* (et al.) in building C. W. Post Athletic Field, Battle Creek, 1961.
Benefactress, Boy Scout Camp, Garza County, Texas.
Benefactress, "Merriweather Post" Boy Scout camp site, Woodrow Wilson Reservation, Lorton, Va.
Benefactress, C. W. Post College, Long Island University.
Private and personal educational and other funds.

American Citations:

Cross of Honor, U. S. Flag Assn., presented in the White House by Mrs. Franklin D. Roosevelt.

American Symphony Orchestra League Award for sponsorship of "Music for Young America," presentation, Providence, R. I., 1956.

Washington Board of Trade Award for Music in Nation's Capital, 1957.

South Plains Council of Boy Scouts of America, in appreciation for gift of Scout Camp near Post, Texas, 1957.

The People of Garza County, Texas, Golden Jubilee Award, 1907-57.

District of Columbia Education Assn., for notable services in the field of education, 1958.

American Nat'l. Red Cross, for services 1960 Fund Campaign.

Nat'l. Soc. Children American Revolution, for Practical Realism, 1960.

C. W. Post College, in Appreciation to Patroness & Benefactress, 1960.

Golden Anniversary Award, Natl. Capital Area Council and Boy Scouts of America, 1960.

Variety Club, Tent #1, for interest in 7 Lively Arts, Pittsburgh, 1961.

American Natl. Red Cross, in Appreciation for Volunteer Services, World War I, presented March 1963, Washington, D. C.

National Federation of Music Clubs, Citation Award, for contribution to Musical, Cultural and Artistic Life, Pittsburgh Conv., April 1963.

American Federation of Musicians, for Distinguished service in behalf of Live Music and Musicians, April, 1963.

National Conference of Christians and Jews, "Brotherhood Award," 1963.

Decorations by Foreign Governments:

Cross of Honor, Order of Adolph de Nassau, Luxembourg, 27 Nov. 1939.

Chevalier of the Order of Leopold, Belgium, 29 Nov. 1939.

Commander of the Order of Juan Puablo Duarte, Dominican Republic, 25 Feb. 1946.

Officer of the Order of the Crown, Belgium, 28 June 1947.

Chevalier of Legion of Honor, France, 7 April 1957.

Chevalier, Order of the Southern Cross, Brazil, 12 Dec. 1958.

Hereditary Societies:

Daughters of the American Revolution.

Vermont Society of Colonial Dames.

Daughters of Founders and Patriots.

James Towne Society (Descendants of Founders).

Descendants of Colonial American Clergy.

The Daughters of the Barons of Runnemede.

Living Descendants of Blood Royal (in America) listed 1963.

World Nobility and Peerage, listed 1962.

Private Clubs:

Established first cabana beach club in this country, Bath and Tennis, Palm Beach.

Field Club, Greenwich, Conn., Life Member.

Colony Club, New York City.

Chevy Chase Club, Washington, D. C.

Sulgrave Club, Washington, D. C.

Everglades Club, Palm Beach.

Seminole Club, Palm Beach.

Gulf Stream, Delray, Florida.

Rolling Rock Club, Pittsburgh.

Duquesne Club, Pittsburgh.

Fox Chapel Country Club, Pittsburgh.

Foreign Decorations Conferred Upon Marjorie Merriweather Post

1. Cross of Honor, Order of Adolph de Nassau, Luxembourg, November 27, 1939.
2. Chevalier of the Order of Leopold, Belgium, November 29, 1939.
3. Commander of the Order of Juan Pablo Duarte, Dominican Republic, February 25, 1946.
4. Officer of the Order of the Crown, Belgium, June 28, 1947.
5. Chevalier of the Legion of Honor, France, April 7, 1957.
6. Chevalier of the Order of the Southern Cross, Brazil, December 12, 1958.

FOUR GENERATIONS

Marjorie (Post) May

Adelaide Brevoort (Close) Riggs
(Mrs. Augustus Riggs IV)

Marjorie (Durant) Waller
Marjorie Post Waller

Post Tradition Carries On

~

The photographs and the reproductions of portraits in this biography capture the personalities of Marjorie Post's family. The Post tradition of intelligence, energy, character, and personal charm is inherent in her three lovely daughters, Adelaide Close Riggs (Mrs. Augustus Riggs IV), Eleanor Close Barzin (Mrs. Leon Barzin), and Nedenia Hutton Rumbough (Mrs. Stanley Rumbough). The pictures also introduce some of Mrs. Post's seven grandchildren and eight great-grandchildren. In them she finds the same joy and pride C. W. and Ella Post found in their three granddaughters.

Adelaide Brevoort Close

Eleanor Post Close

Portrait by Sir Oswald Birley

Adelaide Brevoort Close

Adelaide Brevoort Post
(Mrs. Augustus Riggs IV)

Eleanor Post Close

Eleanor Post Close
(Mrs. Leon Barzin)

Nedenia Marjorie Hutton

Nedenia Marjorie Hutton

Nedenia Marjorie (Hutton) Rumbough

Stanley Hutton Rumbough   *David Post Rumbough*

Genealogical Supplement

Post Genealogy

❦

Ancestors and Descendants

of

Charles William Post
(1854-1914)

and

Ella L. Merriweather
(1853-1912)

COMPILED BY

NETTIE LEITCH MAJOR

Post Lineage

Other charted genealogical lines at end of supplement.

Post

The surname Post, Poste, Poast, Van der Post may be found in early Dutch records. In the year 1376 in the records of Arnheim, Holland, a Van der Post was one of the 24 Burghers of Arnheim. There seems little doubt that the Maidstone, County Kent, England, Post families were descendants of the early Dutch Posts. Panwell Van der Post married Sarah Van Gelder, daughter of Abraham Van Gelder, on February 7, 1571 and removed from Arnheim to Maidstone. The records of the Dutch Church, Maidstone, Kent, list Abraham Post and twin Sarah, born October 6, 1572, to Panwell and Sarah (Van Gelder) Post. This Abraham Post married Anne Hunte on April 26, 1595, at Hollingbourne, Kent. [Canterbury Cathedral Archives, London, England.] The Parish register seems to have been partially destroyed for the listings of the children of Abraham and Anne (Hunte) Post; however, there remain fragments from which one would conclude there were at least two children for this couple. One entry assists greatly in identifying daughter Mary and son Stephen. Mary Post was married March 1, 1632 to Allen Wenn, "with consent of her father Abraham Post, said Mary age 25"; thus Mary was born 1607. With this consent is the bond of her brother, Stephen Post. Abraham Post was buried at Hollingbourne, Church of All Saints, July 22, 1639. Stephen Post was married at Hollingbourne, Parish of Langley, on October 17, 1625 to Ellen Panton. [Canterbury Cathedral Archives.] With the scanty information available in English records for this family, we have only the strong assumption that Stephen Post and wife Ellen (sometimes Eleanor) of Hartford and Saybrook are the same. For further substantiation of this conclusion, we draw attention to the fact that Stephen and Ellen of Hartford and Saybrook named one son Abraham (sometimes called Abram).

This genealogical compilation will deal with the Connecticut Posts and their descendants, with particular emphasis on the direct line of descent to Charles William Post (1854-1914). There will be no attempt to include data on the Long Island Post family, which has been covered in another compilation, *The Post Family*, by Marie C. de Trobriand Post, published 1905, wherein the line is referred to as the Long Island Dutch Posts, tracing the descent from Richard Post of Lynn, Massachusetts, called the founder of the Long Island branch.

For the benefit of searchers seeking additional data on Posts of England, Canterbury Cathedral Archives contain data on other Posts, such as Alienor Post's will, which was proved March 27, 1520, County Kent, and directed that her body be placed beside that of her husband in the churchyard of All Saints, Ulcombe. Her husband was George Post, who named his wife Alienor in his will and named the same sons as those of her will. She named Thomas and daughters, and he named Thomas and George. The will of Thomas Post was proved May 20, 1545 and named sons William, John the younger, George the younger, Robert, George the elder, Sir Rauff Post and Henry Haffynden, son-in-law; the wife of Thomas Post was named as Catherine in his will.

Thomas Hooker and Stephen Post

The life of Thomas Hooker is well enough known that there will be no necessity of including extensive facts herewith, beyond showing any possible association with Stephen Post. Thomas Hooker was born at Marshfield, Parish of Tilton, Leicestershire, on July 7, 1586, and died July 7, 1647. [*History of First Church of Hartford,* by Geo. Leon Walker, pub. 1884.] At the age of 25 he received his M.A. from Emmanuel College, which in 1611 was considered the intellectual center of Puritanism. He began his active career as a preacher in a small parish of Surry, but in 1626 was nominated to lecture at the Church of St. Mary's in Chelmsford, Essex. The moral fervor of his sermons was such that huge crowds flocked from far and near to hear the oracle. The freedom of worship, which had been allowed the Huguenot refugees and the Walloons, was suddenly withdrawn when Bishop Laud came to power. By 1629 the Bishop determined to eliminate all other religions and raise the Church of England as the sole religious power approved by the State. Obviously Thomas Hooker, with his outspoken sermons, would have made powerful enemies. Bishop Laud excommunicated Hooker, and he was placed under bond and forced into seclusion. He went to live in a little hillside parish, known as Little Baddow, just a few miles away. He opened a school there, and his usher, John Eliot, was later to be known as "Apostle to the Indians." There are no records to give us clues as to how and when Stephen Post fell under the spell of Thomas Hooker. Some historians have claimed Stephen Post was a member of the congregation at Chelmsford, but our research reveals factual data to show that more likely he was not a member of the Chelmsford group. Chelmsford was a great market place in Essex. Stephen Post was living in Otham, Kent; therefore, it is not unlikely he could have travelled to Chelmsford on personal business and heard Hooker preach. There is no record that Hooker ever preached at Maidstone or in Kent, but such may have been the case. There is no pure record to show that Stephen Post knew Hooker until Post arrived at Hartford, nor a documented date to show *when* he arrived—September of 1634, thus far, is the only proved date to place Stephen Post in Hartford (one year after the arrival of Thomas Hooker).

The little "Hooker band" began to fear for the life of their idol, and there seemed nothing left but flight. He was accordingly spirited away by his devoted followers across the North Sea into Holland, sometime in the year 1630. His followers found life and times increasingly more difficult at home without the spiritual guidance of their pastor. The first exodus to the New World took place in 1632, known as the "First Band" of Hooker followers, or "The Braintree Company." They arrived at Boston Harbor and were welcomed by Governor Winthrop, who assigned them land at a site which was to be known as Mount Wollaston. But, according to records at Boston, this band was ordered to move to "Newe Towne" by general orders of the Court (1632). New Town was later to be known as Cambridge. There were 47 settlers in this first band of the Braintree Company.

Meanwhile, Thomas Hooker had left Holland in 1633 and was smuggled back to England. It was at the little home tucked away in the Downes where Reverend Samuel Stone was able to hide Hooker and where plans were laid to smuggle him aboard the *Griffin* with a large band of his devoted followers. We do not know by what underground information Stephen Post and his family were able to know, or if they knew, that Thomas Hooker would be aboard. Stephen Post might have been at Gravesend and sailed aboard the *Griffin*, as claimed by past compilers, but it seems more likely that he was not on that sailing, in view of church records uncovered for the first time herewith. Stephen and Ellen baptized, then buried at Otham, their infant son Joseph (*q.v.*) while the *Griffin* was en route to the New World.

The personal diary of Governor Winthrop [Journal of Governor Winthrop, State Library, Hartford] gives the details of the landing: "The *Griffin*, a ship of 300 tons arrived brought in by Captain John Gallop. She brought 200 passengers, having lost four whereof one was drowned two days before landing as he was casting forth a line to take makerl (*sic*). In the *Griffin* were Mr. Cotton, Mr. Hooker, Mr. Stone." In another of his documents it is written: "Between February and October 1633, nine vessels from England arrived with about 700 passengers and many cattle." The *Griffin* was eight weeks in crossing the Atlantic and landed at Boston harbor September 4, 1633.

In the Newtown Records [The *Proprietor's Records*, "Register Book of the Lands and Houses In the Newe Towne," pub. 1896, Edwin H. Jese] is the following: "Mr. Thomas Hooker, Mr. Stone and Mr. Cotton got out of England with much difficulty. On October 11, 1633, Mr. Hooker and Mr. Stone after prayers and fasting took up their work in Newe Towne. Thomas Hooker become the pastor of the souls and young Mr. Stone, a former graduate of Emmanuel College, was named the first teacher of the Colony."

The original records of Newe Towne show: "On the prime of September 1634 lots granted on west side of river to Stephen Post, 12 ackers," which is the earliest documented date for Stephen Post in the New World. By this we see that Stephen Post was established with others of the Hooker Colony in sight of the Charles River. At long last, a New World, a land of liberty and freedom of conscience! But this dream was soon to be shattered. The long-sought religious liberty, freedom of conscience, with freedom of speech, was not to be. These were truly the days that "tried men's souls." The days of witchcraft, burning at the stake, severe punishment for the slightest infraction of rules, and tyranny were rampant. Governor Endicott of Salem was the first to forget he had once been persecuted because of his religion. The Sabbath day was to become a day when no one was allowed to do anything but pray. Heavy fines were imposed, whippings and banishments were inflicted for such offense as "picking peas on Sunday"; a footweary soldier was fined for alleviating the pain of blistered feet, by "wetting a piece of an old hat to put in his shoe." Elizabeth Eddy was severely fined for "wringing out clothes on Sunday." Another maiden was fined for "sitting under a tree on the Sabbath with a young man." Branding in the palm was not uncommon for such offenses as speaking out against a minister or a sermon.

Sir Richard Saltonstall, who had been visiting Governor Winthrop, was shocked at the frightful abuses he had seen. No sooner had he reached England than he sent a letter to the ministers of the city of Boston: "You do not know how I grieve to hear what sadd (sic) things are reported daily of your tyranny and persecution in New England, as that you fyne, whip and imprison men for their conscience."

From the outset there had been a lack of provisions. Corn had to be sent up from Virginia. When potatoes were shipped from Bermuda, the ministers interfered and would not permit their flock to eat them since "potatoes were not mentioned in the Bible." There was an abundance of seafoods, as we learn from the journal of Governor Winthrop the following, dated 1634: "This week great stores of eels and lobsters were brought by 2 or 3 boys. They had brought in a bushel of eels at a time and over 60 huge green lobsters. Wild turkeys dusted themselves in the sand. . . ."

Thomas Hooker was not slow nor quiet in his criticism of conditions and tyranny in the New World. Over and over again he preached that the choice of the magistrates belonged unto the people by God's own allowance, that they are the ones who have the power to appoint officers and magistrates. It is entered in the town records of Newe Towne: "since the coming of Hooker the Newe Towne freemen grow to be very jealous of their liberties." Within one year of their settlement at Newe Towne, Governor Winthrop's journal reflects the start of the movement to leave the Massachusetts Bay Colony. On May 3, 1634, the Governor wrote: "Those of Newe Towne complained of straitness for want of land, especially meadow land and desired lief of the court to look out for either enlargement or lief of removal." On May 14, 1634, the Court decided there was to be "lief granted to the inhabitants of Newe Towne to seek out some convenient place for them, with promise that it shall be confirmed unto them, to which they may remove . . ." though at the same time the Court reminds them that the location which they pick out "shall not be in any place to prejudice a plantation already settled." Shortly thereafter, the records show: "the Newe Towne Congregation accepted the enlargement offered which embraces the Muddy River." (This today is the section of Brookline, Brighton and Newton.) It then becomes apparent that, on more sober thought, Thomas Hooker realized they might be still tied to the tyranny of the Bay Colony, for shortly after this they refused the offer. Governor Winthrop doubtless encouraged Hooker to turn his attention to the "Long River." The treaty with the Mohegans was a reality, and the threat of a Dutch settlement in the Connecticut Valley greatly alarmed Governor Winthrop, who feared the powerful Dutch. There is little doubt the Governor was anxious to induce the unhappy English settlers to settle this new region. On September 4, 1634, Thomas Hooker asked, in his own name and that of his congregation, to move to Connecticut, repeating that it was necessary because "of lack of pasturage for cattle, inability to provide means to support a minister, etc. . . . that the towns are too close together, while space and fertility in Connecticut is abundant." After much deliberation at the Court of the Massachusetts Bay Colony, the matter was put to vote. The Court was divided. Some would not consent to this separation. Others felt it wise that this band of men be allowed to settle the Connecticut River and thus safeguard it for the English. The minister, Mr. Cotton, suggested that the 13th of September be set aside as a day of humiliation and prayer, thus to seek advice of the Lord. Mr. Cotton preached a sermon with a view to pacifying the dissatisfied. Finally permission was granted for the removal to "Connectico." An advance party was headed by Samuel Stone to select land they felt would be suitable ground. Well into the wilderness a band of friendly Indians greeted them, and records show that Sunchquassen, Sachem of the Suckiag Tribe, made out a deed of sale which was signed by Samuel Stone and William Goodwin. On the 6th of May, 1635, the final consent of the Massachusetts Bay Company was secured. Governor Winthrop in person presented the Hooker congregation with "three pieces of canon to fortify themselves in their new settlement in case of attack." On the 31st of May, Thomas Hooker and his band of Newe Towne followers, headed by Samuel Stone with 160 head of cattle, plunged into the wilderness . . . the pilgrimage to Hartford was underway. Mrs. Hooker, the invalid wife of Thomas Hooker, was carried on a litter. For fourteen days this band of pilgrims trudged on foot. An old English chronicle records this event, saying: "the adventure was all the more remarkable as many of this company were persons of high standing, who had lived in England in honor, affluence and delicacy, and were entire strangers to fatigue and danger."

Founding of Connecticut Posts

1. Stephen Post, born *ca.* 1596 at Hollingbourne, Kent England; died August 16, 1659,† Oyster River, Saybrook, Connecticut; married (banns) October 17, 1625, Parish of Langley, Hollingbourne, Kent,* **Ellen Panton,** born *ca.* 1605, possibly Hollingbourne; died November 13, 1670, Saybrook, Connecticut.†

Issue: 5 children.

+2 ABRAHAM POST, birth of whom is in dispute, see text to follow.
+3 JOHN POST, baptized September 13, 1629, Otham, Kent.*
+4 KATHERINE POST, not recorded at Otham, see text under #4.
+5 THOMAS POST, baptized November 1, 1631, Otham, Kent.*
+6 JOSEPH POST, baptized August 8, 1633, buried September 3, 1633, Otham.*

The marriage banns for Stephen Post designated him "carpenter of Otham"; the evidence to follow will show this to have been his occupation in the New World. In view of the date of 1625 at Parish of Langley and no further entry in that parish for them, we have been unable to ascertain where they were until the baptism of John at Otham in 1629. It is entirely possible that they went to Chelmsford, as past compilers have indicated; if this is correct, they were back in Kent by 1629, and through 1633 dates shown above. With the four-year lapse between marriage date and baptism of John, we might assume Abraham to have been the eldest child; however, this point is open for further study (details in text under #**2**, *q.v.*). There is another assumption at this point. With the burial of Joseph in September 1633 at the time the *Griffin* was en route to the New World, one wonders if Eleanor would have remained in England and followed with relatives or friends at a later date, which seems unlikely. While every compiler for many years has stated that Stephen Post came on the *Griffin*, there is no pure record to indicate he *was* aboard. One publication stated that Stephen came to Connecticut in 1631; however, past compilers had not located the parish entries. The first date for a documented record on Stephen at Newe Towne was September 1634, one year after the *Griffin* arrived in the New World, when Stephen was granted the 12 acres (*op. cit.*). The *Griffin* landed September 4, 1633, and Joseph was buried September 3, 1633, in Kent. There is no doubt of the

* Canterbury Cathedral Archives, London, England.
† *Early Connecticut Probate Records,* compiled by Charles Wm. Manwaring, published 1904, Hartford, pps. 22, 83, 144, 148.

Reference:
First Church of Old Saybrook, published 1896, J. S. Stewart Co.

close connection of Stephen Post and Thomas Hooker. Whether this close tie was formed in the New World or in England may never be resolved.

In the Cambridge Town Meeting Records, 1630–1705, the first entry was the 12 acres. Pratt's *History of Cambridge* also shows this as the first date located. The Newe Towne *Proprietors' Records* (*op. cit.*) show that Stephen Post was on "the south side of the Charles River on the highway into the Common, southwest Samuell Wakeman, one northwest of Thomas Dudley, Esq., northeast . . . etc." This Thomas Dudley was the Deputy Governor who, after a bad fire in Boston, had decreed "in our newe towne which we intend to build this summer we have ordered that no man there shall build his chimney with wood or cover his house with thatch."

The foregoing chapter shows the agitation for the movement from Newe Towne Colony into the wilds of Connecticut. In June of 1635 the Hooker Colony headed for Hartford. Stephen Post's name is among those on the monument at Hartford as one of the "Founders of Hartford." Court records show that he was "appraiser of inventory and goods of William Lotta" about 1636. [*Early Connecticut Probate Records, op. cit.*] In 1639 his home lot was in the distribution of lands on the south side of the road from George Steel's to the South meadow. In the records of the First Church of Hartford [*Historical Catalogue of the First Church of Hartford*, 1885, pub. by the Church], Stephen Post was voted to clapboard the first Meeting House. And in 1641 he was to build a porch and stairs in the Meeting House, which is the same year he was elected constable. In the original town records of Hartford, as copied in 1665 by John Allyn, he wrote: "Stephen Post an original proprietor of undivided lands in Hartford . . . ." and then added, "allotted in divisions at two different times according to the proportions payed for the purchase of sayed lands, Stephen Post payed thirty pounds and twenty-four shillings." Here one might take flight into fantasy and conclude that Stephen Post was an excellent carpenter in the New World; this is the same occupation designated with the marriage banns in Kent. This was a trained profession in his day; the art of "clapboarding" and the use of shingles for a roof could not be accomplished by the amateur. From the records of The First Church: "On the 20th of October, 1640, *Goodman* Post should clapboard the building and furnish himself with the clapboards at five shillings, six pence the hundred, thus he to hew, plane and lay the clapboards." The structure of the Meeting House was almost square. The top of the pyramid roof was a turret, where the bell, which was brought from Newe Towne, was hung. There were three entrances, doors on all three sides, and on the fourth was the pulpit area. The height inside was sufficient for a row of galleries. The north side had raised seats, where the guards sat or remained on duty during the services, as look-outs. The porch and staircase, which Stephen built leading to an inside chamber, were the arsenal. Before the order to Stephen in October, 1640, the General Court on the 5th of April 1638 ordered that the Meeting House should be "put into good kelter" and "that there be a guard of men to attend all services with their arms fixed and with a supply of powder and shot." Two men were to oversee same, and one man to stay outside as a sentinel.

About this time, between 1642 to 1645, Stephen Post and his family were looking toward Saybrook. According to the *Collections Of The Historical Society of Connecticut*, published 1912, Stephen made a forage and exploration to Saybrook about 1645. Whether this trip was for his own edification or at the behest of other settlers is not shown. Saybrook is about 38 miles down river from Hartford, and one entry in 1646 shows Stephen Post and family as "leaving Hartford for Saybrook." Saybrook, in old records often spelled Seabrook, was named for Lord Say and Lord Brook. Saybrook was opened up about 1614, and the history of that founding will not be covered here since the details are available in published works. Some compilers of records on Stephen Post have regarded him as one of the earliest settlers there, but evidence disputes this assumption. Not until the Hartford group moved into the area did Saybrook become much of a thriving community. Stephen Post was definitely quite active as Saybrook expanded and attracted more settlers. The town plat of Saybrook for the year 1650 shows his lands to be of the first choice in the town. This plat shows many names of lot and landowners who were Hartford men; thus it becomes apparent that the move there was due to the opening of the lands to public sale. This section was known as Oyster River Quarter. Stephen Post purchased his land there about 1648; judging by the following entry from original town records: "Robert Chapman, Town Clerk of Saybrook, a true copy of the original attested by me, 18 Mar. 1672, Stephen Post paid in the year 1648 the sum of three hundred pounds and was granted 250 acres of land in the Oyster Quarter." Prior to this date, the Pequot depredations made settlement unwanted. In 1637 the "Corte att Hartford" ordered that there be an offensive war against the Pequots. From Hartford 42 men, from Wethersfield 30 men, from Windsor 18 men, under the command of Captain John Mason, were to form the army against them. Reverend Thomas Hooker sent Samuel Stone as their Chaplain. Captain John Mason's diary is on file at the New York State Library concerning his activities, and it is a very interesting document.

From the town records of Saybrook, it seems expedient to set forth here the lands of Stephen Post at Oyster River: "2 akers in the calves pasture abutting south to the lands of Robert Pargo, west to the highway, north to Richard Toosland (*sic*); 3 akers and a half of meadow in the planting field abutting east to Cove, south to Richard Toosland, north to John Bushnell, 7 akers of upland at Pennywise abutting east to land of John Clarke, west to Oxpasture, north to Highway; 5 akers of meadow more or less south end of said upland abutting east to meadow of John Clarke and west to Oxpasture. The commonage in Town Commons belonging to the estate of one hundred and fifty pounds." The original 250 acres granted to Stephen Post were: "his house and home lott in the towne abutting east, north and south to the highway and west to the lands of S. Huntington." The town records of Saybrook also show close association with Alexander Chalker, whom he assisted in building his dwelling. The grist mill operated by Chalker was built by Stephen Post, and the tumbling remains were still standing at Saybrook a few years ago. Stephen's daughter, Katherine, married the son and namesake of Alexander Chalker.

By order of the General Court at Hartford [*The Public Records of the Colony of Connecticut*, by J. Hammond Trumbull, pub. 1850, Vols. I, II, III, etc.—consult index], Stephen Post was named Lieutenant of the Fort at Saybrook on October 10, 1649, and was appointed to finish building the Fort. This order also included his son, John Post. The original town records of Saybrook show that in 1650 Stephen Post bought land on the west side of Oyster River. In 1651, 12th of August, John Lay made over to Stephen Post "all lands at Pochuge, *viz.*, 54 acres of upland. . . ." The Hartford records show that Stephen Post and son John Post were present for Town Meetings. There are entries for him, such as administrator of estates of his neighbors, or appraiser, and such functions common to an outstanding and trusted citizen of the community. And now we come to the demise of this intrepid immigrant.

Original Saybrook Land Records: "Stephen Post died 16th of August 1659." From *Early Connecticut Probate Records* (p. 144, *op. cit.*), the end of August 1659 there is entered "Stephen Post Inventory, four hundred and forty-two pounds, three shillings, six pence." This was signed by John Clarke, Thomas Leffingwell, Christopher Huntington. This was a considerable sum for the year 1659 for "moveable estate"; the inventory did not include the valuation of his lands. Since the exact acreage is not known, and the valuation of the land not completely apparent, we can conclude that Stephen Post exceeded his best dreams of prosperity in the New World. The Thomas Leffingwell, whose signature appeared on the inventory, was to play a very important part in the lives of two of the sons of Stephen Post and in the history of Norwich.

It seems necessary to interject here what other compilers have had to say about Stephen Post. *Genealogy and History of Connecticut,* by Cutter, Vol. I, p. 325 states: "Stephen Post and wife Eleanor came to America in the *Griffin,* arriving September 4, 1633, as a member of Rev. Mr. Hooker's congregation which he led through the wilderness June 1635 to found the Colony of Connecticut. After a time Stephen Post removed to Saybrook Fort at a place called Oyster River, where he died August 5, (*sic.*) 1659. His name is inscribed on the monument in the old burying ground of Center Church, erected by the citizens of Hartford, in memory of the founders of that city. His wife Eleanor died November 13, 1670. They had four children born in England, John 1626, Thomas 1628, Abraham 1629, Catherine 1630." While Cutter's information is substantially correct, we have shown from Parish records that the dates are slightly amiss. The publication *Post Family in America,* by Marie C. de Trobriand Post, states that Stephen had been a member of Reverend Thomas Hooker's Congregation at Chelmsford, Essex. This appears to be an undocumented statement, though not impossible; however, this is entirely unlikely in view of information given herewith above. *Saybrook, At the Mouth of the Connecticut,* by Gilman C. Gates, published 1935, shows "the lands of Stephen Post, his house and home lott in the town. . . . John Post appears to have been a son of Stephen Post who came to Newtown in 1634 and to Hartford with Hooker's Company in 1636. John Post married 1642 Hester Hyde, only daughter of William Hyde of Saybrook." On page 146, Gates stated "Catherine Post, daughter of Stephen Post, married Alexander Chalker." *A Genealogical Dictionary of First Settlers of New England,* by James Savage, published 1860, makes varied claims concerning Stephen Post and his descendants, which data should be used with care in compiling genealogical descent from Stephen[1].

This genealogical account is concerned primarily with Stephen's son Abraham, but perhaps an injustice would be done to family records unless some items from source material are presented on the other three children. Therefore, data are given in numerical order by number borne before each child's name and continued in that fashion through this compilation.

2. **Abraham**[2] **Post** *(Stephen*[1] *and Eleanor),* whose birth date is in dispute, either 1627 in England or at Hartford 1640, details of which are in text below. He died at Saybrook, Connecticut, *ca.* 1694; married *ca.* 1663, **Mary Jordan,** daughter of John and Ann (Bishop) Jordan of

Guilford; she was born *ca.* 1644 and died March 24, 1683/4, buried at Saybrook Point Cemetery.

Issue: 10 children.*

+ 7 Stephen[3] Post, born December 3, 1664, Saybrook; married June 14, 1692, Hannah Hosmer (see text #7).

   8 Ann[3] Post, born May 4, 1667, Saybrook (no further data).

+ 9 Abraham[3] Post, born June 9, 1669, Saybrook, of whom further (text #9).

  10 James[3] Post, born March 14, 1670/71, Saybrook, and died after 1708 and before 1738 (see text #7 Stephen).

  11 Hester[3] Post, born December 14, 1672, Saybrook; died January 16, 1676.

  12 Daniel[3] Post, born November 28, 1673, Saybrook; married Mary Rutty on August 29, 1699 (no further data).

  13 Jordan[3] Post, born May 27, 1676, Saybrook; died Hebron, January 20, 1748.

  14 Joseph[3] Post, born February 6, 1677/78, Saybrook (no further data).

  15 Mary[3] Post, born February 21, 1679/80, Saybrook; married Edward Bull on November 16, 1704, who died August 30, 1717; she married (2) — Pratt.

  16 Eleanor[3] Post, born February 21, 1682, Saybrook; died December 25, 1740; married Jonathan Parker.

At the Connecticut Genealogical Society there was (1939) an extensive handwritten manuscript, faded and worn with age, compiled by Reverend F. W. Chapman, probably intended for a Post genealogy which never came into being. Chapman gives the date of birth of Abraham Post as definitely at Hartford in the year 1640. He gives no references or proof for this statement. There is no entry of this birth in the records of the First Church at Hartford, nor in town records; there is no deposition in Saybrook town or land records whereby Abraham ever stated his age, no tombstone remains at Saybrook Point Cemetery. There is some basis of assumption for the date of 1640 from public records; the first entry for any transactions of Abraham seems to have been in the year 1661, on May 31st [original town records] namely, that "John Paine of Boston owes Abraham Post money." Perhaps he had not long turned 21, the age when a young man was of proper years to transact business legally. However, if this is correct, we do wonder about the possibility of any child of Stephen[1] being born before John was baptized in 1629. There is further strength in the 1640 date in the birth of the first child of Abraham, *viz.,* Stephen[3] born 1664. For that era, the birth of a first child usually indicated the age of fathers to be from 21 to 25 years, whereas, the 1627 birth for Abraham

* Above dates of birth and marriages are from original town records of Saybrook, and from *First Church of Old Saybrook (op. cit.).*

would place him at 37 years of age for his first child, a little out of routine for the era in question. This moot question may never be resolved.

On October 18, 1663, Abraham Post sold a bay mare of seven years to Elias Doughty; on May 11, 1665, Abraham Post was admitted as a Freeman by the General Court at Hartford. There are a number of entries wherein residents of Boston owed Abraham Post money. The record is not clear as to reasons for debts due him. The published *Colonial Records of Connecticut, 1665-1677*, page 60, show: "May 9, 1667, Abraham Post appointed an Ensign of Train Band."

Abraham Post seems to have been one of the most active of the sons of Stephen[1]. The Indian Sachem, Uncas of Mohegans, deeded 4,000 acres of land to Abraham in the year 1670, which was confirmed by Uncas's will. In 1670 Abraham was appointed deputy of Saybrook at the Hartford General Court. Other activities concern many dealings with the Indians. Many appointments are entered for him in the original town records of Saybrook. In 1675, Joshua, the Indian Sachem, granted Abraham Post and a group of other Saybrook residents land, "8 miles broad and 18 miles long." In May of 1680 Abraham was made Lieutenant of Saybrook Fort. [*Hartford Land Records*, Vol. VI, pp. 185, 188] There seems little doubt that Abraham Post was a merchant, though there is no record of what type merchandise was involved; that he needed a warehouse for such is shown as follows: "April 25, 1682, Abraham Post given six rods of land and permission to erect a warehouse and make a wharf along the river front." Doubtless this enterprise explains how men of Boston residence became indebted to Abraham Post [original Saybrook Land Records, Vol. I, p. 52]. One entry in the town records of Saybrook might explain some of the activities of Abraham: "This obligeth me to pay unto Abram (*sic*) Post or his order at 24 shillings a hundred, to the balance of 9 pounds, 5 shillings or in *shop goods* (italics are the author's) to that value to be paid at or before the last of May, the year 1661, by John Pane (*Paine*)."

In the State Library vault at Hartford, Town and Land Series, No. I, Vol. I, is a letter perfectly preserved, though the lettering is at times very difficult to read, in a precise hand and signed by Abraham Post which states: "Mr. Ely, yours per Mr. Chapman being communicated and considered of the Towne together with the award of the gentlemen we returned to you that we doe fully set downe by award, and we allso willing to have their advice in such esteeme as that you shall have the fence now standing in your proposition upon reasonable terms; and if you are not better provided and doe see cause to make use of any of us to helpe repair what is defective, provided it be speedily, we shall be willing to afford to you what help we may, and not require immediate satisfaction, but according to the advice of the Gentlemen in staying our recompence both for the fence and the labor until the next season of payment which with the tend of suitable respects is all from you in what we may. This 20th March 1672." The handwriting and spelling are thoroughly compatible to the date shown, which reflects schooling of Abraham Post beyond the run-of-the-mill townsmen at that period. He looms large in the records for Saybrook and was outstanding in his handling of all Indian affairs. He was on many committees for settlement of boundaries and disputes, evidence bears out the complete lack of difficulty with the Indian Sachems with whom he dealt. In the will of Joshua, son of Uncas the Chief, 16 May 1678, Joshua gave to his son and daughter and to his father Uncas, all of his lands. [*Connecticut Probate Records,* pub., Vol. 3, p. 35.] In the will of Uncas, 1683, he confirms 4,000 acres to Abraham Post.

The death date of Abraham Post has not been definitely determined from town or probate records, but it is believed proof can be adduced herewith to pinpoint a date *ca.* 1694. There have been various claims made for his death date, without citing authority or reference to factual material. J. H. Beers' *History of Middlesex* states he died 1671. The W. A. Post private papers in the vault at Westbrook show the date as 1690. The F. W. Chapman manuscript (*op. cit.*), *The New England Historical and Genealogical Register,* Savage's *Genealogical Dictionary,* Vol. 3, pp. 465 and 234, *Genealogy of Old Fairfield,* by Donald Lines Jacobus, all give the date as 1715. However, in the original Saybrook Land Records, Vol. I, p. 232, is entered: "lands of Abraham Post, late af Saybrook, deceased, datcd 1694." After this date there are numerous entries concerning the lands of Abraham, which were obviously being handled by his son Stephen. In the Saybrook Land Records, Vol. II, p. 238, is the following entry: "Stephen Post states his right to sell lands in Hebron, having inherited from Joshua, Sachem, late of Saybrook, deceased, and in right of my honorable father, Lt. Abraham Post, late of Saybrook, deceased." This instrument was dated July 23, 1707. Then Vol. I, p. 140, Saybrook Land Records, "Received the 5th of March 1720, I, Stephen Post formerly of Saybrook in ye county of New London, administrator upon ye estate of my Hond. father, Abraham Post, late of Saybrook, deceased, by virtue of power given me by the honorable court of Probate do set out unto my brother Daniel Post, one third part of an hundred pound right in the Town Commons of Saybrook, as aforesaid, as witness my hand ye 5th March 1720." Further, in Volume II, p. 217, Saybrook Town Records, a letter dated from Hebron, October 1708 from Stephen Post to Mr. Smll. Willard, Sr.: "These are to desire you to record to my brother Danll. Post, to my sister Mary Pratt, and to my sister Elianor Parker, a third part of an hundred pound right in ye Town Commons . . . it is to be understood it was part of that right which was my honored fathers." From New London Probate Records, Book 5, p. 321, Stephen Post, administrator of Abraham Post, deceased, dated June 5, 1705. In the original Deep River Records, Vol. II, p. 363, there is a letter from Stephen Post, dated at Hebron, 1708, which concerns the division of his father's lands as follows: "desire you record to my brother Abraham Post and James Post of Pachuoge that they did receive part of their portion of Stephen Post, Administrator of Estate of his honored father, to Abraham Post ten acres of land with orchard. . . ." As late as 1738, Stephen Post continued to write Samll. Willard about the lands of his father, this time concerning his brother James, who apparently died after the 1708 entry and before the 1738 date, as follows: "Sir, these lines may inform you that if neither your father nor you have not recorded one third part of one hundred pound right in the Town Commons to my brother James in the time of his life that you would do it now to his heirs in part of that which his fathers right upon their right charge."

This should close the chapter on Abraham Post. Only his eldest son, Stephen, who figured prominently in the settlement of his affairs and as founder of Hebron, and Abraham³ (#9), who is the direct ancestor in this work, will be traced. The balance of the children of Abraham² are dropped from this record.

3. **John**² **Post** *(Stephen*¹ *and Eleanor)*, born Otham, Kent, England, baptized September 13, 1629; died November 27, 1710, Norwich; married March 31, 1653 at Saybrook, **Hester Hyde,** daughter of William Hyde of Hartford and Saybrook. She was born *ca.* 1635; died November 13, 1703, Norwich.

Issue: 9 children.*

17 MARGARET³ POST, born February 21, 1653/4, Saybrook; married Cabel Atwell.

18 ELIZABETH³ POST, born February 22, 1654/5, Saybrook, never married.

19 JOHN³ POST, born April 12, 1657, Saybrook; married at Norwich, December 24, 1685, Sarah Reynolds. He died July 15, 1690. His widow died May 11, 1703.

20 SARAH³ POST, born November 6, 1659, Saybrook; married Captain John Hough of New London.

* Vital Records of Saybrook and Norwich.

21 MARY[3] POST, born *ca.* 1662 at Norwich shortly after the family removed there from Saybrook; married Jonathan Rudd.

22 ABIGAIL[3] POST, born November 6, 1664, Norwich; died young.

23 SAMUEL[3] POST, born March 8, 1668, Norwich; married March 17, 1697, Ruth Lathrop (for issue see *Norwich Vital Records*).

24 HANNAH[3] POST, born October —, 1671, Norwich; married the son of Deacon Stephen Hosmer.

25 LYDIA[3] POST, born March 11, 1674, Norwich; married (1) Abel Moore of New London; married (2) Joseph Harris of New London.

John[2] Post bought lands in Saybrook with his father Stephen. In 1649 he was named by the Hartford Court to assist his father in rebuilding Saybrook Fort. In the year 1652, just before his marriage, he bought two acres on which to build a house close to Saybrook Fort. As previously cited under the chapter on his father, Stephen[1], John was present at Town Meetings in the year 1655. Perhaps greater opportunity came to him with the opening of lands at Norwich, for in the year 1660/61 he removed there. On October 8, 1663, he was declared eligible for the Freeman's Oath. Thereafter the Town Records of Norwich show him in many capacities. In 1674 he was named as Townsman, and again in 1679. And as his father before him, he was named to be in charge of building a Meeting House. In 1685 he was ordered to lay the boundary line between New London and Mohegan Indian Lands. This same year, Owaneco left 2,000 acres of land to John. He was named to run the boundary between the property of John Gallop and T. Minor. In 1690 he was ordered to lay out land of Captain Fitch, and in 1691 was appointed to lay out 150 acres of Nathaniel Niles "because of his poverty due to his losses from the French." It was at this time that he lost his son, John, Jr. In October 1697, Sarah, relict of John Post, Jr., was granted leave to sell 14 acres of land. In the year 1701, John Post, Sr., is listed on the "survivors list of settlers of 1660."

John and his brother Thomas seem to have traveled side by side most of their lives. Retracing the steps back to 1645, the Narragansett Indians invaded the stronghold of the Mohegans. The Mohegans, under the leadership of Uncas, had rendered untold assistance to the English by aiding them to destroy the Pequots, their hated enemy, who for a while threatened the existence of the entire Connecticut Colony. Thomas Leffingwell, who was one of the appraisers of the estate of Stephen[1] Post, volunteered to take a few canoes with sufficient food to prevent the Mohegans from dying of starvation. Because of the fire at Saybrook Fort in 1647, no records are extant prior to that date to show who accompanied Thomas Leffingwell, but it is probable that John Post, then 18 years of age, accompanied him. Leffingwell was able to pack canoes with beef, corn, and peas, and paddle from Saybrook to reach the besieged Mohegans. This generous relief and assistance doubtless kept the Mohegans closely allied to the Saybrook settlers. From then on Uncas did all in his power to encourage the English to settle his lands; he especially aided Thomas Leffingwell. We know that John and Thomas Post made the move to Norwich. In the meanwhile John married the daughter of one William Hyde, another of the Hartford-Saybrook group who, from the founding of Hartford, owned a lot only four lots away from the Post family. Saybrook land records show that John Post's lot was "bounded on the west by William Hyde." *The Hyde Genealogy,* published 1864, by Reuben H. Walworth, Vols. I and II, has many connections with the Posts. This genealogy states that Hester Hyde was a cousin of Ann Hyde who married James II of England when he was Duke of York; however, there is no proof offered for this statement.

In the year 1659 John Post and his brother Thomas applied to the General Court at Hartford for permission to make a settlement at Norwich. The General Court replied: "The Court doe declare that they approve and consent to what is desired by petitioners respecting Mohegan, provided within ye space of three years they doe effect a plantation on ye place propounded." The following June 6, 1659, the three Mohegan chiefs, Uncas and his two sons, Owaneco and Attawanhood, deeded to the white men of Saybrook the nine square miles which was purchased for seventy pounds. Captain John Mason and John Post ran a race to see who could build the first house in Norwich. Some historians claim Mason won, others say John Post finished first. An old document at Connecticut Archives states: "James Fitch with his father-in-law Major Mason with 35 grown men, mostly heads of families, went to this new town in the forest with their wives and belongings in shallops, and were met by some Indians who escorted them to Norwich on the banks of the Yantic (now Thames) River." The Reverend Mr. Fitch was the first pastor at Norwich and was to hold the office for fifty-six years. Cotton Mather called him: "the bold, astute and learned Mr. Fitch."

The Town Records of Norwich reflect the various activities of John and Thomas Post. John is listed in 1660 as one of the original 35 proprietors. On the 3rd of October, 1663, he and his brother Thomas were accepted by the General Assembly to become Freemen; however, they did not take the oath until October 1669. On the 21st of June, 1665, John and Thomas were witnesses to the will of William Backus, Sr. In October of 1671 John was made guardian of the children of Lieutenant Griswold. In the year 1679 he was listed as "Townsman." In 1680, on the 12th of January, he is designated "Selectman John Post," and with two others was given full power to perfect the work of the Meeting House in behalf of the town. In 1681, John Post was appointed on a committee with several others to search the original dates of early grants and acts, and generally to preserve the early town records and keep them in order so as to supplement the Norwich statistics. In 1685, the patent was finally obtained and confirmed for the original tract of "nine miles square" to be the entire township, of which John was one of the original patentees. In that same year, Owaneco, Sachem of the Mohegans, gave to John Post for "love and friendship received from him" two hundred acres of land. The fast friendship of the Mohegan Sachems for the Post heirs is constantly reflected in the deeds of New London whereby vast tracts were granted to the Posts and allied families. Uncas left to John's younger brother, Abraham, considerable land. In 1689 he parted with four sizeable plots of ground, which later formed the township of Lebanon where other Posts were to aid in bringing that community into being.

In 1685 John Post and Thomas Leffingwell jointly signed the following letter: "We being appointed and ordered by the General Assembly to finish running the boundary line of Stoningham. . . ." When John Post was appointed to lay out the land of Captain Fitch, he was called "Captain John Post"—October 1690. Then on October 10, 1690, the General Court held at Hartford noted that "John Post accomplished the work entrusted to him about the making of Stonington north bounds, to Preston south bounds, according to the former order of the court, and the court approved the same." [*Public Records of Connecticut*, published 1850, Trumbull, *op. cit.* Vol. IV, pp. 57, 132, 235.]

The 1710 list of survivors of first Norwich settlers reads: "Now surviving on January the 31st, 1710, John and Thomas Post." (This Thomas Post was the son of Thomas Post, Sr.) Shortly thereafter John Post was no longer a survivor—his tombstone at Norwich reads as follows: "Here Lies the Body of Mr. John Post who Dyed Nov. 27, 1710, aged 84 years." Whether the survivors of John Post erred in his age, or if this is correct, can only be assumed as follows: he was baptized at Otham in 1629 (*op. cit.*), which would have made him 81 at death; therefore, was the baptism not performed until he was 3 years of age? Such could have been, but in this regard there are many known errors on tombstones showing that the survivors assumed an approximate age, particularly when the deceased had attained venerable years.

For the benefit of future compilers we list herewith the following records which cover many of the facts given above. These records would aid in compiling material on other of the Post and allied families: *The Public Records of the Colony of Connecticut*, Vols. III, IV, V, consult index. *Early Connecticut Probate Records* (*op. cit.*), Vols. III, IV. *History of Norwich, Connecticut,* by Francis M. Caulkins, published 1874, pp. 1, 5, 6, 53, 60, 66, 74, etc. Barbour collection of Connecticut Vital records, card file, State Library, Hartford, or on microfilm at most large libraries.

4. **Katherine**[2] **Post** (*Stephen*[1] *and Eleanor*), born *ca.* 1630 in England, date of death unknown; married September 29, 1649, Saybrook, Connecticut, **Alexander Chalker,** born *ca.* 1627; killed by the Indians in the Narragansett War.

> *Issue:* 7 children **Chalker.**
> 26 STEPHEN[3] CHALKER, born September 8, 1650, Saybrook; died 1711.
> 27 MARY[3] CHALKER, born April 27, 1653, Saybrook; married Richard Cozens of Block Island.
> 28 ABRAHAM[3] CHALKER, born November 8, 1657, Saybrook.
> 29 KATHERINE[3] CHALKER, born November 8, 1657, Saybrook; became second wife of John Jordan, brother of Mary Jordan, wife of Abraham Post.
> 30 SARAH[3] CHALKER, born October 19, 1659, Saybrook.
> 31 JANE[3] CHALKER, born March 25, 1662.
> 32 ALEXANDER[3] CHALKER, born February 25, 1666; died May 27, 1727.

Some historians claimed that Katherine Post was born in Newe Towne. If this were the case, she would have been 13 years of age at marriage. It seems more likely that she was born in England, *ca.* 1630; even as late as 1634 would place her marriage at 15 years. Pure records have not been sought for this child of Stephen[1] beyond the vital records of Saybrook. [Barbour collection, *op. cit.*] Alexander Chalker was one of the first settlers of Guilford. He was made a Freeman on May 22, 1648. When Stephen Post died, Katherine inherited land from her father in the Oyster River Quarter. On October 3, 1661, Alexander Chalker bought of Thomas Post of Mohegan, "half that farme that was Stephen Posts lyieing on the west side of the Oyster River . . . in consideration whereof the aforesaid Chalker doth promise to pay one mare of about six years of age, and one halter, to be delivered forthwith as also forty shillings to be payed either in corn or cattel next March." It is reported that Katherine married (2) John Mills, but this compiler has not sought additional data on this line. Katherine is included herein for benefit of those interested in all children of Stephen[1]. The publications* listed below will aid greatly in following the Chalker line of descent, as well as for additional material on the Post family.

* *New England Historical and Genealogical Register,* published Vol. II, p. 133; original town records of Saybrook; Savage's *Genealogical Dictionary, op. cit.*; original Saybrook Land Records.

5. Thomas[2] **Post** (*Stephen*[1] *and Eleanor),* was baptized at Otham, Kent, November 1, 1631; died at Norwich, Connecticut, September 5, 1701; married January 1, 1656 (1) **Mary Andrews** (recorded variously as Mary, Margaret, and once as Sarah), she died March — 1661, Norwich. Thomas Post married (2) **Rebecca Bruen,** September 2, 1663; she was born *ca.* 1640 and died at Norwich, April 15, 1721.

Issue: 6 children by 2 wives.

By **Mary Andrews:**

33 SARAH[3] POST, born November —, 1657; married Thomas Vincent.

By **Rebecca Bruen:**

34 THOMAS[3] POST, born December —, 1664.

35 HANNAH[3] POST, born February —, 1666; died unmarried, age 70 years.

36 MARY[3] POST, born June —, 1669.

37 OBADIAH[3] POST, born —; died *ca.* 1703 without issue.

38 JOSEPH[3] POST, born 1681; married November 20, 1733 to Mary Post of Saybrook. He died April 23, 1749.

Various activities and details about Thomas Post have been given under the section concerned with his brother, John #3. The reader is referred to many compilations for Thomas Post. Much guesswork has been done as to his birth; however, consideration must be given to the fact such compilations were done before the finding of the Church records at Otham, Kent. Previous assumed dates have been *ca.* 1628, which is close enough without benefit of Kent records. Caulkin's *History of Norwich,* original town and land records of Norwich, and many vital records would lead one to the solution of the descendants of Thomas. Doubtless the first wife died at Norwich before a burying ground was laid off. The Town Records of Norwich show: "The Towne hath purchased a burying place"; dated December 16, 1661. This plot was purchased from Thomas Post, "a parcel of land eight rods one way and five and a half the other way, in the home lott of said Thomas Post, adjoining a highway, six feet from the road to the burying place." The plot adjoined that of *Goodman* Gadger, and henceforth was to be known to the settlers of Norwich as the Post-Gadger Burial Ground, and many of the earliest inhabitants of Norwich are buried in the plot. By a deed of Thomas Post to Alexander Chalker [Saybrook Land Records, Vol. II: 77] he disposed of his Saybrook land after removal to Norwich. In this same land record is the following: "I give Segt. Richard Baskett, my kinsman, a tract of land adjoining that of Daniel Tracy, I also give him 4 acres of land at Yantic District, by that of Thomas Post, to the north and east." In the Town Records of Norwich is the following entry dated October 13, 1698, "Thomas Post is released by this court from the fyne that was imposed upon him for retailing liquor." This is the first record wherein a Post was guilty of an infraction, but since his fine was remitted, he doubtless proved himself innocent. The Thomas Leffingwell who had been in association with the family, the hero of the Mohegans, was settled in Norwich as neighbor to Thomas Post and John Post. Leffingwell, his son and grandson began the weaving of stockings on a loom. Later he acquired more looms until he was producing 1,500 pairs of stockings annually. It was in front of the Leffingwell shop that many years later the inhabitants of Norwich assembled as troops for their march to Lexington in the Revolutionary War. The trend to manufacturing in New England had begun, and the vicinity was less and less one of agrarian economy. By 1705 the New England colonists were raising sheep for wool and were manufacturing their own woolens with a great deal of success, thus imposing a real threat to the mother country. The distilling of liquor was an honorable business, and the local sale of rapidly increasing quantities was another added threat to England's exports—and perhaps the reason why Thomas Post was fined for retailing without a license. The mother country had imposed laws of strict taxation on the Colony. When Thomas Post died, he was interred in the old burial plot. The house he erected remained in possession of the family for over 125 years, and then was sold by Joseph Post, Jr., who moved to Lebanon, to one Ezekiel Barrett. This deed was dated April 14, 1775, and in part reads as follows: "excluding about 32 rods of land within said bounds, belonging to the town of Norwich being the old burying ground, with liberty of a pathway across my other land, from the Town street to the above bargained premises, to pass and repass. . . ." The descendants of Thomas Post have not been traced for this compilation; however, the references given are helpful for further search.

7. **Stephen**[3] **Post** (*Abraham*[2], *Stephen*[1]), was born December 3, 1664, Saybrook; died May 16, 1752, Hebron; married June 14, 1692, Saybrook, to **Hannah Hosmer,** born *ca.* 1672; died January 25, 1752, Hebron, Connecticut.

Issue: 11 children.

39 HANNAH[4] POST, born Saybrook, March 29, 1692; married (1) David Barber; married (2) B. Trumbull. She is mentioned in her father's will as Hannah Trumbull, wife of B. Trumbull.

40 STEPHEN[4] POST, born Saybrook, September 6, 1695; reputed to have died at Hebron February 26, 1775.

41 MARY[4] POST, born Saybrook, March 13, 1696/7; married Hezekiah Hutchinson.

42 HESTER[4] POST, born Saybrook, March 19, 1698/9; married Obadiah Dunham; she died May 7, 1752.

43 THOMAS[4] POST, the Deacon, born Saybrook, February 10, 1702; married July 1, 1730, Dinah Brown. Thomas died at Hebron December 2, 1782; Dinah died October 28, 1775.

44 GIDEON[4] POST, born Saybrook, February 10, 1703; died at Hebron, January 1, 1752; married Anna Terry.

45 PHINEAS[4] POST, born Saybrook, December 2, 1704; died March 21, 1787; married Anna Post, December 25, 1741.

46 SIBYL[4] (CIBELL) POST, born Saybrook, October 10, 1706; died January 26, 1737, before her father; not mentioned in his will; married William Buell.

47 DOROTHY[4] POST, born Saybrook, January 29, 1708; mentioned in her father's will as "Dority" Beckwith, husband Reynol Beckwith.

48 ISRAEL[4] POST, the Deacon, born Saybrook, May 13, 1709; died May 21, 1776 at Hebron; wife Phoebe ————, who died June 2, 1786.

49 RACHEL[4] POST, born Hebron, September 25, 1713; married September 4, 1735, Benjamin Bissell of Hebron.

Stephen[3] (of Abraham and Mary Jordan Post), is not in the direct line of descent traced in this particular genealogy; however, it would be interesting to descendants to learn facts concerning the various sons and grandsons of the first Stephen in the New World. This Stephen[3] cannot be ignored in his importance in the records. When only eleven years old, Joshua, the Indian Sachem, willed to Abraham, his father, four thousand acres of land which Stephen was to inherit. In the chapter on his father, it was seen that Stephen[3], as eldest son, was given the task of dividing the lands of the estate; and various other of his transactions were noted. Just before his marriage, Stephen bought 5 acres of land in Saybrook from Samuell Lord; his father being alive at that time, he therefore independently started his own life. The Saybrook Land Records (Vol. I, pp. 232, 233, etc.) show entries such as in May, 1700, he was given permission by Thomas Dunk to cart hay through his meadow and in June of that year, bought of Samuel Chalker for 66 pounds, meadow land at a place called "Upper Planting Field." In 1701, John Pratt exchanged 5 acres of Ox-Pasture for land known as Pennywise (what better name for property of a thrifty Yankee!). John Pratt was also to make a pair of plow irons, with Stephen to furnish the iron.

The New London Probate Records, original (Book A:321), show Stephen Post as administrator of the estate of Abraham Post, as previously cited in the section on his father. Stephen Post was one of a committee chosen on May 8, 1707, to name Hebron. That same year he sold to Ebenezer Page a home lot in Hebron from land that was willed to him by Joshua. Various entries in the Saybrook Town Records show him selling lands of

Saybrook after he became a resident of Hebron. The 18th century citizen had the same troubles as beset the 20th century man—his taxes annoyed him. In 1718 he petitioned the court and stated that his personal tax should be cut. Stephen seems to have engaged basically in farming and agriculture—he complained of his corn being trampled by oxen and entered his cattle mark in 1730. In December of 1738, it seems that the lands of his father were still not entirely settled, for on that date he wrote to Saybrook from Hebron requesting that his brother "James Post to have a third right in the Town Commons, as set forth in my father's will." This is the only evidence that his father, Abraham, left a will, which has not been located; obviously with Stephen appointed as administrator, rather than executor, the will was either lost, or for other reasons it was not filed for probate.

Stephen Post's activities in the founding of Hebron are found among the parchment records in the vault of the State Library at Hartford. These old records are a jumble, torn and yellowed, and in tremendous volumes. There is no chronology, many words are crossed out and changed, but some are clear and show the problems that beset the founders or original proprietors of Hebron—"Stephen Post, Samuel Jones and Daniel Bushnell, of Hebron, proprietors of the undivided lands. . . ." claimed that the grant and patent to Wethersfield gave them about 5 miles in breadth, one mile on the west side of the river and 8 miles (long?) on the east side of the river, to be measured at the north and south bounds. One document shows as follows: "On the third of October 1736, petition of Stephen Post (*et al.*), of Hebron, County of Herford (*sic*), and proprietors of Hebron and the rest of the proprietors . . . that in the year 1675 Joshua, Sachem, gave unto Capt. Robert Chapman, Robert Lay, Abraham Post, Abraham Chalker, William Bushnell and their heirs. . . ." Stephen Post was more or less "bell-cow" of the Hebron group. Under "Estate of Stephen Post, of Hebron, dated 1752, number 2471, Colchester Probate District" the will and estate matters for him are found at the Connecticut State Library. His will was dated the 5th of October 1748, inventory filed June 15, 1752. He mentioned his "loving wife Hannah; son Stephen, £20 and what he had already, with other pieces of land and books; to son, Thomas, £20; son Gideon, £20; son Phineas, £20; son Israel the other half of my buildings with lands on which they stand, he providing substantial maintenance for me and for my wife during our natural lives with £20; daughter Hanner (*sic*) Trumbull, £40; daughter Mary Huchason (*sic*) £40; daughter Esther Dunham £40; daughter Dority Beckwit (*sic*) £40; two sons Phineas and Israel Post sole executors." It is to be hoped that various references given within this work will aid future compilers of the descendants of this Hebron group of Posts. No other research was attempted on this line.

250

9. Abraham³ Post *(Abraham², Stephen¹),* was born June 9, 1669 at Saybrook; died at Westbrook, January 31, 1747/48, buried at Saybrook Point Cemetery. The wife of this Abraham has been cited variously. One compilation names her as Hulda, which doubtless is a grave error. The Westbrook Church Records in the vault at Clinton show that Abraham's wife was **Elizabeth.** The F. W. Chapman ms. (*op. cit.*) shows she was **Elizabeth Stevens,** daughter of Thomas and Mary (Fletcher) Stevens, which also is the tradition passed down in various branches of the family. The Stevens Genealogy* shows that Elizabeth, daughter of Thomas and Mary (Fletcher) Stevens, married Nathaniel Chittenden. There is no pure record by which this dispute might be resolved beyond the tradition and records of Westbrook Church for her given name; her identity will be assumed on best possible authority as **Elizabeth Stevens,** born July 14, 1668, at Killingsworth; she died after 1733 at Westbrook.

Issue: 8 children.

  50 ANNE⁴ POST, born July 7, 1693, Saybrook.
  51 ELIZABETH⁴ POST, born September 2, 1695; married Lt. Daniel Buell.
+52 ABRAHAM⁴ POST, born February 14, 1698, Saybrook, of whom further.
  53 JOHN⁴ POST, born June 16, 1700, Saybrook; married Lydia Bushnell on September 2, 1723 at Westbrook Congregational Church.
  54 NATHANIEL⁴ POST, born April 2, 1702, Saybrook (Westbrook section).
  55 NATHAN⁴ POST, born August 17, 1707; died October 19, 1802, aged 96 years, buried Westbrook; married Hannah Barnes who died March 3, 1752, age 45. This Nathan is reputed to have left records to the family which showed his mother was Elizabeth Stevens. Issue of Nathan and Hannah: I. Hannah; II. Nathan; III. Hester; IV. Joseph; V. Phoebe; VI. Christoper (all above children of Nathan are recorded in the Westbrook Church record).
  56 MARY⁴ POST, born June 3, 1711, Westbrook (no further data).
  57 MINDWELL⁴ POST, born November 14, 1714 (no further data).

Abraham Post³ was generally known as Deacon Post. He was the first Deacon of Westbrook (a few miles northwest of Saybrook), but unfortunately very few records are extant for the founding of Westbrook Congregational Church, nor are the earliest town records extant. There are fragmentary documents of the Church in the vault at Clinton. Abraham Post was listed in Saybrook land records as "Farmer Post" and as "Deacon Post" after the settlement of Westbrook. He purchased one piece of land in Saybrook from Peter Cross in the Oyster River Quarter, which deed is dated June 25, 1703, as follows: "I, Peter Cross, with my wife Mary, the only surviving child of Robert Wade, sometime inhabitant of Saybrook, deceased, I, Peter Cross of the town of Mansfield, County of Hartford, with

* *Genealogy of John Stevens,* by Charlotte S. Holmes, published 1906.

free consent of my wife Mary . . . for £3 to me in hand paid by Abraham Post, farmer of Saybrook, doe convey. . . ." The land records of Saybrook show a number of entries for Abraham Post; they show that he used the "cattle mark of my brother Jordan Post," this mark was a swallow's tail cut in the right ear, and Daniel also used the same mark, with half-penny cut out of under side of left ear. James Post entered the same mark. Abraham recorded his mark on May 13, 1708.

In 1716, the land records show that Abraham had 20 acres in Westbrook Center on which was his dwelling, a barn and an orchard. This house was reputed to be the first Post home in the area known as Westbrook and was built on a knoll at the head of the Pochogue River. Across from Abraham Post, on the east side, was William Bushnell, into which family the Posts married on several occasions. These were large "Salt-box" type houses. Around the home of Abraham was a slim, high picket fence, and against each side of the front door stood lilac bushes which remained in good condition for several generations, by word of later descendants. This Post homestead stood until 1837 when it was destroyed by fire. On October 25, 1705, Abraham was named to settle a dispute concerning opposing groups in a land controversy; one side Thomas Avery, and the other James Jordan, Stephen Post and others: "it is said the meadow descended from Mr. Stephen Post and is now in possession of his grandchildren Abraham Post and others. . . ." In 1722 is found the following land entry: "Husbandman Abraham Post received from his brother husbandman Jordan Post, a tract of land situate near and lying in said Saybrook River Quarter at a place commonly called Pond Meadow . . . estimation 10 acres . . . bounded east upon Abraham Post's land, southwardly upon Daniel Post land . . . ," recorded May 7, 1722 and signed by Jordan Post.

The settlers of Westbrook apparently had been making the trek to Saybrook for church services, but as the settlement grew with the constant inflow of new inhabitants, a petition was sent to the General Assembly at Hartford, dated May 13, 1724, asking "for power and privileges common to distinct societies." The petition was granted on May 28 of the same year, and the Ecclesiastical Society of West Saybrook was founded. In June of 1726 the church was organized with six men and eight women. In January of that year the group had voted to proceed "to the building of a Meeting House for God's Publik worship"; the dimensions were to be 40 x 32 x 18 feet. This building stood until 1828, and three other buildings were to be erected on the same site. The original fourteen members of Westbrook Church were Samuel Chapman, Abraham Post, James Post, John Post, Jared Spencer, Thomas Spencer, Margaret Chapman, Elizabeth Post, Lydia Grinnell, Sarah Spencer, Margaret Chapman, Mary Denison, Sarah Booker, and Mary Waterhouse. Abraham Post was named Deacon; he was to keep that position for seven years alone, after that time he was assisted by Jedediah Chapman. Though the earliest records are destroyed, from 1733 forward a most detailed account was kept. From 1733 to 1739, twenty-four Posts are recorded. From 1767 to 1770, there are 47 Posts listed by Reverend Wm. Worthington; from 1731 through 1741, twenty-one Post babies were brought forth for baptism. Then from 1757 through 1802, there were eighty-eight Post babies baptized and recorded by Reverend Jno. Devotion. Under the heading of June 25, 1733, is a list of "those added since at the Lord's Table: Mary Post, Elizabeth Post, Daniel Post, Jr., Sarah Post, Elizabeth Post." In 1755, Mindwell Post appears "at the Lord's Table." In Reverend Jno. Devotion's handwriting he entered: "whereas I find no mention of appointment of any Deacon before Mr. Robert Lay, I have made diligent enquiry of several aged fathers in this church and especially Mr. Nathan Post and Mr. Post informs me the Church first nominated Mr. Abraham Post who accepted the office and served almost seven years alone. Deacon Jedediah Chapman was chosen and served with him. Deacon Jedediah Chapman and Deacon Robert Lay were in office at the time of my Ordination which was October 26, 1767."

In the records of the Connecticut Probate, one finds that on May 11, 1727, Abraham Post was named by the General Assembly as Lieutenant of a Company of Trainband of Saybrook. No estate settlement has been located for Abraham Post. His death is recorded in the Westbrook Church records as given at the beginning of this section. Footnote references* below will aid further research for this particular line.

52. Abraham [4] **Post** (*Abraham* [3], *Abraham* [2], *Stephen* [1]) was born February 14, 1698, Saybrook; died after 1767, see text to follow. The wife of this Abraham has been a point of debate with all compilers. Outlined in the text below one will find various claims, explanations, and conclusions. This genealogy concludes that he married on November 16, 1726, at Easthampton, Long Island, **Elizabeth Barnes,** who was born either May 13, 1705, or November 10, 1706. She died after 1767.

Issue: 7 children.
+58 Roswell [5] Post, born *ca.* 1727, Westbrook, Connecticut, age obtained from his tombstone, of whom further.

* *Men of Mark in Connecticut*, Vol. III; 367; Original town records of Saybrook; Ms. of Westbrook Congregational Church, Clinton, Connecticut; *Connecticut Colonial Records*, Vol. VII: 102; *New England Historical and Genealogical Register*, Vol. LXII: 333; *American Lineage of Hoyt Post*, Detroit, published n.d. (to be used with caution).

59 MARGERY[5] POST, baptized February 3, 1733, Westbrook; no data.

60 ABRAHAM[5] POST, baptized December 12, 1736, Westbrook Church.

61 HULDA[5] POST, born *ca.* 1738; went to Vermont.

62 REBECCA[5] POST, born *ca.* 1740; no further data.

+63 WILLIAM[5] POST, born *ca.* 1742; see brief data under #63 to follow.

64 NATHAN[5] POST, born *ca.* 1744. No attempt has been made to trace the life of this Nathan, beyond the data in the Westbrook Church records. He seems to be the same Nathan who was in command of the sloop *Revenge* as mentioned in *Maritime Connecticut During the Revolution.* Apparently he settled in Vermont after the War.

In view of the fact that the wife of Abraham has been disputed and variously cited, we give herewith several of the sources regarding the subject. *The Hoyt Post Genealogy (op. cit.)* states that she was Elizabeth Roswell, daughter of Richard and Lydia (Trowbridge) Roswell. The F. W. Chapman manuscript (*op. cit.*), and all descendants, have assumed her to be a Roswell; however, the *Trowbridge Genealogy* states that Elizabeth, daughter of Richard Roswell and Lydia Trowbridge married on December 22, 1726, Francis Brown. *Families of Ancient New Haven,* by Donald Lines Jacobus, states the marriage to Francis Brown concerned this Elizabeth Roswell. The published vital records of New Haven show *Mrs.* Elizabeth Roswell married Francis Brown. The use of the *Mrs.* in this instance may not indicate a widow, but the possibility presents itself. The strongest proof against the Roswell connection is that Elizabeth Roswell was born to Richard and Lydia on September 5, 1690, by the New Haven Vital Records, therefore if she had married Abraham Post, she would have been age 36 when their first child was born. This seems a little out of routine for the era in question, and to bear children until age 54. The will of Richard Roswell does not clarify the matter since he died in March of 1702 before the marriage of his daughter Elizabeth. No will has been found for Lydia Trowbridge Roswell, who died December 10, 1731, which might clarify the identity of the husband of Elizabeth. More substantial information comes to light from the Church records of Easthampton, Long Island, which give the following: "Married November 16, 1726, Abraham Post of Saybrook and Elizabeth Barns of Uptown." One Elizabeth Barnes was baptized at Easthampton May 13, 1705, daughter of William and Mary (Rogers) Barnes; another Elizabeth was baptized November 10, 1706, daughter of Samuel and Elizabeth (Dyke) Barnes. While this does not entirely explain the eldest child of Abraham and Elizabeth named as "Roswell," proof seems to be satisfactory that Elizabeth Barnes married this Abraham Post.

There is very little to be done for pure records on Abraham and Elizabeth. The Westbrook Church records for this period being in very poor condition and not complete, only scattered entries can be collected. For instance, Reverend William Worthington made an entry without date, but which appears before entries dated 1731, as follows: "Roswell Post, son of Abraham and Elizabeth Post, was brought to church to be baptized." From the Town Records of Tinmouth, Vermont, where Roswell died, his death is dated January 3, 1814 in the 88th year of his age; thus he was born 1727. The entries of baptism for the next two children, Margery and Abraham, Jr., appear complete as given above. There are no dates for Hulda and Rebecca, or William and Nathan, but in a communion list somewhat later the minister gives: "Abraham Post and wife Elizabeth, and children Roswell, Margery, Abraham, Jr., Huldah, Rebecca, William and Nathan." Until Reverend Jno. Devotion took up his labors at Westbrook Church there is very little that is complete. However, he made an entry which gives some clues: "Elizabeth and Abraham Post were both members and living and remaining in the Church when I was ordained on October 26, 1767." After that date, Reverend Devotion's records are quite complete; however, there is no death date nor further entry for Abraham and Elizabeth. Just how much longer they lived or remained in the community is not known. There were no probate matters for either of them. All of their children removed to Vermont during the period of the Revolutionary War; it is not unlikely that they may have made the move also. One public function of Abraham can be confirmed: "On October 12, 1749, the General Assembly confirmed the appointment of Abraham Post to be Lieutenant of the 10th Company of 7th Regiment of the Connecticut Colony." About 1770, the Norris family acquired the property of Abraham Post. F. W. Chapman's manuscript indicated that Elizabeth died about 1767, and that Abraham went to Vermont with his children, doubtless to Rutland.

58. **Roswell**[5] **Post** (*Abraham*[4], *Abraham*[3], *Abraham*[2], *Stephen*[1]) was born Westbrook, *ca.* 1727; died at Tinmouth, Vermont, January 3, 1814, age 88th year; married (1) November 29, 1750, Westbrook, **Mehitabel Jones,** daughter of Nathaniel Jones of Saybrook; she was born *ca.* 1731 at Saybrook, died November —, 1778, Rutland, Vermont. He married (2) on June 14, 1779, at Rutland, **Esther Meeker,** who was born *ca.* 1755; date of death unknown, living 1800.

Issue: 12 children

By **Mehitabel Jones:**

65 MEHITABEL[6] POST, born October 12, 1751, Westbrook; died July —, 1779.

+66 Roswell⁶ Post, Jr., born May 10, 1753 at Saybrook; of whom further.

67 Jared⁶ Post, born June 26, 1755, at Westbrook. F. W. Chapman ms. states he married and had a family. He and two sons were drowned while boating on Lake Champlain in 1827; no further data.

68 Huldah⁶ Post, born April 25, 1757, no further data.

69 Reuben⁶ Post, born October 25, 1759, Saybrook; served as corporal in Captain Saml. Adams Company, Colonel Meade's Regiment of Vermont, and in 1781 on the payroll of Colonel Eben Walbridge's Regiment for defense of Vermont frontier. Data are given here to assist further search; he was possibly of Dorset, Vermont, where a Reuben Post recorded births of children during the 1780's. [Card File, State Library at Montpelier. One Reuben Post was residing in Addison County, town of Bristol, on the 1800 census of Vermont]

+70 Elias⁶ Post, born January 27, 1763, baptized June 19, 1763, by Reverend Jno. Devotion at Westbrook; see data under following #70.

71 Edmond⁶ Post, born March 1, 1765; died May 27, 1768, Saybrook records.

72 Martin⁶ Post, born August 12, 1767, baptized September 21, 1767, by Reverend Jno. Devotion; died January 15, 1777.

+73 Amanda⁶ Post, born August 13, 1771, baptized September 15, 1771, by Reverend Jno. Devotion; see data under #73 to follow.

74 Temperance⁶ Post, born June 8, 1774, and baptized July 16, 1774, by Reverend Jno. Devotion.

By **Esther Meeker:**

75 Russell⁶ Post, born June 19, 1781, at Rutland, Vermont. [Vital Records].

76 Levi⁶ Post, born February 9, 1783, at Rutland, Vermont. [Vital Records].

It is believed that the date of movement of Roswell Post from the area of Saybrook and Westbrook to Rutland, Vermont, can be proved. That he resided in Saybrook part of the time has been proved by the Bible and data left by his son, Roswell, Jr., who stated that he was born in the town of Saybrook on May 10, 1753; however, that date is not recorded in the Westbrook Church record, nor the town records of Saybrook; nor is Mehitabel recorded for the year 1751. Saybrook Land Records [Vol. I, p. 34] show that Roswell Post entered his cattle mark on May 28, 1746. During the years 1754 to about 1760, he served in the French and Indian Wars and was commissioned a Lieutenant in Colonel James Meade's Company engaged in guarding the Vermont frontier. [*Connecticut Colonial Records*, Vol. XIII, p. 435] It seems likely that he decided on Vermont while on these expeditions and then formed his opinion about settling there. His children continued to be baptized in the Westbrook Church through 1774. Under date of May 12, 1774, the Connecticut Assembly "do establish Roswell Post to be Lieutenant of the 10th Company of Trainband in the 7th Regt. of this Colony. [*Connecticut Colonial Records*, Vol. XIV: 274] Thereafter, he was known as Lieutenant Roswell Post. The Westbrook Church records also show him as Lieutenant Roswell Post until he left the community.

In the meantime, his brother William had established himself at Rutland and the Town Records of Rutland [Vol. I, p. 22] show: "August 11, 1775, William Post sells 50 acres of land to Roswell Post for £38 in the township of Rutland." It has been shown that Roswell's daughter, Temperance, was baptized by Reverend Devotion in July 1774; the land in Rutland was bought in August 1775, and the Town Meetings for Rutland show that Roswell Post was present at the 1775 Meeting; therefore it is assumed the move from Westbrook to Rutland occurred between those two dates. Prior to the Revolution, in the year 1771, Roswell Post had been with Colonel Allen in the land controversy between New York and New Hampshire over Vermont lands. Vermont had not been a separate Colony, and had been known as New Connecticut when the Hampshire Grant was settled in 1724 by colonists from Massachusetts Bay in the belief that it was part of Massachusetts Bay Colony. During the French and Indian War, hundreds of soldiers were called to march to Fort Dammer, which today is Brattleboro, Vermont. Many came from New Hampshire, Connecticut, and Massachusetts to help drive the enemy from Lake Champlain. In 1758, when scurvy broke out at Crown Point, the soldiers stationed there were helpless, and 800 New Hampshire troops, with axe, shovel, and hoe, worked night and day to cut a road from Charlestown, New Hampshire, along the Black River and Otter Creek through to the center of what is today the town of Rutland. As soon as the road was broken through, five droves of over 400 head of cattle were hurried along to the scurvy-ridden soldiers stationed there.

A heated controversy arose over Vermont which lasted for many years. Roswell Post was an active participant in this controversy for the next twenty years. From manuscripts at Middlebury College, the *History of Old Rutland,* and Town Records of Rutland, Roswell Post appears in many capacities. From 1777 through 1790, Lieutenant Roswell Post was a member of the Assembly and represented Rutland County, then known as Otter Creek. In the year 1778, he made the decision (among others) that Rutland would become headquarters of the State Troops, and he saw to the erection of a fort. In the middle of the War and his many activities, his wife Mehitabel died, and being left with ten children, he took a second wife, Esther Meeker. The Town Records of Rutland show that he was married in his own home to Esther on June 14, 1779. On November 22, 1779 "Roswell Post, the senior, on payroll of Captain Simeon Wright's Company of Militia in Colonel Gideon Warren's Regiment for alarm at Neshobe for three days in month of November." [Adjutant General's File, Montpelier, Vermont] Another compiler has assumed the following entry to concern Lieutenant Roswell Post, Sr., but it certainly is evident that this applies to his son Roswell, Jr., since being a lieutenant before this date and after, would indicate he probably was not likely to be a sergeant: The Adjutant General's Files at Montpelier show "June, 1780, Sergeant on pay roll of Captain Thomas Lee's Company in Militia of Colonel Gideon Warren's Regiment, at Ticonderoga and Crown Point, 7 days." Roswell, Jr., was then 27 years of age, and his father 54, therefore there is no reason to assume the sergeant to be the senior Roswell. In the year 1781, the General Assembly of Vermont ordered a Committee to be appointed to hold a conference concerning the removal of a garrison at Pittsfield and to make a report, on which committee Roswell Post was a member. This same year he was named by the General Assembly to a committee for the convention held by New York State and Vermont, concerning land title claims.

In 1782, he was Town Clerk and Selectman. In 1787, his name, along with William Post, is listed as connected with the Meeting House-On-The-Hill in the center of Rutland. In a list made in the year 1788, he was called an original member of the First Congregational Church of Rutland. About this time Roswell was doubtless feeling the urge to slow up and take life a little easier; he was sixty-three years of age; his youngest child was born six years prior. So, in 1789, on February 12, he sold one half of the buildings on his farm and 40 acres of land for the sum of 150 pounds to his kinsman Elias Post. [City Clerk's Office, Book 2: 127] Perhaps political fortunes displaced him since records show him active and of importance in Rutland until Vermont officially became a state. Nothing intimate is known of reason why, but soon Roswell was to pull up stakes and head for Tinmouth. Most of his children had long since established themselves, and perhaps he wished to go once again to new fields before the sun should set on his life's career. We have just one entry to tell us that he moved on. In the First Congregational Church Records for Rutland his name is transferred to the Church at Tinmouth in the year 1803. There are very few entries for him in Tinmouth town records; however, the Tinmouth Congregational Church book shows that he died January 3, 1814, in the 88th year of his age. The date of death of his second wife, Esther Meeker, has not been ascertained. The following works will be of assistance for further research on this branch of the family.*

* *Genealogical Dictionary*, Savage, Vol. III: 465; Original Westbrook Church Records; Archives of Middlebury College; Saybrook Land Records, Vol. I: 34; Original Town Records of Rutland, Vermont, Vol. I: 220; Vol. V; Vol. II: 127; Adjutant General's File, State Library, Montpelier; *Connecticut Colonial Records*, Vol. XIII: 435, Vol. XIV: 274; *History of Old Rutland*.

63. William⁵ **Post** *(Abraham⁴, Abraham³, Abraham², Stephen¹)* was born *ca.* 1742, Westbrook; married on July 16, 1766 to **Keziah Jones,** as entered by Reverend Jno. Devotion in the Westbrook Church records. The first two children are entered by Reverend Devotion; the family disappears from the records of Westbrook after 1771. Rutland Town Records show one child born in that place; however, the complete list of his children has not been sought for this genealogy. We give information with the thought that material gathered in passing will benefit future researchers.

Issue: (total not known).

77 Noah⁶ Post, baptized December 4, 1768, Westbrook.
78 John⁶ Post, baptized January 6, 1771, Westbrook.
79 Major⁶ Post, born October 26, 1783, Rutland, Vermont. Town Records show that Major Post died in Rutland, May 18, 1882, aged 98.7. 19.

William Post was a Revolutionary War soldier. Much material may be found about him in the Vermont records, as well as *Revolutionary War Soldiers of Vermont,* by Goodrich. William Post served in Colonel Meade's Regiment, "scouting after Tories and guarding in time of trial such as were taken supposed to be enemies, commencing May 6, 1777 and ending the 26th of same month." Vermont Rolls show that he was "Lieutenant Wm. Post, August 29th to September 20, 1780." On February 5, 1782, he sold land in Rutland to Joseph Post of Woodbury in the County of Litchfield, Connecticut, as follows: "Know all men that I, William Post, of Rutland, for the sum of 15 pounds to me paid by Joseph Post of Woodbury, tract of land in Rutland bounded by and as follows, from my home farm at a hemlock . . . 30 acres." The deed was witnessed by Abraham Post, doubtless his brother, and one Joel Post. This deed alone shows the migration of other Posts from Connecticut to Vermont. The Vital Records on file at the State Library in Montpelier show many Posts recorded for birth, death and marriage, which entries were not germane to this particular genealogy and have not been included. The 1800 census of Vermont shows William Post was living in the town of Georgia, Franklin County, Vermont. As heads of house in that town, appearing along with William Post, are Noah Post, Jesse Post. We give these data for benefit of future searchers.

66. Roswell⁶ **Post, Jr.** *(Roswell⁵, Abraham⁴, Abraham³, Abraham², Stephen¹),* was born May 10, 1753 at Saybrook, Connecticut, and died May 5, 1826, age 73, buried Congregational Church, Cornwall, Vermont. Roswell married three times: (1) **Hannah Johnson,** July 14, 1776, at Rutland; (2) **Martha Mead,** on July 14, 1777, at Rutland; she was born, probably, at Little Nine Partners, New York; she died on September 12, 1807, age 50, buried at Congregational Church, Cornwall, Vermont (see text). He married February 10, 1808 (3) **Rebecca (Stevens) Bascom,** by whom there was no issue. She died in 1854, by a Bible entry of her step-son Truman Post.

Issue: 9 children **Martha Mead.**

+80 MARTIN[7] POST, born November 11, 1778, Rutland (see data under #**80**).

+81 ELIZABETH[7] POST, born April 2, 1781, Rutland (see data under #**81**).

+82 MEHITABEL[7] POST, born April 10, 1783, Rutland (see data under #**82**).

83 MERCY[7] POST, born June 23, 1785, Cornwall, Vermont, married September 23, 1803 at Cornwall, to Samuel Blodgett; died at Malone, St. Lawrence County, New York. Had issue, not traced here.

84 ROSWELL[7] POST, born March 30, 1787, Cornwall, Vermont; married November 23, 1815, Cornwall, Vermont, to Martha Holmes; thought to have died in New Orleans.

Issue:
I. Edward
II. Elizabeth

+85 PHOEBE[7] POST, born June 8, 1789, Cornwall, Vermont (see data under #**85**).

+86 REV. REUBEN[7] POST, born January 17, 1792, Cornwall, Vermont (see data under #**86**).

87 CLARINDA[7] POST, born August 24, 1794, Cornwall, Vermont; married December 1, 1811 at Cornwall, to Henry Carr Green. They removed to Parishville, New York, where Clarinda died August 12, 1837.

Issue:
I. Martha Post Green.
II. Meribah Carr Green, born in Cornwall; married David Daggett and died at Potsdam, New York, on July 4, 1903.
III. Henry Green, married Mary Perkins and died in Michigan.
IV. Rollin Sanford Green, married Sophia Coll and lived at Parishville, New York.
V. Clarinda Lucretia Green, married Martin Welch and lived at Pierpont, New York.

+88 TRUMAN[7] POST, born December 11, 1796, Cornwall, Vermont, of whom further.

The original Bible of Roswell Post is in the hands of his great-great-granddaughter, Marjorie Merriweather Post May, and information therefrom is used regarding the children and dates of Roswell Post. His marriage to Hannah Johnson is entered as follows: "my first born son by my first wife was born February 11, 1777." Under deaths he has entered "my first born son by my first wife died about 19 days old on the 26th of February 1777. [If the dates are correct, the baby was 15 days old] Apparently a premature birth of this child resulted in the death of mother and child, as he entered "Hannah my consort died February 19, 1777." Just one year from the date of the first marriage, Roswell married Martha Mead. The dates are entered in the Bible, and also may be found in the town records of Rutland and of Cornwall. The second marriage is recorded in the Land Records of Rutland: "To whom it may concern, I joined in marriage on the 14th of July, 1777, Roswell Post and Martha Mead, by Benjamin Root." According to the birthplaces of the children, Roswell Post evidently remained in Rutland until 1784.

The parentage of Martha Mead has long been in dispute, but obviously it is now resolved. *History and Genealogy of the Mead Family*, by Spencer Mead, published 1901, shows that Martha (Patty) Mead was the daughter of Zebulon Mead and his wife Mercy (should be Mary) Carey. Other publications have shown that Martha (Patty) Mead was the daughter of Colonel James Mead of Rutland, which is entirely in error. The Mead family appears on the Barbour Collection of Vital Records of Connecticut as being of Greenwich until about 1750. From there, the family migrated to Nine Partners, New York, and about 1765 removed to Rutland. Timothy Mead and his five sons were early settlers of Rutland. The Rutland, Vermont, Probate District (microfilm copy at Montpelier), Vol. IV, pp. 150 to 153, has the full settlement of the estate of Colonel James Mead, naming all heirs; Martha (Patty) is not among those listed. Vol. III, p. 160, *ibid*, shows that administration of the estate of Captain Zebulon Mead was granted Zebulon Mead, Jr., and Henry Mead, at the Court of February 2, 1797. No final accounting of the estate is shown in the probate records; however, Land Records of Rutland, Volume IV, p. 170, contains a deed of partition of the estate of Zebulon Mead, *viz*.; "Zebulon Mead, Jr., Cary Mead, Martin Mead, Zerah Mead, Seth Mead, Roswell Post and Martha, his wife, Nathaniel Blanchard and Mercy, his wife, Moses Boardman and Abigail, his wife, Francis Hewit and Phoebe, his wife, Benjamin Platt and Chloe, his wife, heirs of Captain Zebulon Mead, for two thousand dollars deed to Henry Mead all claim upon the estate, except one-third part of the estate which is reserved for our honored mother, Mary Mead." This instrument was dated June 8, 1797. This Mead family, through Zebulon, his father, Timothy, etc., may be traced back from Rutland, to Nine Partners, New York, and into Greenwich, Connecticut, for the very earliest of the Mead family. Spencer Mead's published work must be used with care for data on this family. At the State Library in Montpelier, there is the *Life of Lafayette Wilbur*, an autobiography published 1881, Jericho, Vermont, which gives the descendants of Zebulon Mead and Mercy Carey as Patty, who married Roswell Post, Zebulon, Jr., Henry, Carey, Seth, Zarah, Phoebe, Mercy, Chloe and Abbie. The Bible of Roswell Post does not show the birthplace of Martha Mead. The Barbour Collection of Vital Records does not show the marriage of Zebulon Mead, nor the births of any of his children, though the records show entries for Timothy and his children. Since they obviously left Greenwich about 1750, and Martha was born 1757, we believe the births of the children of Zebulon probably took place at Nine Partners, New York.

Vermont Revolutionary War Rolls show Roswell Post was a scout in the year 1779 in Captain Simeon Wright's Company. In March of 1780 he served as a Sergeant in Captain Simeon Wright's Company and went to Five Mile Point and Bridport, Vermont, and on to Ticonderoga and Albany. In 1781, he was Clerk in Captain Nathaniel Blanchard's Company in Colonel Ebenezer Allen's Regiment. During this time, doubtless he was preparing for the move to Cornwall. It has already been established that his father moved from Westbrook to Rutland between 1774 and 1775. At that time Roswell, Jr., was about 21 or 22 years of age, and troubled times were beginning. He evidently went along with his parents to Rutland, but there is always the possibility that he had forged on ahead. Factually, we know that he was in Vermont in 1775. He had married his first wife, Hannah Johnson, in Rutland in 1777, and by the following deed acquired lands in Cornwall: [Rutland Land Records, Vol. 1: 3] "I, William Post, of Rutland, for the consideration of £50 do sell Roswell Post, Gentleman, 100 acres of land in the township of Cornwall, it being the second division lot to the original Right of Joseph Williams." This deed was dated November 6, 1783. By this time, Roswell was designated "Gentleman," indicating prestige for the era in question. His father was now married to his second wife and had his 12th child this same year. Roswell, Jr., had already sold Rutland land several years before: [Rutland Land Records, 29th of May 1780] "in consideration of £3 gold money, Roswell Post, Jr., to Samuel Beach, a half lot of pines lying in Rutland, containing 14 acres."

There are no records of Cornwall (Otter Creek) showing the original 65 patentees of the land when they received their charter. The Original Grantee list included Roswell Post, Chapmans, Hydes, Lathrops, and other kinsmen. By the deed of William Post, Joseph Williams shows as an original patentee. In the year 1783, Roswell entered his cattle mark in the Cornwall Records [Cornwall Land Records, Vol. I, p. 3]—the same mark as used almost one hundred years before in Saybrook by the sons of Stephen[1]. Thereafter, the town records and Land Records of Cornwall show some 35 entries of land transactions for Roswell Post, Jr. He sold lands to his sons as they matured: "To Martin Post one and one half acres for $30.00, year 1803." [Vol. IV, p. 335] This land was deeded by Martin back to his father on January 11, 1811. [Vol. V: 90] On April 4, 1818,

Roswell deeded to his son Truman Post 52 acres and 27 rods of land. [Vol. V: 368] He was an active and devoted member of the Congregational Church of Cornwell. On the 12th of March, 1812, the town of Cornwall voted an appropriation of twelve dollars with which to purchase of Roswell Post the burying ground west of the Baptist Church. The old Baptist Church was still standing within the last few years, but had not been used in many years. This was on the site of the original ground of Roswell Post when he settled at Cornwall. He was a devoted Christian man, sincere and complete in his belief. He had one son who became an outstanding minister, and grandsons whose ability in the ministry had wide recognition. These are covered in this compilation. In later years, when he would recount the early days, he was proud of the facts and retold his story many times. Roswell said that when he left his father's home in Saybrook, his only property was his axe, a clean shirt tied in a pocket handkerchief, and a determination to succeed. He did succeed in many ways. He became active in Town Meetings, and was trustee of schools. In 1803, he was Selectman. His handwriting in his Bible is extraordinary, and indicates penmanship and education above the average for that era. The records searched reveal no man in the Post family who signed with his mark, a singular distinction in the Colonial era.

Roswell Post, his wife Martha Mead, and their son Martin are buried near the Meeting House, high on a lovely hill, overlooking the rolling countryside. The tombstones at one time had fallen over, and in 1937, were repaired and cemented into position. They were the original stones, however. This restoration was done by Roswell's great-great-granddaughter, Marjorie Merriweather Post, now Mrs. Herbert A. May. The dates on the stones are the same as recorded herewith, and are from the Bible and the Town Records of Cornwall. (For additional information, see footnote.*)

70. **Elias**[6] **Post** *(Roswell*[5]*, Abraham*[4]*, Abraham*[3]*, Abraham*[2]*, Stephen*[1]*)*, was born January 27, 1763, baptized on June 19th, Westbrook Church; died September 4, 1851, Mount Holly, Vermont; married *ca.* 1788 at Rutland, Vermont, **Martha Porter,** daughter of Thomas Porter of Rutland; she was born March 9, 1763, and died about 1837.

> *Issue:* 8 children.
> 89 Eli[7] Post, born November 5, 1789, Rutland, Vermont.
> 90 Electa[7] Post, born March 1, 1791; died July 19, 1875.

* *History of Cornwall,* by Rev. Lyman Matthews, published 1862; Original Congregational Church Records, Cornwall; Original Rutland Town and Land Records; Original Town and Lands Records of Cornwall.

91 EDMUND⁷ POST, born November 26, 1792; died May 21, 1794.
92 THEODA⁷ POST, born November 17, 1795.
93 JAMES ALEXIS⁷ POST, born December 20, 1797.
94 SALLY⁷ POST, born January 13, 1800; married Dan Peck; died November 3, 1873.
95 JOHN JACKSON⁷ POST, born January 19, 1802.
96 EDMUND RUSSELL⁷ POST, born February 3, 1808; died at Birmingham, Michigan, November 5, 1891; married June 6, 1836, Almira (Collins), Colvin.

Issue:
I. Hoyt Post, born April 8, 1837.
II. James Post.
III. Vernon Post.
IV. Julia Post.
V. Xenia Post.

Elias Post is given herewith for reason of the *Hoyt Post Genealogy,* (*op. cit.*). This particular genealogy can be found in many libraries, and the reader is cautioned to use it with care; there are many errors in the work when placed against factual material. Hoyt Post was the son of Edmund, son of Elias, as given above. Other than his baptismal date, Elias has not been proved by this compiler; the balance of the data herewith are from the genealogy in question. Hoyt Post stated in this genealogy that Elias Post served in the Revolution with his brother, Roswell, in Captain Samuel Adams' Company of Colonel Meade's Regiment. As a possible aid to further research, there is an Elias Post on the 1800 census of Vermont, living in the town of Rutland, with the eldest male in the household between the ages of twenty-six to forty-five years. In 1820, the census of Vermont shows an Elias Post living in Tinmouth, Vermont. Elias Post made an application for Revolutionary War Pension on January 29, 1834, at which time he was residing in Rutland, Vermont. (Pension not read by this compiler.)

73. Amanda⁶ **Post** (*Roswell*⁵, *Abraham*⁴, *Abraham*³, *Abraham*², *Stephen*¹), was baptized September 15, 1771, Westbrook Church, Westbrook, Connecticut; married February 25, 1789, at Cornwall, to **Eliphalet Samson,** of Cornwall.

Issue: 12 children **Samson.**
97 TEMPERANCE⁷ SAMSON, born November —, 1790; married H. Linsley.
98 AMANDA⁷ SAMSON, born August 18, 1792; married L. Lamb.
99 BETSEY⁷ SAMSON, born June 14, 1794; married ———— Lamson.
100 REUBEN⁷ SAMSON, born July 1, 1797.
101 HERMAN⁷ SAMSON, born July 25, 1799.

102 WILLIAM⁷ SAMSON, born June 20, 1801.

103 POLLY⁷ SAMSON, born June 11, 1803; married R. T. Bingham.

104 SALLY⁷ SAMSON, born June 25, 1805; married Reverend Luther Goodyear Bingham, who was a graduate of Middlebury College and 13 years a pastor of the Congregational Church at Marietta, Ohio. He died at Middleburgh, New York, January 23, 1878.

105 THOMAS⁷ SAMSON, born September 22, 1807.

106 MARTIN⁷ SAMSON, born August 31, 1809.

107 ELIPHALET⁷ SAMSON, born September 15, 1811.

108 ASHLEY SAMSON, born May 2, 1814, was graduated from Middlebury College and was ordained in 1839; died October 15, 1850 at Fayette, Missouri.

This compiler has not attempted to expand any data beyond that given here, as concerns the Amanda Post Samson family. The information given comes from the F. W. Chapman Ms., the *Hoyt Post Genealogy* (*op. cit.*), and vital records of Cornwall, Vermont. Eliphalet Samson was the son of William Samson who settled in earliest days of Cornwall (Otter Creek) from Londonderry, New Hampshire. William Samson was elected Deacon of the Congregational Church of Cornwall in 1788; reared a large family of sons, and died in 1798 at the age of 66 years. Eliphalet bore the title of Captain and Esquire, rearing a large family in punctual observance of religious ordinances, conducting weekly prayer meetings at his home. To those who are interested in tracing the descendants of this Samson family, perhaps data given here will benefit. There is no question that additional information could be expanded through the Town Records of Cornwall, and vital records on file at the State Library at Montpelier.

80. Martin⁷ Post (*Roswell⁶, Roswell⁵, Abraham⁴, Abraham³, Abraham² Stephen¹*), was born November 11, 1778 at Rutland, Vermont; died February 2, 1811 at Cornwall; married October 6, 1803 at Orwell, Vermont, to **Sarah Hurlburd** (daughter of Ebenezer Hurlburd of Orwell). Date of birth of Sarah not known; she married (2) Captain Augustus Hand, and by him had Augustus T. Hand, Oliver Hand, and Sarah Jane Hand. Sarah (Hurlburd) Post Hand died at Ferrisburgh, Vermont, December 2, 1839.

Issue: 3 sons.

109 MARTIN MERCILLIAN⁸ POST, born December 5, 1805, at Cornwall; died October 11, 1876 at Logansport, Indiana. He was graduated at Middlebury College in 1826, and passed through a theological course at Andover. At age 25, he went to an Indian Trading Post at Logansport and remained there until his death. He was ordained pastor of the

oldest Presbyterian Church in Logansport in 1829 and held the post for 40 years; he was founder and principal of Logansport Seminary; founder of Wabash College and trustee for 38 years. He married (1) Lucretia Hobart of Homer, New York, September 9, 1832, who was born June 9, 1811, and died March 5, 1840 at Logansport. He married (2) on December 1, 1841, Eliza Mellon Breed, who was born April 11, 1818, at Keene, New Hampshire, and died March 22, 1884, at Logansport. All of his children were born at Logansport.

Issue:

    I. Rev. Martin Post of Sterling, Illinois.
    II. Rev. Aurelian H. Post of Milton, Wisconsin.
    III. Rev. Alfred B. Post, who died at Santa Clara, California.
    IV. Rev. Edmund Post of Lowell, Indiana; missionary to Japan.
    V. Rev. Roswell Post of Logansport, Indiana.
    VI. Mary Post who married ———— Ely.
    VII. Lucy Post who married Professor Coulter of Logansport.

110 AURELIAN HURLBURD[8] POST, born February 26, 1807, at Cornwall, was graduated at Middlebury College in 1832 and commenced a theological course at Andover, but illness prevented his continuing. He established a private school at Medford, Massachusetts, but again illness forced him to leave school and all work. He went to Mississippi for his health and from there to visit his brother at Logansport, where he died on October 15, 1834. Never married.

111 TRUMAN MARCELLUS[8] POST, born June 3, 1810, at Middleburry, was named for his father's brother. The life of this man was quite outstanding, and a complete biography was done by his son, T. A. Post, published in 1891 under the title *Truman Marcellus Post, a Biography.* He was graduated at Middlebury, valedictorian of his class, and taught at Addison County grammar school. He had intended becoming a lawyer; Judge Lockwood of the Supreme Court of Illinois signed a certificate in June, 1833, admitting him to practice law in the State of Illinois. He was appointed professor of ancient history at Illinois College in Jacksonville, where he remained fourteen years. He then began his pastorate at the First Trinitarian Congregational Church (Third Presbyterian) at St. Louis, Missouri, where he remained until his death on December 31, 1886. On a return visit to his home in Vermont, he married Frances Henshaw, on October 5, 1835, at Middlebury; she was the daughter of Daniel Henshaw, and sister of Bishop John P. K. Henshaw of Maryland, Delaware, and Rhode Island.

Issue:

    I. Frances Henshaw Post.
    II. Truman Augustus Post.
    III. Henry McClure Post.
    IV. Catherine Harriett Post.
    V. Clara Harrison Post; all of above born at Jacksonville, Illinois.
    VI. Martin Hayward Post, born at St. Louis, Missouri.

Martin Post, father of #109, #110, #111, studied law with Seth Storrs, prominent Middlebury lawyer; he was admitted to the bar early in 1802, and for a time, practiced law at Jericho, Vermont. While there, he married Sarah Hurlburd of Orwell Village. They returned to Cornwall where they built their small home near his father (Roswell[6]). Martin is buried in the same plot with his parents. He was Town Clerk in 1802 and in 1804, Clerk of the House of Representatives in 1804 and 1808, and Clerk of the Addison Court in 1808 and 1810. Additional data will be found concerning his estate settlement under the details of his youngest brother, Truman, #88. In the intimate account of *Truman Marcellus Post,* (*op. cit.*) the author states that Captain Hand, a retired sea captain, possessed such a temper that the step-sons left home. T. M. Post returned to Middlebury to live with relatives while attending school. This son of Martin Post kept close family ties with his uncle Truman, and the families of both these men were closely associated in the West. T. M. was a wise and just counsellor for Charles William Post, the subject of the foregoing biography. C. Rollin Post and his sons visited frequently at Jacksonville, and at St. Louis, with Truman Marcellus Post. For complete details see later herein.

81. Elizabeth[7] **Post** (*Roswell*[6], *Roswell*[5], *Abraham*[4], *Abraham*[3], *Abraham*[2], *Stephen*[1]) was born April 2, 1781, at Rutland, Vermont; died May 25, 1853 at South Farms (Litchfield), Connecticut; married December 28, 1798 at Cornwall, **Simeon Sanford,** of Litchfield; he died on June 23, 1846, and both are buried at South Farms, now Morris.

Issue: 4 children **Sanford.**

112 ORAN[8] SANFORD, born October 29, 1799, Cornwall, Vermont; died age 3.

113 RHODA[8] SANFORD, born July 7, 1801, Cornwall, Vermont; married William Harrison of Litchfield on November 6, 1822; he died March 17, 1830. She married (2) Edward Cowles on September 22, 1839; he died April 4, 1849. Rhoda died July 7, 1893 in Morris, Connecticut, aged 92 years. Rhoda Cowles became crippled in later life and engaged her time by filling 24 scrapbooks with family data. It was she who compiled the Post family notes in circular form, which have been used by many of the family as a basis for genealogical information. In her 90th year she wrote the history of Morris. She had two children by William Harrison, and one child, who died young, by Edward Cowles.

114 CLARINDA[8] SANFORD, born February 2, 1804, Cornwall, Vermont; married on November 12, 1823 to William Harrison. They both died at Baltimore, Maryland, and are buried in Greenmount Cemetery. Clarinda died on May 21, 1875, and William Harrison died on January 25, 1870, aged 70. It is reputed that they had two children.

115 ROLLIN[8] SANFORD, born March 27, 1806, Cornwall, Vermont; married (1) on May 25, 1835, to Maria Seymour, who was the daughter of Ozias Seymour, and sister to O. S. Seymour, Chief Justice of Con-

necticut. Maria died April 5, 1836. Rollin Sanford married (2) Lucy Ann Wright of Brooklyn, New York, on September 10, 1839, and she died April 20, 1843. Notes on Rollin Sanford were from the papers of his sister, Rhoda Cowles, and the information contained therein seems confused and without proof. She places him at Hastings-On-Hudson as late as 1862, which data are not verified by this compiler.

There has been no effort made to establish, or authenticate, the above information on Elizabeth Post Sanford and her descendants. Information given here is with the thought that it might be helpful to future researchers; however, we caution the reader to use with care.

82. Mehitabel[7] **Post** *(Roswell*[6]*, Roswell*[5]*, Abraham*[4]*, Abraham*[3]*, Abraham*[2]*, Stephen*[1]*)* was born April 10, 1783, Cornwall, Vermont; died at Crown Point, New York, on September 16, 1872, buried at Cornwall; married April 22, 1802, Cornwall, **David Foote, Jr.,** of Cornwall.

> *Issue:* 4 children **Foote.**
>
> 116 Betsey[8] Foote, born at Cornwall; married Truman Ellis, had issue.
> 117 Colonel Abram[8] Foote, born May 5, 1805, Cornwall, Vermont; died at Middlebury, Vermont, on June 10, 1876, buried at Cornwall. He was prominent in Cornwall, three times a member of the legislature, and Deacon of the Baptist Church; married Orpha Williamson and had four children.
> 118 Martha[8] Foote, born at Cornwall; married Henry Davis of Crown Point, New York; had issue.
> 119 David[8] Foote III, born April 13, 1813, Cornwall, Vermont, was graduated at Middlebury. Principal of the Academy at Moriah, New York; pastor at Nassau, New York, and Hamilton, New York; married Esther Lamb; had one daughter. David Foote III, died June 10, 1848.

Mehitabel Foote is reputed to have married three times, (2) to a Reynolds, and (3) to Samuel Murdock of Crown Point; proof not sought here for above data. In the letters of Truman Post (her brother) to his sister Clarinda Green he mentions a proposed trip to Crown Point to see his sister Mehitabel; however, there is very little information about this sister in any of the letters of Truman Post.

85. Phoebe[7] **Post** *(Roswell*[6]*, Roswell*[5]*, Abraham*[4]*, Abraham*[3]*, Abraham*[2]*, Stephen*[1]*)* was born June 6, 1789, at Cornwall, Vermont; died May 31, 1864, at the home of her daughter in East Cambridge, New York; married July 2, 1807, Cornwall, Vermont, to **Dr. Hosea Brooks,** and moved to Parishville, New York (St. Lawrence County), where Dr. Brooks died.

Issue: 5 children **Brooks.**

120 MARTHA POST⁸ BOOKS, born March 16, 1808, Cornwall, Vermont; married R. S. Hawthorne; died November 8, 1833 at Parishville. Issue: 2 daughters.

121 MARY PARSONS⁸ BROOKS, born September 10, 1810, Cornwall, Vermont; died March 4, 1831, Parishville, New York.

122 CAROLINE LOUISE⁸ BROOKS, born April 20, 1815, Parishville, New York; married May —, 1837 to Dr. Henry Newman and had two children who died young; married (2) Herman Morse of E. Cambridge, New York, *ca.* 1854.

123 EMMA ELIZABETH⁸ BROOKS, born August 6, 1816, Parishville, New York; married October 7, 1840, to Phineas Denslow Gurley, D.D., who was born at Hamilton, New York. He was a well-known minister, first preaching in Indianapolis, Indiana, then in Dayton, Ohio. He was called to New York Avenue Presbyterian Church, Washington, D. C., and was at the bedside of Abraham Lincoln when he died. He served as Chaplain of the U. S. Senate. Issue: 5 children (not sought).

124 ERASMUS DARWIN⁸ BROOKS, born March 6, 1818, Parishville, New York; married Pamela Sanford. Issue: 5 children (not sought).

86. Rev. Reuben⁷ Post (*Roswell⁶, Roswell⁵, Abraham⁴, Abraham³, Abraham², Stephen¹*) was born January 17, 1792, Cornwall, Vermont; died September 24, 1858, Charleston, South Carolina; married *ca.* 1827 to **Harriott Moffitt,** of Alexandria, Virginia, who was born 1805, and died May 30, 1857, age 52, Charleston, South Carolina.

Issue: 5 children.

125 DR. WILLIAM MOFFITT⁸ POST, born May 16, 1828, Washington, D. C.; married Mary Stuart of Alabama, reputed to be a great-granddaughter of Eleanor Calvert Custis Stuart. After the Civil War, Dr. Post was a physician at Beaufort, South Carolina, and Baltimore, Maryland. He died November 3, 1870 at the home of his sister, Mrs. Harriott Pinckney, in Sumter, South Carolina; he was buried in Alexandria, Virginia. Issue: 6 children.

126 HARRIOTT LEE⁸ POST, born at Charleston; married Henry Laurens Pinckney of Statesburg, South Carolina.

Issue:

I. Harriott Frances Pinckney, born August 12, 1863.
II. Rebecca Elliott Pinckney, born October 29, 1865; died same year.
III. Charles Post Pinckney, born January 16, 1867.
IV. William Reuben Pinckney, born March 1, 1872; died same year.

127 FRANCES ANN⁸ POST, died at Charleston, April 13, 1852, aged 18 years.
128 EMILY⁸ POST, died in infancy.
129 RICHARD HENRY⁸ POST, died in infancy.

Reverend Reuben Post had wide acclaim as a minister. He was graduated from Middlebury College and studied theology at Princeton. In the year 1818, he was called to the First Presbyterian Church, Washington, D. C., and served there for 18 years. He was Chaplain of the Senate for a short time. John Quincy Adams chose him as pastor in Washington and considered him one of the greatest preachers of his time. Reuben Post's wife, Harriott Moffitt, was a grandchild of Richard Henry Lee, her mother having been a half-sister to Robert E. Lee. [Not verified by this compiler, information from letters of Truman Post, who was her brother-in-law] She was reared in Alexandria, Virginia, and is reputed to have met her future husband while he was serving the First Presbyterian Church in Washington. He was called to Charleston as pastor of the Independent Congregational Church (Circular Church), remaining there until his death.

While they were serving the Circular Church, Charleston, Reverend Reuben Post contracted yellow fever and died there. The Congregation of the Circular Church (First Presbyterian) erected a fine monument to him, and the following is inscribed thereon: "Our Faithful and Beloved Pastor, Reverend Reuben Post, D. D., born January 17, 1792, died September 24, 1858—For Me to Live in Christ and to Die Is to Gain." Next to his stone is that of his wife, "Harriott Post, wife of Rev. Reuben Post, D. D., Fell Asleep May 30, 1857, aged 52 years. Thanks Be To God Who Giveth Us the Victory Through Our Lord Jesus Christ." With these two stones is that of their daughter Frances, who died April 13, 1852, aged 18 years and 7 months. Reverend Reuben Post and his brother Truman Post kept in close touch by correspondence until Truman Post died in 1847. The same entries as appear on the stones at Charleston are recorded in Truman Post's Bible in the handwriting of his wife Betsey.

88. Truman[7] **Post** (*Roswell*[6], *Roswell*[5], *Abraham*[4], *Abraham*[3], *Abraham*[2], *Stephen*[1]) was born December 11, 1796, Cornwall, Vermont; died October 29, 1847, Waverly, Illinois, where a tombstone remains in excellent condition. He married on March 19, 1820, at Granville, New York, **Betsey Atwater** (daughter of Stephen and Anna (Moss) Atwater), She was born December 9, 1794, Cheshire, Connecticut; died August 18, 1861, Springfield, Illinois (tombstone).

Issue: 10 children.*

130 a daughter was born December 7, 1820 and died January 7, 1821.

+131 REUBEN LARNED⁸ POST, born December 15, 1821, Cornwall, Vermont, (see data under #131).

+132 LAFAYETTE⁸ POST, born August 20, 1823, Cornwall, Vermont, (see data under #132).

+133 CHARLES ROLLIN⁸ POST, born January 15, 1826, Cornwall, Vermont, (see data under #133; this is the father of the subject of the foregoing biography).

134 HERBERT⁸ POST (twin) born December 27, 1827, Cornwall, Vermont; died September 12, 1920, Kansas City Missouri; married (1) on August 27, 1851, Emorette E. Peck, at Parishville, N. Y.; she was born August 10, 1830; died August 30, 1860, Springfield, Illinois. He married (2), August 30, 1862 as her third husband, Julia E. (Hyde) Bunker Havens, born April 1, 1824; died January 12, 1889, Fort Worth, Texas. Herbert Post, brother to Rollin, was closely associated with his brother and nephew Charles William Post, and travelled with them from Springfield, to Forth Worth, Texas, later settling in Kansas City, Missouri, near his married children.

> *Issue:* by his first wife only.
>
> I. WILLIS HERBERT⁹ POST, born June 15, 1854, Springfield, Illinois; died November 27, 1930, Battle Creek, Michigan; married Emma E. Reed. Willis Post was the *"father"* of *Instant Postum* for his cousin, C. W. Post. Issue of Willis H. Post not traced.
>
> II. MINNIE HELEN⁹ POST, born June 8, 1857, Springfield, Illinois; died May 19, 1946, Kansas City, Missouri; married August 18, 1880, Nathaniel T. Green, born August 30, 1855, Danville, Virginia; died August 15, 1916, Kansas City, Missouri.
>
> > *Issue:*
> >
> > i. Herbert Post Green, born July 7, 1881, Marion, Alabama.
> >
> > ii. Natalie Green, born December 11, 1883, Postburg, Alabama; living (1963) Kansas City, Missouri.
> >
> > iii. Julie E. Green, born January 9, 1888, Birmingham, Alabama, living (1963) Kansas City, Missouri.
> >
> > iv. William S. Green, born November 3, 1893, Kansas City, Missouri.
>
> III. GEORGE HAWTHORNE⁹ POST, born May 14, 1859, Springfield, Illinois; died October 21, 1898, New Orleans, Louisiana; married Fannie Caspari. Had issue: Ruth and Myra Post.

135 HARRIOTT⁸ POST (twin), born December 27, 1827, Cornwall, Vermont; died April 3, 1849; married May 24, 1848, Gustavus A. Hull, who was born April 18, 1827 (printer and publisher of Louisville, Kentucky).

136 ERRA ANNE⁸ POST, born November 20, 1831, Cornwall, Vermont; died November 16, 1865, Springfield, Illinois; married May 27, 1857 to Paul Selby, editor of Illinois State Journal.

* All dates of birth, death and marriages for these children are found in the Bible of Truman Post, now in the hands of his great-granddaughter, Marjorie Merriweather Post, Mrs. Herbert A. May.

Issue:
    I. Emily Selby, born May 23, 1858.
    II. Erra Selby, born October 18, 1865; married Rev. Harmon Johnson.

137 HENRY MARTYN[8] POST, born March 30, 1834, Marietta, Ohio, killed April 6, 1862, by accidental gunshot while hunting. Married Elizabeth Rayburn.

138 EMMA BROOKS[8] POST, born July 20, 1836, Marietta, Ohio; died November 7, 1847, Waverly, Illinois. Buried by her father, tombstone in good condition.

139 TRUMAN SANFORD[8] POST, born December 7, 1839, Marietta, Ohio. He served in the Civil War for four and a half years, was Captain of the 7th Illinois Regiment, went to Texas for a time, then removed to Washington, D. C., where he worked in the Post Office and Treasury Departments until his death. He married about 1874 Fannie Dibble Wilson, daughter of Commodore Wilson of the U. S. Navy.

Issue:
    I. Truman Wilson Post, born January 27, 1875.
    II. Margaret Post, born about 1877 and died 1889.
    III. Julia Alice Post, born January 9, 1880; married Harry J. Genslor, of Washington, D. C.

Truman[7] Post, father of the above ten children, numbered from #130 through #139, was reared at Cornwall, Vermont, where he was a farmer from maturity until his removal to Ohio and Illinois. It is quite probable that he married Betsey Atwater at Granville, New York. The date of their marriage is recorded in his Bible, but the place is not given. Marriages for Cornwall do not reveal this marriage, and judging by his extant letters, Betsey lived at Granville for a time, as did her family.*

Cornwall Land Records reveal many transactions under the name of Truman Post. One deed shows that "the most convenient place across Roswell Post's land," is deeded to Truman, and it is the first deed of purchase by him. [Land Records, Vol. V, p. 418, June 19, 1818] In the town clerk's office at Cornwall was found a small slip of paper in the handwriting of Truman Post which lists "1 poll, 5 horses, 7 cows, and 2 two-year olds," dated 1824. His land purchases run through Cornwall Land Records, Vol. V, pp. 69, 570, and through Vols. VI and VII. On

* *Atwater Genealogy,* by Frances Atwater, published in several editions, gives very good data on the ancestors of Betsey Atwater. Her father, Stephen Atwater, was a Revolutionary War pensioner (Pension S-12014, Connecticut); he was born May 13, 1758, Cheshire, Connecticut, to Stephen and Hannah (Hotchkiss) Atwater; he married on March 13, 1780, Cheshire, Connecticut, Anna Moss, daughter of Barnabas and Ann (Hollingsworth) Moss. Anna (Moss) Atwater was born November 29, 1757; died November 23, 1801, or 1811, either in Cheshire, Connecticut, or Granville, New York. The pension of Stephen Atwater is not clear as to her death or place. After her death, Stephen migrated to Crawford County, Pennsylvania, where he died November 26, 1836.

272

October 24, 1827, he took over the lands of his deceased brother Martin, who died February 2, 1811, purchasing same from the heirs of Martin, as follows: "We, Martin M. Post, Aurelian H. Post, Truman M. Post, for $550.00 to Truman Post, quit-claim, being the same lands of our father, Martin Post, late of Cornwall, deceased, which he bought of James Parker." [Land Records, Vol. V:639] There were many deeds for Truman Post until his decision to move to the western country, after which the land records reflect his selling off as rapidly as possible. Vol. VI, p. 237, shows the following: "I, Truman Post, of Cornwall, County of Addison, State of Vermont, appoint Reuben P. Bingham, of Cornwall, my sufficient and lawful attorney for me and in my name . . . to such persons for such considerations as my said attorney, shall deem most to my advantage and profit certain parcels in Cornwall; one piece bounded on west by highway containing 18 acres, also two other pieces of undivided land Elizur Peck and myself bought of Colonel John Chip, lying in the swamp near the Creek; also my share in the pew in the Congregational Church Meeting House in this town, it being one-third; also six-tenths of a pew in the Baptist Meeting House, formerly owned by Reuben Hall. . . ." The original of this document is in the hands of his great-granddaughter; the signature thereon is identical to his Bible entries though the balance of the document is apparently the penmanship of the clerk of the court. Truman was preparing to depart for Ohio.

The journey to Ohio was not especially easy for Betsey; she was expecting her next child, Henry Martyn Post, who was born shortly after arriving at Marietta. They left Cornwall by wagons with a number of possessions, and their first destination was Troy, New York, where they transferred their goods to a barge and were taken via the Canal to Buffalo, following the water route for Erie. Here they once again unloaded family and possessions and transferred to teams for the journey to Pittsburgh, thence embarking by boat for a trip down the Ohio River to Marietta. The entire journey took well over a month from Cornwall to Marietta, and with six small children, this was quite a journey. This was the year 1834; their son Charles Rollin Post was not quite 8 years of age, but many years later he could recount many of the details of the journey.

At this point, it seems wise to insert correspondence of Truman Post; letters addressed to his sister, Clarinda Green, Hopkinton, New York, have been preserved in the family and are now in the hands of Marjorie Merriweather Post May. These letters should prove of interest to the descendants since they give an excellent light on the character of Truman Post and reveal his deep religious feelings, as well as his reasons for leaving Cornwall. The first of these extant letters is dated from Cornwall, September 9, 1821, and reads as follows:

"My dear Sister: After writing you two pretty long letters I have one little short one in return, but notwithstanding I return you many thanks for that, and I confess I am not a little influenced to do so by the hope that I may have more.

"When I last wrote you, I could say sinners here were flocking in multitude to the standard of the Cross. O, that I could say it now. But, alas, facts speak for themselves and I must write facts. The work of Divine Grace progressed but a short time, a great many were under serious impressions, and instances of hopeful conversion were very frequent when some came forward to unite with the Baptist Church. The minds of the people were turned to the subject of Baptism and points of difference between B. and C. [ed.: Baptist and Congregational] immediately, and in spite of all the exertions of those that were disposed to keep such things in the background, the effect became general. Christians lost their fervor and sinners their concern and the work has gradually declined. Who is the most to blame I will not say—but I express my opinion and I believe it to be the general opinion that the work would, in all probability, have been continued yet had no one united with either Church and nothing said upon principles. There has not been much disputing—but it has been telling what this and that one said. Twenty-four, I think, have united with the Baptist Church and thirty-nine with Mr. Bushnell's.*

"I meant when I began this letter to have written lengthy, but I can not. All well, write soon. T. Post."

The next extant letter of Truman Post was to the same sister, and was dated at Cornwall, July 13, 1828:

"My dear Sister: I am just informed that Mr. Pettibone leaves Middlebury tomorrow for St. Lawrence County, which allows me but a few moments to write you. We are all well, our babies grow finely, just begin to sit alone. [ed.: These are the twins, Herbert and Harriott]

"The state of revival in this town is pretty much as it has been for some weeks past. It continued a still but powerful work. The great mass of people in the town are affected by it, but where it takes hold of a person's mind, conviction is pungent and they are almost all led to close in with the terms of Salvation. At first, some express a small degree of hope, that hope brightens and in a short time they come forth decided and active advocates of the religion of Jesus. More than 50 in town are reckoned as fruits of this revival. Last Sabbath, 14 united with Mr. Bushnell's Church—Julius Long and wife, Mrs. Hamilton, two of Uncle Samson's boys, Mr. Rockwell's boys, D. Matthews, N. Lewis, L. Post, were among the number. It was a solemn and interesting day.

"As respects myself, I wish I could say that I was more heartily engaged in the service of Christ. I think I do feel some little engagedness, but I come far short of what I ought to be. Other things seem to have control of my mind and press me down that I

---

* Rev. Jedediah Bushnell's pastorate began in 1803 and continued 33 years; he was finally dismissed because he disapproved of the evangelistic methods of Mr. Burchard, the same revivalist whose labors were the cause of serious dissension among supporters of Middlebury College.

do not rise to the work of religion as I ought. I hope, my dear sister, that you will pray for me that the world may not have too much of my heart, but that I may be active in the service of Christ.

"I wish you to inform mother or rather I would inform her (as I intend this letter as much for her as yourself, but direct it to you not knowing where she is) that her brother from Georgia [ed: Vermont] has called here since she has been gone, he stayed about a moment or two and went to Orwell. He stayed there about 5 days and has returned home. None of his family came with him except a son, who he has left in Massachusetts at school. I was at Orwell two or three days since and they are all well.

"Reuben says in his last letter—'now prepare for some good news! On the 16th of May at 5 minutes past midnight God blessed us with a fine boy, both Harriott and the child are remarkably well, I expect he will be a prodigy if he lives!'

"That is all, so good-bye, your aff. brother. Truman Post."

From the above letter, proof is given that Reuben Post, brother of Truman, had a son born on the date given, and in the chapter on Reverend Reuben Post (#86) his son William Moffitt Post was indicated as born in Washington, D. C., on this date. Truman also mentions "mother" in this letter. His own mother died in 1807, and his father married in 1808 widow Rebecca Bascom, who became a devoted mother to the children of Roswell Post.

The next extant letter from Truman Post to this same sister gives a very clear picture of preparations to leave Vermont for the Ohio country. Notice the reference to Granville, New York, and his wife Betsey:

"Cornwall, Vermont, April 27, 1833: My dear Sister, I have written to sister Brooks [ed: his sister Phoebe, married Dr. Hosea Brooks, Parishville, N. Y.] and Reuben and now I will write you on an entire different subject. If you have not already heard, you will probably soon hear, if I do not inform you, that I am anxious to sell my property and leave this section of the country, and you may hear such vague stories about it that I think it best to write you particularly my motives in doing so.

"Rev. H. H. Shepherd called on us about 5 weeks since. He was an early friend of my wife, formerly from Granville, and for some years an intimate friend of mine, but now resides in Ohio. He, with some others have formed a plan for establishing a Manual Labor School. They have organized, appointed a Board of Trust and appointed him their agent. After much deliberation they have concluded to locate the school in the north part of Ohio about thirty miles from Cleveland on an entirely uncultivated tract. In the outset they have the good fortune to obtain a gift from the landholders of 500 acres as a farm for the school and a contract for 5,000 acres more at $1.50 per acre, which is $1.00 less by the acre than the land can be bought for in that vicinity. Mr. Shepherd is now in the East soliciting funds and enlisting colonists to go and settle that 5,000 acres at $1.50 per acre and give in addition $1.00 on each acre for the School. So you see should that land all be taken at that price the school will start with a capital of $5,000 and a good large farm without any sacrifice to anyone. With this, and $10,000 more which he hopes to raise from the public, they hope to go forward in their hopes. Mr. Shepherd is a man I think well qualified for such an undertaking and his labors had been very successful when here. The plan was so agreeable to my mind that I did not hesitate, but after examination of the subject with all the scrutiny I was capable and I hope with earnest supplication for Devine direction, I came to the full decision that Providence permitting I would sell and go help build up in the wilderness an institution which we hope will eventually cause the hearts of many of the sons of God to rejoice, and many sinners to tremble and submit. I have yet seen no occasion to repent my decision. How soon I may be able to go I know not, having as yet succeeded in selling only some pieces of land.

"I think some of going to see the spot for myself in the course of the season. If I do, it will be doubtful whether we visit you the coming fall or not. I could write more particulars and no doubt, could you see me, you would make many inquiries about it, but I have given the outline of the plan. The Colony is to be a Christian Colony, and going there for similar purposes I think we may confidently expect agreeable society and kind friends.

"I suppose the labor of clearing up a new farm will be severe, and as it respects myself it matters but little whether I stay here or go there, but I think I can do more for my children there than I can do here. I feel very differently now than formerly, when I have talked of going West—more decided. I may not be able to dispose of my farms at all, but think I shall, at least I intend to make every honorable effort to sell.

"We are all well, mother is quite well, or at least would be if it were not for an occasional shaking spell. I hope you will write soon. Where is Martin? I have heard nothing direct from him. Tell him I do not forget his promise. A letter from brother Reuben not long since, all well. Truman M. has been some time with him during the winter. He has now probably gone to Jacksonville, Illinois, to engage in the profession of law. Let me know all about my boy there when you write. Your aff. brother, Truman Post."

Such letters as these should be included within the text of a genealogy, in the opinion of this compiler, since originals might become lost to posterity, nor can they be otherwise shared with numerous descendants. The Martin to whom he referred was Martin Mercillian Post, son of his brother Martin, who at the date of the letter had already arrived at Logansport, as a missionary minister. Truman M. was also the son of brother Martin, and at this date had arrived at Jacksonville, per data given previously herewith.

Either Truman Post erred in the location of the new school, by stating it was thirty miles from Cleveland, or his plans were altered for other reasons, since evidence is produced that he immediately went to Marietta and became interested in the school there. Family tradition states that he took over the experimental farm station at Marietta, but this has remained unverified by extant records. Rollin Post (his son) stated that his father was at Marietta a very short time and from there went to West Virginia near Wheeling for a very short stay; not liking the area, he then took his family to Waverly, Illinois, where he settled. His son Reuben Larned Post was entered at Marietta College as a student in 1842. Luther Bingham of Cornwall was pastor of the Congregational Church at Marietta, and one of the principal founders of the college; he had married Truman's cousin, Sally Samson. This may have been a motive for the stop at Marietta.

Court records indicate that Truman Post acquired land at Waverly, Illinois, in 1844, where he remained until his death in 1847. His estate matters are also recorded at Sangamon County adjoining Morgan County in which Waverly lies. "On the 17th of October 1848, Homer Curtis and Lafayette Post appeared as executors of Truman Post, deceased. Betsey Post, widow, Herbert Post, Harriott Post, Erranne, Henry M., heirs at law of Truman Post, whereas there is a deficit of personal assets to pay the claims filed against the estate of Truman Post to the amount of twenty-four hundred and thirty dollars, it is ordered that so much of the following described lands and real estate, or right, title and interest of same, be sold at public vendue."

Lafayette Post and Homer Curtis, executors, sold the land at the door of the Post Office in the town of Waverly. At this sale, C. Rollin Post bid-in the sum of eleven hundred and one dollars for the tracts lying in Sangamon County. [Sangamon Deed Books BB: 421, 422, 423, 424] In the personal correspondence of Rollin Post, he stated that he farmed near Waverly until the gold rush venture, remaining near his mother, and with the help of brother Herbert, took care of both properties. At that time, Reuben L. Post was attending school in Marietta, later settling in Louisville, where he died. When Lafayette and Rollin went to California in 1849, Harriott was married and settled in Louisville; Reuben lived there, too, consequently the mother and Truman S. joined them to await the outcome of the gold rush venture. Lafayette had sent his wife and baby back to Connecticut to her family. The Posts did not again settle in Waverly, though Sangamon County became their home for many years. The tombstones of the father Truman and Erranne are still standing in good condition at Waverly.

131. Reuben Larned[8] **Post** *(Truman*[7]*, Roswell*[6]*, Roswell*[5]*, Abraham*[4]*, Abraham*[3]*, Abraham*[2]*, Stephen*[1]*)* was born December 15, 1821, Cornwall, Vermont; died September 25, 1871, Louisville; married April 20, 1847, (1) **Hannah Louise Mason** (niece of Lowell Mason, the composer); she was born September 18, 1826; died July 18, 1850, Louisville. He married on April 28, 1853, (2) **Mary B. Anderson,** born ——; died May 21, 1895, Indiana, Pennsylvania, buried in Louisville.

Issue: 5 children

By **Hannah Louise Mason:**

140 ERMA FAYETTE POST, born November 24, 1848; died February 26, 1850.

141 EMMA LOUISA POST, born July 16, 1850; died age 21 days.

By **Mary B. Anderson:**

142 LOUISA MASON POST, born ——, 1854; married John W. Sutton.

143 EDMONIA POST, (no data).

144 WALTER POST, born *ca.* 1858, (no data).

This compiler has not been able to ascertain additional data on Reuben Larned Post but used the above data as found in the Truman Post Bible. In the Gold Rush Journal of Rollin Post (see #**133**) we learn that Reuben was living in Louisville, as given above.

132. Lafayette[8] **Post** (*Truman*[7], *Roswell*[6], *Roswell*[5], *Abraham*[4], *Abraham*[3], *Abraham*[2], *Stephen*[1]) was born August 20, 1823, Cornwall, Vermont; died December 22, 1863, Middletown, Illinois; married June 18, 1846, Waverly, Illinois, to **Huldah Elizabeth Root,** of Oakville (Waterbury), Connecticut; she was born December 3, 1821, Waterbury; died May 26, 1869, Springfield, Illinois.

Issue: 8 children.

145 HERBERT G. POST, born November 22, 1848, Waverly, Illinois; died December 23, 1884, Beardstown, Illinois; married April 24, 1879, at Springfield, Adaline Barney, born August 19, 1849, Rochester, New York; died October 5, 1918, Springfield, Illinois. Adaline Barney Post married (2) Hiram Gardner, a widower with one son, John, by his first wife.

Issue:

I. Herbert Earl Post, born February 20, 1880, Beardstown, Illinois; died March 21, 1947, Tacoma, Washington; married October 21, 1902, Elizabeth Berry, born August 9, 1878; died June 22, 1955.

II. Georgiana Post, born February 18, 1882, Beardstown, Illinois; married December 26, 1903, John Gardner, son of her stepfather. [Information covering Herbert G. Post and heirs was supplied by his daughter, Mrs. Georgiana Post Gardner, of Springfield, Illinois]

Issue:

i. Jane Catherine Gardner.

ii. Lucia Gardner.

iii. George Post Gardner.

146 EMMA POST, born December 6, 1851, Middletown, Illinois; died unmarried, December 15, 1927, Springfield, Illinois.

147 CAROLINE POST, born January 15, 1854, Middletown, Illinois; died February 19, 1928, Kansas City, Missouri. Caroline Post was a medical doctor, a much loved and respected person. She married (1) on January 15, 1884, at Beardstown, Illinois, John Bates, who was born September 16, 1850; died May 18, 1884, no issue. She married (2) on June 7, 1887, at Springfield, Illinois, Samuel Richard Guyer, who was born May 22, 1851, Towanda, Pennsylvania; died April 22, 1915, Kansas City, Missouri.

Issue:
    I. Julia Guyer, born December 23, 1890, Springfield, Illinois, living at Kansas City, Missouri, 1962.
    II. Robert Guyer, born September 21, 1897, Kansas City, Missouri; married on November 16, 1931, Ann Hurd, at St. Louis, Missouri.

148 HARRIOTT POST, born May 12, 1858, Middletown, Illinois; died April 7, 1926, Waterbury, Connecticut; married John Maccauley and lived at Waterbury, Connecticut.

149 ERRAMETTE (MITTE) POST, born May 12, 1858, Middletown, Illinois; died May —, 1929, Corbettsville, New York; married Charles Phillips and lived at Brooklyn, New York, later removed to Corbettsville.

150 FAYETTE POST, born April 19, 1860, Middletown, Illinois; died —, 1921, Beardstown, Illinois; married Minnie B. Knight.

151 SYLVESTER POST, died 1861, aged 2 weeks.

152 EDWARD ROOT POST, born and died, 1863.

Lafayette Post, father of the children numbered from 145 through 152, accompanied his brother on the gold rush trek, and a better account of him may be found in the section on Rollin Post, which follows. The dates for Lafayette Post, wife and children are recorded in the Truman Post Bible.

Charles Rollin and Caroline (Lathrop) Post

The genealogical section covering Charles Rollin and Caroline (Lathrop) Post is set apart with special heading in view of the fact that they are the parents of the subject of the opening biography. This section will be a detailed coverage of their lives, since many of the factors in their lives greatly influenced the life of their famous son. It is the desire of the family to preserve for posterity the personal letters, Bible entries, and accounts of this beloved couple. Their private papers, family data and photographs are in the hands of their granddaughter, Marjorie Merriweather Post May. It is her desire to pass on to future generations the contents of various letters and journals by publication of this account . . . the detailed genealogy and accounts follow.

133. Charles Rollin[8] **Post** (*Truman*[7], *Roswell*[6], *Roswell*[5], *Abraham*[4], *Abraham*[3], *Abraham*[2], *Stephen*[1]), was born January 15, 1826, Cornwall, Vermont; died July 15, 1919, Los Angeles, buried in Oak Ridge Cemetery, Springfield, Illinois. He married on October 10, 1853, at Hartford, **Caroline (Lathrop) Parsons,** widow of Abner Parsons. She was born November 27, 1824, Ashford, Connecticut; died October 17, 1914, Fort Worth, Texas, buried Oak Ridge Cemetery, Springfield, Illinois.

Issue: 3 sons.

+153 CHARLES WILLIAM[9] POST, born October 26, 1854, Springfield, Illinois, of whom further, in addition to biography.

154 AURELIAN (AURRIE) ATWATER[9] POST, born October 18, 1856, Springfield, Illinois; married June 16, 1892, Mary Lee Johnson, at Fort Worth, Texas. Lived and died at Fort Worth.

> *Issue:*
> I. Nellie Caroline Post, born May 15, 1893, Fort Worth.
> II. Charles Lathrop Post, born June 7, 1896, Fort Worth.
> III. Mary Ella Post, born April 6, 1898, Fort Worth.

155 CARROLL LATHROP[9] POST, born September 9, 1859, Springfield, Illinois; died April 24, 1948, California, buried Battle Creek, Michigan; married October 15, 1879, Mary (Mollie) Lee Staley, at Springfield, Illinois; she died May 25, 1925, buried at Pasadena, California. He married (2) June 2, 1926, Fannie Grace Hanchett, who outlived him.

Rollin and Carrie Post were a devoted couple, loving and much loved. They were affectionately referred to as "Uncle Rollin and Aunt Carrie" by the vast group of cousins, relatives, friends and neighbors. To know a man well is to know something of his parents. C. W. Post owed much to the splendid background and environment afforded him by the union of these two people. They were one of those godly New England families. They were, in every sense of the word, spiritually complete. Their Christian principles were strong and mature, their sense of humor clearly defined, and their love of life, and fellow man, followed them to the grave.

Caroline Lathrop was a direct descendant of Reverend John Lathrop who came to America with Reverend Thomas Hooker. Caroline was the daughter of Erastus Lathrop, who was born at Norwich, May 18, 1784, and died July 3, 1851 at Hartford; married at New London, September 21, 1807, to Sarah Bailey, born January 13, 1790, New London, and died July 6, 1856, in Illinois.*

The personal letters of Rollin and Carrie date back to their courtship and have been carefully preserved. Since some of these might interest the descendants in days to come, we shall quote liberally within the text. As stated in the genealogical data on his father (Truman Post), Rollin remained near Waverly until the Gold Rush fever reached the area of Waverly. The account of that venture can be best given in his own words many years later, when he wrote these recollections for his niece, the daughter of Lafayette:

"My dear Niece: In your letter to your Aunt Carrie received yesterday you wished me to give you some reminiscenses of the trip in 1849 to California with your father in search of gold. It was not a very eventful one, so that I do not know that I can entertain you with any hair-lifting or blood-curdling events. In the 57 years that have intervened, I have forgotten many of the minor happenings, yet I recall the most impressive features of the trip with a great deal of pleasure.

"The news of the discovery of gold in California in 1848 came slowly drifting through the papers, and early in the winter of 1849 the gold fever struck Waverly, Illinois, pretty hard. So, Fred Curtiss, James Godfrey, your father and myself decided to make the venture. Your father was living on a farm about four miles east and I was on one about a half-mile south of Mr. Curtiss. We gathered our crops, sold the farms and gathered together 4 yoke of oxen, one cow and two small mules, fitted up a wagon and made everything ready for one long trip of over 2,000 miles. Our mother, and

* *The Lathrop Genealogy*, by Huntingdon, pub. 1884, shows Erastus as the son of Azel[5] and Elizabeth (Hyde) Lathrop; John[4] and Elizabeth (Abel) Lathrop; Israel[3] and Rebecca (Bliss) Lathrop; Samuel[2] and Elizabeth (Scudder) Lathrop; Reverend John Lathrop[1]. An improvement can be made in this published work by consulting the vital records of Connecticut. Errors are in evidence in the published genealogy, but these may be resolved with a little work.

The Bible of Reverend John Lathrop is now in possession of the Sturgess Library, Lathrop Room, Barnstable, Massachusetts. The Bible was given to the library in 1958 by Grace Lathrop (Dunham) Luling. See text for complete description, page 291.

brother Truman, went to Louisville to live with brother Reuben and sister Hattie, and your mother, with baby Herbert, went to Waterbury, Connecticut, to your Aunt Newton's. About the 27th of February, 1849, Fred and myself, the two unmarried ones, left Waverly with the team and wagon to drive across the country to St. Joseph, Missouri, where your father and Godfrey joined us about April 1st, having gone up the Missouri River by boat. There we remained about one month, resting up the stock, laying in provisions, etc., waiting for grass to grow so that the cattle could live on it. About May 1st, we ventured to make the start.

"We joined a company as a measure of self-protection from Indians, etc., of about 100 men with 350 head of cattle. They bought rubber boats, fire arms, beads, etc., for trade with the Indians; also had a guide to pilot the caravan across the wide plains. We soon found that the guide did not know anything about the country more than we did, and that sufficient grass could not be had for so large a body of cattle, consequently we were obliged to travel too slowly, so after travelling about 100 miles together, one bright morning, 24 men with 6 wagons and about 40 head of oxen, pulled out, leaving the rest of the company in camp with their guide, rubber boats, beads, etc., and pushed out along the already beaten trail for California and gold. As events proved, we beat them to the 'diggins' about one month.

"We pushed along over the country, then a vast wild prairie, but now settled with homes, to Fort Kearney on the Platte River, where the soldiers were stationed to protect the migrants. We followed up the south side of the river until we came to the junction of the South Platte with the North Fork. Here we crossed the South Fork and followed up the North branch to Fort Laramie where another small regiment was stationed. On our way, we had seen large herds of buffalo grazing along their northward annual migration, as well as deer, antelopes, etc., so that we had an abundance of fresh meat. I know of a train of wagons detained one whole day just waiting for buffalo to pass, as it was dangerous to drive through them, for if they should happen to take fright, they would rush pell mell over teams, wagons and any other obstacle. Fortunately we were not detained by them. We occasionally came across tribes of Indians, Pawnees, Sioux, Crees, Arapahoes, Snakes and Shoshones, but they were then peaceable and did not molest us, although the Pawnees and Sioux were at war with each other. In fact, we travelled all one day with a village of Sioux and camped at night within half a mile of them. After supper we went to their camp and they entertained us with their Tom-Toms and a sort of music. Not more than a month after, having been badly treated by following emigrants, they became quite hostile and caused a great deal of trouble.

"After leaving Fort Laramie, we followed up the Sweetwater River to where we crossed the South Pass, a low point in the Rocky Mountains, where on one side the water flowed to the Atlantic and on the other side to the Pacific. At one place we found a spring with hot water and a few hundred feet away was another with very cold water. Near it we found a marshy spot where a foot below the surface was ice, which I think never melted. Passing on, we struck Bear River, and instead of keeping on a very straight westward course to Salt Lake City, we made a detour to the northwest around the bend of the river to Fort Hall, passing Soda Springs. Here we saw the first gold which was brought by a returning Californian. This was on Snake River, a tributary of the Columbia. Here we turned southward over the desert to the Humboldt River, down which we followed to the Sink, a place where the stream disappears into the sands. At that point, we found that we must cross a stretch of a desert of 45 miles

282

with no water except a hot spring about midway. We filled every available vessel with water from the river, filled up our stock and ourselves, and about sundown started out for an all night drive through to Hot Springs, which we reached early in the next morning. Here we were obliged to camp for the day. All the water given to the stock had to be taken out of the spring, hot enough to boil an egg, and cooled. About sundown, we left there with a small amount of water in canteens and kegs for ourselves for another all night travel to the Truckee River. Along toward morning, after pulling along our wagons through the heavy sand with all men walking, our cattle began to give out and lay down by the roadside. We were obliged to stop and allow the cattle to rest awhile. I then took some canteens and went on over the intervening 3 or 4 miles to the river. You can imagine how refreshing was the sight of that water to me as I came to the banks and saw it tippling along so clear and cool. It seemed in some measure to satisfy my thirst just to look at it, and I sat on the banks and looked and looked and looked and looked for at least five minutes before I went down for a drink. When I felt sufficiently refreshed I filled my canteens and hurried back and found the cattle unyoked and resting in the shade of the wagons. All drank as sparingly as possible, but two or three were no nearly famished that we had to deny them all they would have drunk at first. We then hitched up all the cattle which could rise and crawled along the river. In a few hours the 2 or 3 exhausted oxen, left behind, came straggling in. We stayed here until all were filled up with water and grass and other provisions and thoroughly rested up, thankful that we had all lived through.

"We soon came to the foothills of the Sierra Nevada Mountains. Here we came to the place where so many of the Donner party perished. The Donner family lived 5 or 6 miles east of Springfield and in 1848 a company of 34 persons started for California and were belated in the season so that heavy snows caught them on the east side of the mountains. Here they stopped and built log cabins, while they sent two or three men across the range to settlements in California for help. When help arrived, all their cattle had died and been eaten, and it was said that one man had sustained life by eating the bodies of his friends who had perished. The rescuers succeeded in getting the few survivors to the settlement. When we passed there, there were two or three cabins still left with logs about 5 feet high and poles upon which they had stretched the hides of cattle to protect them from the severe weather. There were stumps of trees still standing about 15 feet high, showing the depth of the snow where they had stood to cut them. I picked up the skull of a child with some hair still left on it. We then crossed the Sierra range, passing through snow although it was then about the 10th of August. In 3 or 4 days we arrived at the diggings where we decided to stop and prospect for gold. As there was but little grass in the mountains, we were compelled to send the stock down to the valley and turn them loose in the luxuriant grass. Two of our men started with them but during the succeeding night the miserable 'Digger' Indians stole our mules and three head of cattle, which was the only loss we had on the entire trip. I hope the Indians enjoyed their mule steak and poor cattle, as they must have been awfully tough.

"After staying in the mines until cold weather set in, we moved down to the valley and by accident came across 2 or 3 of our cattle which were as fat as butter. We butchered them and the meat was as tender as chicken, having taken on fat very quickly from their lean condition.

"We all went down to Sacramento, where Mr. Godfrey, almost beside himself with homesickness, left us for San Francisco and home, via Panama. After looking around awhile, your father, Fred Curtiss and myself, bought a whale boat, which we loaded with provision for the mines about 300 miles up the Sacramento River. We made some money out of the venture and then returned down to the junction of the Sacramento and Feathers Rivers, where we decided to spend the winter. We built a small house and went to making shingles at $15.00 per 1,000.

"In the Spring of 1850, Fred Curtiss decided to go up to the mines, and your father and I bought 10 mules and an old white bell mare for a leader and went to packing provisions into the mines, at which we did very well. We paid $37.50 for 100 pounds of flour at Sacramento, and after packing it on our mules into the mountains about 80 miles, we sold out for $1.00 per pound, and other articles in proportion. This made somewhat expensive living but when restaurants charged $2.00 per meal, they managed to survive. Then a company of ten was formed and we went to the north fork of the north fork of the Yuba River near Downieville, where we staked off claims and sawed lumber with a whipsaw by hand for a flume, by means of which we could carry the water overhead and work out the bed of the stream. After working out our 10 claims, we took the flume down stream and worked out some claims for other parties, one of which was called 'Tin Cup Diggins'—so called because the owner took a tin cup full of gold from the bank above the water. In this claim was a rock about 10 feet in diameter in the middle of the stream on the lower side of which considerable gold had accumulated. In order to see what there was, I took a shovel and scooped up out of the water at one trial, $200.00 of gold. We found $6,000 worth around that rock. As all our men were not needed in working out the claims, I took one of them with a whipsaw and went down to Downieville where we began to run a human sawmill to supply as far as we could the demand for lumber. We would cut our logs and roll them on the skids, and with myself as top sawyer, and the other man as pit sawyer, we could cut upon an average of 200 feet per day. This we could sell as fast as made, at $1.00 per foot for lumber and 50 cents per foot for slabs. We continued at this until finally a man worked his way over the mountains with an ox team loaded with a portable sawmill. He employed us to cut sufficient lumber to enable him to get his mill in operation; when he put the price down to $500 per 1,000 feet, we retired from the sawmill business in disgust at such low prices.

"About the middle of October, your father got pretty homesick and wanted to see the wife and baby Herbert, so he and Fred went down to San Francisco and sailed for New York. I remained in the mountains until January 1st, 1851, when I sold out and went to San Francisco for home. I was on a slow vessel, being 28 days to Panama. From the Isthmus we went to Havana, thence to New Orleans, thence to Louisville to visit your uncle (my brother) Reuben, thence to St. Louis and Naples. Here we took the old strap rail Wabash R. R. to Jacksonville and Waverly.

"While in the mountains (in California) we could get letters from home only at long intervals, and the postage was 40¢ each, and we had to pay express messengers $1.00 each, making $2.00 (sic) for each letter. I remember paying $10 one day for 5 letters, and I did not begrudge the money in the least. Newspapers, a month old, sold for $1.00 each, but as wages were in proportion, and we were greedy for home news, we bought them as freely as we do now for 5¢.

"I should have said above, upon leaving Havana, I found that Jenny Lind and her company, P. T. Barnum and daughter, were fellow passengers to New Orleans; also the elder James Gordon Bennett of New York Herald, with wife. Upon our arrival at New Orleans, we found the levee black with people who had come to see Jenny Lind.

Barnum found that it would be difficult to take her from the vessel to her hotel, so he sent his daughter's maid to a carriage, hoping that the crowd would follow the carriage, but they soon discovered their mistake and returned to the wharf. Then his daughter took a carriage, and the crowd followed her, and before they could discover their mistake, Jenny Lind soon followed in another. But they were not satisfied as to her identity and one of them poked his head into her carriage and shouted 'Be you Jenny Lind?'—to which she replied, 'Yes, I am Jenny Lind.'

"After leaving Louisville I went by boat to St. Louis and visited your Uncle Herbert, who was employed in a dry-goods store, also saw Cousin Truman's family. [ed. Truman Marcellus Post] While there, I was first introduced on the sidewalk by brother Herbert to your Aunt Carrie. I always insist that she went from Jacksonville to St. Louis just to meet me. Be that as it may, events proved that I then and there met my fate, and I have always felt that a good Providence sent her, and over 50 years of happily married life together have only confirmed my choice.

"In the following Spring, your father, myself, and (your) Uncle Herbert decided to open a dry-goods store in Jacksonville, where we lived until the fall of 1852, when we moved to Springfield where we went into the grain business. As the Chicago and Alton R. R. was just finished from Alton to Springfield, we shipped the first grain ever sent over it south of Springfield. Soon after, your father moved to Middletown, where I suppose you first became acquainted with him!

"I should have said earlier, that in our travels we made it a rule to camp over Sunday wherever the conditions would justify, in order to give ourselves and our cattle the necessary rest after the week's hard travel, and our experience proved that very little, if any time, was lost thereby, as our ordinary travel was 18 or 20 miles with ease. On different occasions while resting on Sunday, other trains whose captains thought it necessary to travel seven days in the week, would drive by us, but almost invariably we would overtake them before the end of the week with their teams fagged out for want of rest, and often left along the roadside to die, thus showing the wisdom of our Heavenly Father in requiring one day's rest in seven. In passing through the mountains, grass was not so plentiful and sometimes it happened that when darkness overtook us, we could not find grass and water, consequently we were obliged to proceed until it could be had, for our safety and perhaps our lives depended upon keeping our teams in condition for travel. On two or three occasions Saturday night overtook us and we were obliged to go into camp where grass was not sufficient and we found it necessary to break camp on Sunday morning and travel until we found a suitable place. In our mess, there was one man who occasionally showed a very disagreeable, obstinate disposition, so much so that we accused him of being one half mule or two thirds mule; however, we usually succeeded in getting along very well with him. On one occasion, after hitching up on Sunday morning to hunt grass, Godfrey said he would not travel on Sunday, but would spend it 'then and thar'—so taking a day's rations, his blanket, Bible and mule, he spread his blanket on the ground under the shade of a big pine, hitched his Bible to the tree and sat down facing his fellow mule to meditate, contemplate, and study the mule. Leaving him in this situation, we drove on until about 10 o'clock, where we found a good camping ground and pitched our camp for the day. Along about sundown, much to our amusement, Godfrey and the other mule came along slowly straggling into camp, tail between legs, looking very sad and dejected, disgusted with themselves and all mankind, neither of them having anything to say in any language that we could interpret. As there were some wild animals around, he thought that it might not be perfectly safe to spend the night there and thought the Lord would excuse him if he cracked a little part of the Sabbath there was left. I do not know what he did with his Bible, as we never saw it afterwards, nor did we ever after hear a peep from either of them about Sabbath travel or any further protests.

"It sometimes happened that we could not get our supplies until quite late and we would turn into bed leaving our tin dishes around the fire. Upon waking we would find them scattered around the ground 40 or 100 feet away, having been carefully, nicely washed clean by cowardly coyotes that came prowling in the darkness. Written to Mrs. Mitte Phillips by her special request, C. R. Post."

This account, mostly from memory, fifty-seven years later, shows that clarity of mind and 'sly-wink' in personality which never departed the nonagenarian. Nor, for that matter, did the perfectly erect, over six-feet-two-inches of height wilt or sag with the years. While the above Gold Rush story is rather fulsome for inclusion in any book, we feel that the firsthand account needs be preserved; most especially should it interest the many descendants of the participants..

Among the personal papers and accounts of Rollin Post is a small memo book, doubtless started upon returning to Illinois. This shows the rugged trip necessary across the Isthmus before the completion of the Panama Canal. The memorandum account also gives an expansion of the details as recounted by Rollin Post for his niece, as follows:

"Jan. 1, 1851, left San F. at 4 o'clock on the *Columbus,* arrived Seapulco Friday Jan. 10; Saturday 11th left at dusk for Panama; Monday we encountered severe gale, which blew us off course; Sunday 19th turned our course to Realejo, where we arrived Monday noon. I went up to the town six miles up the bay. In course of the day several of us hired horses and went down to Chinadonga, nine miles distant. Tuesday started again for Panama, arrived Jan. 25; journey lasted 28 days. On the 26th started for Gorgona. Hired a mule for $12.00, arrived at Gabout at 3 o'clock on the 27th; left Gorgona at daybreak in a canoe for Chagnes, arrived about 5 and immediately went on board the *Georgia;* left 28th at noon. Sat. night the 31st arrived Havana; Sunday went in; Tuesday night 5th of February, left in the *Falcon* for New Orleans, arrived Friday evening the 7th at New O. Jenny Lind on board. 8th left New O. board the *Chief Marshall* for Louisville. Sat. 22nd went to Cincinnati, returned to Louisville on 26th; left on the *Genesee* for St. Louis, arrived Mar. 3rd, remained until 4th; arrived Alton. Wednesday went to Monticello, left Alton on 6th for Naples, there took the cars for Jacksonville; took cars for Berlin, Ill. Arrived home at 8 in the evening. This trip from California to home took 105 days."

With the spirit of adventure somewhat appeased, and a goodly share of profit from the venture, Rollin's thoughts seriously turned to settling down. His brother, Herbert, and their mother were now in Jacksonville where the boys planned to start the dry-goods business. John Lathrop (brother of Caroline) was living in Jacksonville, and Rollin knew Caroline would be there visiting. It was there the serious courtship began. Carrie had married Abner Parsons, of Pittsfield, Massachusetts, at Hartford on March 27, 1844. [Connecticut Vital Records.] Their marriage was a short and sad one, with the death of Abner and their infant child. After returning to Hartford to be with her family, her father died in 1851, followed by the death of her sister Sarah. Brother John Lathrop then persuaded her to go West for a complete change of scenery to get away from painful reminders. That Rollin courted Carrie at the home of John Lathrop is revealed in one of Carrie's letters written to Rollin several years after their marriage while visiting her brother at Jacksonville. She wrote:

"These blessed walls and the old sofa keep their silence well, the place seems almost sacred to me, for here my guiding star first arose, by whose light I am to be guided over life's waters."

Carrie returned to Hartford in the summer of 1852, leaving Rollin to pine away for the presence of the girl for whom he had very serious intentions. He wrote to her on September (—), 1852, as follows:

"These five weeks you have been gone are long ones. I look forward with pleasant anticipation to the time when I may have my gentle Carrie ever with me."

His letters were ardent, reassuring her that the entire family, including his mother, loved her as their own. It was at this time his mother gave him a Bible, inscribed with loving tenderness, and signed B. A. Post. In this Bible, he carefully recorded all dates of birth, death and marriages until he died. He assured Carrie he would come to Hartford to claim her just as soon as brother Herbert returned from the East and they could complete the sale of the dry-goods business. Their plan was to make the move to Springfield, where commercial business possibilities were far more promising at the time, in view of the newly completed railroad. They finally sold the dry-goods business and made the move, entering into grain and agricultural implement business. The course of history for Charles William Post might well have been different had this move not been made; however, from the boundlessness of the son, any location would have been a springboard to success, he was destined that way.

Herbert Post was already married (1851), and the new implement business was now able to support two families. By October of 1853 the brothers felt secure when Rollin left for Hartford to claim Carrie; they were married there on the 10th of the month.

The next purely factual record available in the private life of Rollin and Carrie comes from letters she wrote from her old home grounds around

Hartford, the first of which were dated in the summer of 1858. By this time, Charlie, their first born, was 4 years old and Aurrie was 2 years old, and doubtless this was the first visit to her family and friends since her marriage. In the first letter of the 1858 series, she recounts the train ride with the two boys. Charlie was obviously a constant source of amazement to her in his seriousness of thought at such tender years. She explained to Rollin that Charlie spent most of his time looking out the train window and mumbling prayers to the Saviour and asking Him to explain what he saw, and his added prayers for papa are all carefully retold. The letters contain news of all members of her family and reflect her joy at being near the sea and the old family remembrances, but with grave longings for her "dear, devoted husband." Throughout each of her letters there is revealed an utter devotion to husband, family and friends. There was nothing in her nature that permitted her to think of Carrie first. She showed her concern for the welfare of each member of the family, near or far, exhorting Rollin to refrain from such long hours and hard work for her benefit, saying: "you are far too kind and generous at all times."

In those days of the late 1850's, boarding was quite fashionable, and young married couples often lived in private boarding homes. This Carrie and Rollin did for a few years after marriage, living with the Barrows family of Vermont origin. [1860 census of Springfield, Illinois] By the time Carroll was a few years old, with Charlie and Aurrie growing to be very lively, romping boys, it was necessary to think of more spacious living quarters. They therefore bought the large mid-Victorian house in Springfield, which today is known as *Carrie Post and King's Daughters' Home.* The new and ample residence became the center of family life, to which visiting kinsmen came from far and near, to find a warm welcome under its roof. It housed sons and their wives as they joined the family circle and grandchildren as they came along. Their beloved granddaughter, Marjorie Merriweather Post, was born under that roof, in the little back room; visitors to the Rest Home today are shown the birthplace of their fond benefactress. The residence was not far removed from the home of Abraham Lincoln, and Rollin Post well recounted his acquaintance with the Great Emancipator. Since his account in that regard is not too well known, as written and published by the *Colorado Springs Gazette,* December 1, 1912, it might be of interest here. It is entitled: *"Personal Recollections of Abraham Lincoln,* by a Summer Resident of Colorado Springs—C. Rollin Post." Space here would not permit inclusion of the lengthy story; however, brief abstracts follow:

"In response to oft-repeated requests that I give some reminiscences of my early acquaintance with Abraham Lincoln, I trust I may be pardoned if the personal pronoun is frequently indulged in, as I am introducing the personal features of the case, rather than the historic. . . .

"The first time I had an opportunity to see Mr. Lincoln was in 1844 when he, with a number of other candidates for office, was stumping his Congressional district as a candidate for Congress. This was at Waverly, in Morgan County, about 20 miles from Springfield. I well remember that when the time came for him to address the crowd of 2,000 people, he uncoupled his long legs and rose to his height of six feet four, clad in an old linen duster, with a rent down the back and out at the elbows, to tell the people how he loved them and how they needed him to be sent to Washington. . . .

"In 1852, I moved to Springfield, Illinois, and there made his acquaintance, frequently meeting him in the streets, in the stores and now and then in the courthouse, where while court was in session he, with a number of other lawyers, sat around the large open Franklin stove, regaling themselves with fun and anecdote, with boisterous laughter, in which the sedate judge was often a hearty participant. . . .

"In those days, his eldest son Robert was a callow, irrepressible kid, some 10 or 12 years of age, with little home culture or restraint, who was often sent uptown upon errands to his father. Upon one occasion I met him in the streets, hatless, coatless, and barefooted, with one very uncertain suspender holding his ragged pants in position and he yelled out—'Say, have you seen old Abe Lincoln around here this morning?' This from a future Secretary of War, Ambassador to England, and President of the Pullman Company! Not long after that, I had occasion to call upon Mrs. Lincoln on an errand, I rang the doorbell and while awaiting an answer, I heard from the rear—'Bob, Bob, you little scamp, why don't you behave yourself, I am going to give you a licking, just wait until I get the door!' She appeared at the door, calm and placid as a May morning. I do not know whether Bob got the promised licking, but I'll bet 30¢ he did not."

Here, Rollin Post recounted the famous Lincoln-Douglas debates, and recalled one in particular which he had heard:

"It would seem Mr. Lincoln was a student of the Bible, and knew well the story of the Martyr Stephen, for at the close of one of the debates when Stephen A. Douglas had the opening, Mr. Lincoln quietly arose, taking off his duster, threw it into the lap of a young man, saying, 'Here, young man, hold this while I stone Stephen.' . . . ."

Rollin moved his story along with many well-known and published accounts of Lincoln's life in Springfield, calling attention to Mrs. Lincoln's aspiration for a more elegant home, the one which they had being a small one-story affair, and now that her husband was becoming famous, she felt the need of something more pretentious and accordingly added an upper story and extensive expansions while Mr. Lincoln was away on the circuit. Rollin recounts the Republican Convention in Chicago in 1860 and how Mr. Lincoln remained at home though thoroughly aware of his name being placed in nomination. According to Rollin Post, Lincoln loved a game of ball, and contented himself during the balloting by vibrating between playing ball and running to the *State Journal* offices, where he made his headquarters. The news of that nomination will be told in Rollin's own words, drawn from his personal recollections:

"About noon, my brother Truman S. Post, now of Washington, D. C., on his way to lunch, was standing at the head of the stairway leading to the editorial rooms, in conversation with another gentleman, when a telegraph messenger came bounding up the stairs, and handed a dispatch to Edward L. Baker, the editor; realizing this must be an important message, they followed the boy into the office where Mr. Lincoln was at the time seated alone with Mr. Baker. Opening the telegram and reading its contents, he turned to Mr. Lincoln and grasping his hand, said: 'I congratulate you, sir, as being the next President of the U. S.' The next congratulations were tendered by my brother and his friend, while the room was immediately filled up with others who had heard the news. Lincoln, with the dispatch in his hand, turned and said, 'Boys there is a little woman up on Eighth Street who will be interested in this. Please excuse me and I will go home.' . . .

"On New Year's day, two months preceding the time for him to assume office, in company with friends, I made the President-elect a New Year's call. We were very cordially received, although Mr. Lincoln looked jaded and worn. Mrs. Lincoln appeared with sweetest smile and chatted quite familiarly. She was richly dressed without any profuse ornaments, standing in the broad hoop-skirts so popular in those days, as shown in her pictures."

Next of importance in this article, C. R. Post recounted a personal conversation with Lincoln's old law partner, Wm. Herndon, who told C. R. of the farewell between them; Rollin quoted Herndon's words as follows:

"He (Lincoln) came down to our law office and settled final affairs, after which he threw himself on the sofa for a spell, presently he inquired, 'Billy, how long have we been together?' and I answered, '16 years and never a cross word.' He then gathered up a bundle of papers and books and said: 'that old signboard which hangs on its rusty hinges at the foot of the stairs should remain there undisturbed, give our clients to understand that the election of a President makes no change in the firm of Lincoln & Herndon.' . . . ."

The article deals fully with the farewell of Lincoln when he left Springfield for Washington, a reenactment of which was done in the centennial year of 1961. C. R. tells in the article that his next close association with Mr. Lincoln occurred when he was asked to be one of the escorts to return Mr. Lincoln's body to Springfield for burial, which is told as follows:

"I can never forget the morning of April 15, 1865. On my way to business, I was shocked to learn that the President had been shot the night previous. About nine that morning the announcement came. Going into the streets, I found them filled with excited crowds, many sobbing. In the Spring of 1865, I had been elected Alderman by the voters of the 4th ward. Previous to the death of Mr. Lincoln, the city bought 10 acres of ground not far from the center of town, upon which to build the new $4,000,000

Capitol. Upon the announcement of Mr. Lincoln's death, it was decided to erect a mausoleum upon those grounds, in which his body was to be placed, and it was almost completed when, owing to strong remonstrances from Mrs. Lincoln and some others, it was decided to abandon the plan and to place the remains temporarily in the receiving vault at Oak Ridge Cemetery, there to await the final completion of the new monument already projected.

"Upon arrival of the funeral train at Chicago, on its way from Washington to Springfield, the officials of the Chicago and Alton Railroad tendered the mayor and the city council a special car for their use as escort. Early in the morning of May 4th, accompanied by a number of state officials, we arrived at Springfield about 9 a.m."

Rollin Post then tells the entire story of the funeral, which need not be retold here. Also, he deals with the attempt of ghouls to rob the tomb of Lincoln and hold the body for ransom, their near success, and ultimate conviction. When he wrote this article, he stated that as nearly as he could ascertain, in December 1912, he was the only survivor of the special escort with the body of Mr. Lincoln.

The Springfield days for the Post family were happy ones, and many of the endeavors of their son Charlie are told in his biography in this volume. Throughout childhood the Post boys were pranksters, full of fun and tricks, just normal, healthy boys. They bedeviled the lives of visiting old-maid aunts and cousins, but they lived under a roof of deep religious convictions and principles, with strict observance of the Sabbath, sometimes rebelling, but always obeying discipline.

Rollin and Carrie were life-long members of the Congregational Church, as were their forebears. The First Congregational Church of Springfield was their seat of worship during thirty-six years of residence there. The old church burned in recent years, and a new church was built some few miles distant, in keeping with the trend of the city's outward expansion. Rollin and Carrie, with their sons and subsequent wives of the sons, retained membership in that church until some years after moving to Texas in 1887.

Rollin continued in the agricultural implement and grain business from 1852 through 1887 with his brother Herbert and included his sons as they became of age. He made a very nice living and the family was comfortably situated. Many vacations were taken East to New England, as well as to nearby towns and the homes of relatives. A substantial library was acquired through the years, and Carrie guided her boys through home studies in the arts, music and literature. As the boys married, it was characteristic of Carrie that she never referred to her daughters-in-law other than as "my dear daughter." The sons brought the wives home to live under the roof of Carrie and Rollin, and there is no record or memory of any discord at any time; her saintly nature would have dispelled any conflict. When the boys tried their hands in various ventures, or roamed off to the western country, she understood and gave them full support. Rollin never lost his zeal for a good business deal, and to the consternation of his sons, late in life he would try various schemes for making money, often with less than satisfactory results. After he was financially able to do so, C. W. maintained his parents in every ease and comfort, and there was no reason for Rollin to engage in any business activity, but, as he explained sheepishly when he lost a little money in late years, he just "wanted to keep a hand in."

The pleasure of compiling this work has been made possible by the existence of excellent account books, copies of old letters and original documents, along with a vast number of scrapbooks of newspaper accounts. For the sake of genealogical information, Carrie's letters and notes on the subject shall be quoted. She stated her mother, Sarah Bailey Lathrop, had two sisters, whom she recalled very well: Aunt Harriett Bailey Parkhurst who lived at Coventry, Connecticut; and Aunt Mary Bailey Hoskins who visited in the family home in Hartford. There was another aunt who married a Chapman and lived in Portland, Maine, whose Christian name she did not record. Rollin wrote letters for his sons, outlining his family connections, all of which have been proved to be correct from public records available. He mentioned seeing his grandfather's (Roswell Post) epaulettes, sword and hat, used in the Revolution, "but when we moved to Ohio when I was a boy, they got lost in the shuffle." Rollin kept in close touch with his relatives, those who remained in Cornwall, as well as those who settled at Parishville, New York and other locations; he visited frequently with his cousins around Jacksonville, Logansport, and St. Louis.

Among the letters kept by the family is one written by John Lathrop (brother of Carrie) to his daughter while he was visiting in the East. This letter plagued the curiosity of this compiler until the Bible in question was located. John Lathrop wrote his daughter, in 1871, as follows:

"I stopped to visit with Reverend D. W. Lathrop, at New Haven, my cousin, he brought out the ancient family Bible, printed in England in 1605, and the original property of Reverend John Lathrop, the emigrant. Reverend John Lathrop graduated at Oxford, was imprisoned at London, and finally exiled to America, his wife having died while he was in prison. There are holes burned where Reverend Lathrop dropped fire, apparently; there are family births recorded and a diary of each generation with it, it is bound in fine leather, repaired with cloth and well preserved. The margins of the text show notes made by Reverend Lathrop while studying the scriptures. They say he knew it by heart. The Historical Society at Yale has been trying to buy the Bible from Reverend D. W. Lathrop, but he would not part with it for love or money. I was pleased to see all the names of cousins, aunts and uncles so carefully recorded, and it was brought down to my father. The manuscript with it made room for all the Lathrops who could not be crowded onto the entry pages."*

When the Post family left Springfield, it was for the benefit of the health of C. W. Post; a full account is given in the opening biography. Texas and Fort Worth were very much to the liking of the family, especially Rollin, Carrie and Aurrie, who never removed from there. When the family first settled at Fort Worth, they again sought to affiliate with a Congregational Church. The first group of members met in a tent in the town, but by 1903 C. W. had become an internationally known Battle Creek millionaire, and through his generosity the First Congregational Church of Fort Worth was built, and dedicated in April 1903. This church was constructed in the Spanish style, using tile roof and stucco with loggia on one side, and remained in constant use for forty years. It was located at College and Pennsylvania Avenues and on its outside wall a dedicatory plaque read: "This Church was erected as a testimonial of esteem for Mr. and Mrs. C. R. Post, and dedicated to the services of God." Rollin served on the board of supervisors, and as first Deacon, and his brother Herbert was first Church secretary and superintendent of Sunday School.

In March of 1950, a new Church, a magnificent quarried-stone building, was constructed at 3563 Manderly Place, in order to accommodate the fast-growing congregation. In the parlor of the new building are large portraits of Rollin and Carrie; the plaque is no longer in evidence. Though both have been deceased nearly fifty years, their memory remains with the present congregation. Rollin and Carrie spent at Fort Worth happy years of a life fulfilled, and it is sad to contemplate that they both outlived their devoted Charlie. Carrie lived not many months after the untimely death of her son. Her little diary reflects comfort found in spiritual guidance, her devoted friends and remaining family. She died on October 17, 1914, age 90, and was taken to Springfield for burial in Oak Ridge Cemetery.

After Carrie's death Rollin was extremely lonely. His health was excellent, but he found himself lost without his companion of so many years. He spent time at a winter home in California, and there, on New Year's day, 1917, was married by Reverend Post, a cousin, to Mrs. Nellie J. Moore, his wife's long-time friend, whose first husband had died ten years before in Fort Worth—this marriage to take place in his 91st year was a delight to his family. His granddaughter, then Marjorie Post Close, furnished the bride and groom with a car and chauffeur for a long-desired trip to

---

* This compiler, after difficult search, located the Bible in the Sturgess Library, Barnstable, Massachusetts, where it is preserved under sealed glass and may not be handled.

Vermont and eastern resorts. They toured through Connecticut and up to Cornwall, but as he recalled, "fate played a trick, there was not one soul living near my age who could remember any of the incidents associated with my childhood." He remained in good health and found a great deal of comfort with his new companion for two and a half more years; he died on July 15, 1919 at Los Angeles. His remains were removed to Springfield for burial beside his beloved Carrie. The eulogy given at his services reflected some of his philosophy of life. It was recalled then that he had said many times, though he had been a pioneer of the Gold Rush, "I never carried a gun in my life and never saw the time when I wished I had one, gun-toting is a chip on the shoulder, it is inviting trouble." He went through life with a ready wit and engaging smile and closed the chapter in the same even tenor of his ways.

References:
Barbour Collection of Connecticut Vital Records (*op. cit.*).
C. R. Post's Bible.
Lathrop Genealogy, by Huntington, 1884.
Library of Congress, Newspaper morgue.
C. W. Post scrapbooks (property of Mrs. Marjorie Post May).
Private Letters, Account Books and Journals (property of Mrs. May).
U.S. Census, 1850, 1860, 1870, 1880.
Sangamon County, Illinois, Court Records.

153. Charles William[9] Post *(C. Rollin[8], Truman[7], Roswell[6], Roswell[5], Abraham[4], Abraham[3], Abraham[2], Stephen[1])*, was born October 26, 1854, Springfield, Illinois; died May 9, 1914, Santa Barbara, California; buried Oak Hill Cemetery, Battle Creek, Michigan; married on November 4, 1874, (1) **Ella Letitia Merriweather**, at Pawnee, Illinois, by Rev. Albert Hale. She was born September 18, 1853, Springfield, Illinois; died October 21, 1912, Washington, D. C., buried Oak Ridge Cemetery, Springfield, Illinois. He married (2) **Lelia Young**, 1904, who survived him and married L. J. Montgomery of Battle Creek. No issue by Lelia Young.

Issue: 2 children.

— Rollin Tracy Post, stillborn, December 17, 1883, Springfield, Illinois.
+156 Marjorie Merriweather Post, born March 15, 1887, Springfield, Illinois.

Charles William Post is the subject of the biography in this volume; with an account of his daughter and of his father being also included it is not necessary to include further details within the genealogical supplement. Data are given as concerns the genealogy of Ella Letitia Merriweather. The father of Ella was John Hood Merriweather, born July 2, 1808, Anne Arundel (now Howard) County, Maryland. He was a direct descendant of Nicholas[1] Meriwether of Virginia. The line of descent for John Hood Merriweather[7] was as follows: Nicholas[1], Nicholas[2] and Elizabeth Crawford; David[3] and Anne Homes; Nicholas[4] and Frances Morton; Reuben[5] who came to Maryland and married Sarah Dorsey; Nicholas[6] who married Elizabeth Hood of Maryland; John Hood Merriweather who supplied the extra "a" in the name, married Elizabeth Hummel in Clark County, Ohio and settled near Springfield, Illinois. Through his mother, Elizabeth Hood, he was descended from Hoods, Worthingtons, Warfields, Ridgeleys, Hammonds and other fine families of Colonial Maryland. His grandmother, Sarah Dorsey, daughter of Thomas Beale Dorsey, was descended from the outstanding Dorseys and their connections in Colonial Maryland. John Hood Merriweather was married on March 5, 1835 to Elizabeth Hummel; he died at Springfield, October 15, 1863, and his wife died August 18, 1868, age 55 years, both are buried at Springfield, Oak Ridge Cemetery. He was a very successful merchant of Springfield and left a very comfortable sum of money to his children upon the death of their mother. At the present time a new and completely documented Meriwether genealogy is in process of being prepared for publication by this compiler.

156. Marjorie Merriweather[10] **Post** (*Chas. Wm.*[9] *and Ella L. Merriweather Post*), was born March 15, 1887, Springfield, Illinois; married December 3, 1905 (1) **Edward Bennett Close,** at New York City; he was born January 23, 1882, New York City; died February 5, 1955, Greenwich, Connecticut; married July 7, 1920 (2) **Edward Francis Hutton,** at New York City; he was born September 7, 1875, New York City; married December 15, 1935 (3) **Hon. Joseph E. Davies,** at New York City; he was born November 29, 1876, Watertown, Wisconsin; married on June 18, 1958 (4) **Herbert Arthur May,** at Woodbine, Maryland; he was born June 27, 1892, Watertown, Wisconsin.

Issue: By **Close:**

+157 Adelaide Brevoort Close, born July 26, 1908, Greenwich, Connecticut.

+158 Eleanor Post Close, born December 12, 1909, Greenwich, Connecticut.

By **Hutton:**

+159 Nedenia Marjorie Hutton, born December 29, 1923, New York City.

Marjorie Merriweather Post's life is dealt with here in biographical form, following the life of her father. It would be impossible to cover the many activities of her crowded life in any genealogical account.

157. Adelaide Brevoort Close[11] *(Edward Bennet Close and Marjorie Post*[10]*)* was born July 26, 1908, Greenwich, Connecticut; married January 19, 1927 (1) **Thomas (Tim) W. Durant,** at New York City; he was born October 18, 1899, Waterbury, Connecticut, son of Harold and Mary (Walker) Durant; married on July 26, 1936 (2) **Merrall Mac-Neille,** at Roslyn, Long Island; he was born May 3, 1909, New York City, son of John R. and Ada (Merrall) MacNeille; married on June 8, 1948 (3) **Augustus Riggs IV,** at Washington, D. C.; he was born August 11, 1913, son of Augustus Riggs III and Amalia de Murguiondo Riggs.

Issue: By **Durant:**

160 MARJORIE MERRIWEATHER DURANT[12] born April 20, 1928, New York City; married April 19, 1956, at St. Thomas Episcopal Church, Washington, D. C., to Ronald Bowles Waller, born February 14, 1933, Hastings, Florida, son of Roland H. and Elvira (Bowles) Waller; married (2) Peter Weinrich Dye on April 2, 1962.
Issue:
  I. Marjorie (Wendie) Post Waller.
  II. Post Stevens Waller.
  III. Ronald Timothy Waller.

  By **Dye:**
  IV. John Philip Patrick Dye

  By **MacNeille:**

161 ELLEN BREVOORT MacNEILLE[12], born June 4, 1937, New York City; married June 15, 1957, at Woodbine, Maryland, to Captain George Dudley Iverson V, USA., who was born February 7, 1936, Baltimore, Maryland, son of George Dudley IV and Gertrude Rausch Iverson.
Issue:
  I. George Dudley Iverson VI.
  II. David MacNeille Iverson.

162 MELISSA MERLE MacNEILLE[12], born February 1, 1939, New York City; married September 24, 1960, at Woodbine, Maryland, to Lieutenant Commander Rodion Cantacuzene, USN., who was born October 22, 1928, son of Prince Michael and Clarissa Curtis Cantacuzene.
Issue:
  I. Michael Cantacuzene, born July 12, 1961.
  II. Rodion Cantacuzene, Jr.

Adelaide (Close) Riggs has long been known as a breeder of fine dogs and horses. She became known as one of the youngest judges in the dog show ring, and as a breeder of Fox Terriers, Great Danes, Airedales, Scottish Terriers, Standard Schnauzers and Dalmatians. She was owner of the International Champion, Laurieston Loraine, Scottish Terrier. Her champions in all classes are far too numerous to list here. Her horses included Best Contract Winner of Maryland Futurity; Sidney won the Brook Cup at Belmont and broke the track record for 2½ miles. McCarthy More won the Meadowbrook Cup and the Long Island Hunt Cup. St. Francis won the Temple Gwathmey in race record time and best horse over hurdles in New York for two years. Augustus Riggs and Adelaide now reside at Woodbine, Maryland, where their interests are centered in the field of country life. "Gus" Riggs is the personification of the Maryland country squire, horseman, MFH, breeder, and himself a descendant of Maryland's oldest families, Riggs, Dorseys, Worthingtons, et al., which families produce a common ancestor with his wife's ancestry, though neither was aware of the fact when they met. Mrs. Riggs is a delightfully charming woman of simple taste and a love of the outdoor life.

158. Eleanor Post Close[11] *(Edward Bennett Close and Marjorie Post*[10]*)* was born December 12, 1909, Greenwich, Connecticut; she married April 22, 1942, **Janos de Békessy** (Hans Habe) after an unhappy previous marriage experience. Her only child is by this husband. She married on September 2, 1954, **Leon Eugene Barzin,** who was born November 27, 1900, Brussels, Belgium, son of Leon Barzin and Marie de Bacher Barzin.

Issue: By **De Békessy.**

163 ANTAL MIKLAS POST DE BÉKESSY[12], was born July 14, 1943, New York City.

Eleanor (Close) Barzin was educated at Spence School, Mount Vernon Seminary, and Miss Porter's School, Farmington, Connecticut. She was introduced to society at a ball given by her mother and step-father, Edward F. Hutton, in New York in 1927, and was presented to King George and Queen Mary at Buckingham Palace in 1926. She is a very discerning collector of antique objects of art, showing a quality of taste and selectivity second only to her mother. Devoted to music, Eleanor was once a student of voice with great promise, but the proposed career was abandoned because of health. She and her husband, Leon Barzin, make their home in Paris, and the career of Leon Barzin is worthy of mention here. His father was his first teacher of the violin, but later Leon Barzin studied with Henrotte, Deru, Maergerlin and Ysaye. At nineteen, he joined the old National Symphony Orchestra of New York, and a year after that was engaged as violinist with the Philharmonic Society. In 1925 he became first violinist with that Society, later joining the Philharmonic String Quartet. He received his first break as a conductor when Toscanini walked out of a Philharmonic recording session and Barzin was asked to head a major orchestra. When Barzin turned down the offer to go into teaching, the Maestro stopped speaking to him. In addition, Barzin has served as musical director of the Hartford Symphony (1938-1940) and as orchestral director of the Minneapolis Symphony, New York Philharmonic, St. Louis Symphony, Buffalo Philharmonic and N.B.C. Symphony. In 1946, he received the Alice M. Ditson Award, and in 1950, an honorary doctorate from the College of Music at Cincinnati. As of 1958, he has been Musical Director of the Orchestre de la Société Philharmonique de Paris.

159. Nedenia Marjorie Hutton[11] *(Edward F. Hutton and Marjorie Post*[10]*)* was born December 29, 1923, New York City; married on March 23, 1946, **Stanley M. Rumbough, Jr.,** son of General Stanley M. Rumbough and Elizabeth Colgate; he was born April 25, 1920, New York City.

Issue: By **Rumbough.**
> 164 STANLEY HUTTON RUMBOUGH[12], born May 24, 1948.
> 165 DAVID POST RUMBOUGH[12], born September 27, 1949.
> 166 NEDENIA COLGATE RUMBOUGH[12], born September 30, 1952.

Nedenia Hutton Rumbough is known to the public as Dina Merrill, television and motion picture star. She was educated at Greenvale, Mount Vernon Seminary, George Washington University, American Academy of Dramatic Arts, Berghof Studios, and Stella Adler Studios. Her affiliations with charitable organizations are numerous, she having been a director of New York City Mission, 1954, and other organizations. Her theatrical accomplishments include *The Man Who Came to Dinner; Mermaid's Singing; Butterfield 8; Don't Give Up the Ship;* et al; T. V. Playhouse 90; Westinghouse show; Manhattan Sunday Showcase; U. S. O., South Pacific, World War II; numerous T. V. starring roles. Stanley Rumbough received the A. B., Yale, 1942, N. Y. U. School of Business Administration, 1947–51. Military: 1942–45 Captain USMCR, Pilot; 2 DFC's, 8 Air Medals. Politics and government: Founder and Vice Chairman, IKE DAY, 1956. Charitable Organizations, etc.: Member President's Council for Youth Fitness, 1957;

Founder and Hon. Chairman Washington Area Tennis Club; Patrons Foundation, 1955. Member Davis Cup Committee, 1955–57, and various other organizations too numerous to list here. He is President of the Rumbough Foundation, 1959—; Trustee of International House, 1959—. Business: Director, Secretary, White Metal Mfg. Co., Hoboken, New Jersey; V. P. and Dir., Willis Air Service, Teterboro, New Jersey; Pres. Dir., Metal Containers Corp., Indianapolis, Indiana; Pres. Dir., American Totalisator, Baltimore, Maryland; Dir., General Register Co., New York; Dir., Welding Engineering, Nassau, British West Indies; President, Rumbough Company, New York; Chm. Board, Extrusion Dev. Co., Hawthorne, New Jersey.

The foregoing genealogical account gives the descent from Stephen Post[1] in a direct line unto the latest grandchild and great-grandchild of Marjorie Merriweather (Post) Close Hutton May.

Charted Ancestral Lines

of

Marjorie Merriweather Post

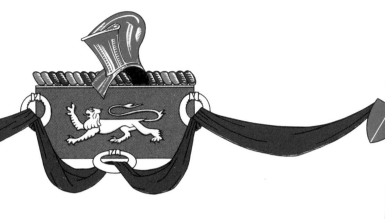

Rurik, the Viking
unto
Marjorie Merriweather Post
(direct line of descent)

31 Rurik, The Viking (reign 862–879), Prince of Russia, came from Upsala, Sweden.

30 Igor, son of above, born 875, died 945, Grand Duke of Kiev, married Olga, who assumed the Regency in the name of her son, Sviatoslaf.

29 Sviatoslaf, son of above, Grand Duke of Kiev, Reign 964–972.

28 St. Vladimir, born 965, died 1015, Reign 972–1015, Grand Duke of Kiev and Prince of Russia; married Anne, daughter of Romanus II, Roman Emperor.

27 Jaroslav I, Grand Duke of Kiev, born 978, died 1054; married Ingegard, daughter of Olaf III, King of Sweden.

26 Anne of Russia, daughter of above, married Henry I, King of France (1005–1067), Reign, 1031–1061.

25 Hugh Magnus, son of above, died 1101, Duke of France; married Adelaide Vermandois.

24 Isabel de Vermandois, married (1) 1096 Sir Robert de Beaumont.

23 Sir Robert de Beaumont (1104–1168), married Amice de Gael (Montfort).

22 Sir Robert de Beaumont (1135–1190), 3rd Earl of Leicester; married Petronilla de Grantmesnil.

21 Margaret de Beaumont; married Saier de Quincy (1155–1219), 1st Earl of Winchester; Magna Charta Surety and Crusader (Baron of Runnemede).

20 Roger de Quincy, 2nd Earl of Winchester, died 4.24.1264, Constable of Scotland; married Helen, daughter of Alan, Lord of Galloway.

19 Margaret de Quincy, married *ca.* 1238, died 3.12.1280, married William de Ferrers, Earl of Derby, buried, 5.31.1321.

18 Joan de Ferrers, died 1309, married 1267, Thomas de Berkeley, Lord Berkeley, (1245–1321).

17 Maurice de Berkeley, Lord Berkeley, Chief Justice of South Wales; married 1316, Eva la Zouche, daughter of Eudes la Zouche.

16 Sir Thomas de Berkeley, Lord Berkeley, Knt. (1296–1361); married (2) 5.30.1347, Katherine, daughter of Sir John de Clyvedon.

15 Sir John Berkeley of Beavertone, born *ca.* 1351, married (1) Elizabeth, daughter of Sir John Bettishorne.

14 Elizabeth de Berkeley, died 12.8.1478, married 1408, (2) Sir John Sutton, K.G., Baron Dudley, born 12.24.1400, died 9.30.1487.

13 Jane Sutton married Thomas Mainwaring of Ightfield.

12 Cecily Mainwaring married John Cotton, born 1509, died 1546, Eq. to Henry VIII, King of England.

11 Sir George Cotton of Combemere, 2nd son, married Mary Onley.

10 Richard Cotton, Esq., died 6.15.1602, married (2) Jane Silliard.

9 Frances Cotton married George Abell of Stapenhill, County Derby, died *ca.* 1630.

8 Robert Abell, born County Derby, died 6.20.1663, Rehoboth, Massachusetts, married Joanna. (He was the immigrant to America.)

7 Joshua Abell married (2) Bethiah Gadger, both died at Norwich, Connecticut. Joshua 1649–1722; Bethiah 1660–1723.

6 Elizabeth Abell, born 10.-1695, married 4.7.1715, John Lathrop (1690–1752), both of Norwich, Connecticut.

5 Azel Lathrop married Elizabeth Hyde, born 4.11.1755, daughter of Phineas and Ann Rodgers Hyde; after death of Azel, she married (2) Ezra Huntington.

4 Erastus Lathrop, born 5.18.1784, Norwich, died Hartford, 7.30.1851; married Sarah Bailey of New London, she was born 1791, died 1856.

3 Caroline Lathrop (1824–1914) married Charles Rollin Post (1826–1919).

2 Charles William Post (1854–1914) married Ella Letitia Merriweather (1853–1912).

1 Marjorie Merriweather Post (1887–) married (1) Edward B. Close; (2) Edward Francis Hutton (issue by these two husbands only).

(References for Rurik, The Viking on page 310)

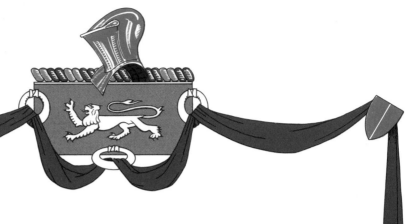

House of Capet

unto
Marjorie Merriweather Post

Capet is the surname of that family to which, for nearly nine centuries, the Kings of France and many rulers of the most powerful French fiefs belonged, and which intermarried with most of the royal houses of Europe. The original significance of the name remains in dispute, but the first to whom it was applied was Hugh, who was elected King of the Franks in 987. The real founder of the House, however, was Robert the Strong, who received from Charles the Bald, Carlovingian, King of the Franks, the countship of Anjou and Blois, and who is sometimes called Duke, as he exercised some military authority in the district between the Seine and the Loire.

31 Robert the Strong, Count of Anjou and Blois, son of Witichin, was slain in 867. He was rector of the Abbey of Marmouttiers in 853, and was also *Missus,* or governor of the counties of Maine, Anjou and Corbannais. He had a son Robert, who follows.

30 Robert I, King of Franks, was born in 865, and was killed in battle near Soissons, June 15, 923. In the year 922, he took up arms against Charles the Simple, and having achieved victory, was proclaimed King of the Franks at Rheims on June 29 of that year. He married (1) Adele, whose parentage is not known; and (2) Beatrix of Vermandois. (Charlemagne and William the Conqueror to Vermandois). Among his children was Liegarde of France, who married Heribert II, Count of Vermandois, and Hugh, who follows.

29 Hugh the Great, also called Hugh le Blanc, Duke of the Franks and Count of Paris and Orleans, son of Robert I and Beatrix of Vermandois, died June 16, or 17, 956. He took the title of his father, King of the Franks, but allowed it to pass into temporary disuse. He married, 936, Hedwiga of Germany. Their son was Hugh Capet who follows.

28 Hugh Capet, King of the Franks, son of Hugh and Hedwiga, was born about
938, and died in Paris, October 24, 996. He succeeded to his father's
numerous fiefs in 956, thus becoming one of the most powerful feuda-
tories of France. When the son of Lothair, Louis V, the last Carlovingian
King of France, died, Hugh Capet was proclaimed King of the Franks
in 987. His kingdom included all present-day France except Brittany and
Aquitaine. Hugh Capet married Adelais or Adelaide, daughter of William
III, Duke of Aquitaine, Count of Poitiers of Auvergne, and his wife
Gerloc, Heloys, Adele or Adelaide of Normandy. A son of this marriage
was Robert, who follows.

27 Robert II, called the Pious, was born in Orleans about 970 and died about
1031. He won his sobriquet from his humility and charity, but despite
these qualities he was a good soldier and a statesman. He married (1)
in 988, as her second husband, Susanna, daughter of Berengar II, King
of Italy. He married (2) Bertha, daughter of Conrad the Peaceful, King
of Burgundy or Orles. He married (3) in 1003, Constance of Toulous.
By the third marriage he had Henry I, who follows.

26 Henry I, King of France, son of Robert and Constance, was born May 15,
1008, and died August 4, 1060. He was anointed king at Rheims in 1027,
at the suggestion of his father, in order to assure his succession. The
reign of Henry I, who warred with William the Conqueror over the
latter's domain in Normandy, marks the height of feudalism in France.
Henry I married (1) Maud, niece of the Emperor Henry III, and (2)
Anne of Russia, daughter of Jarsolav, Grand Duke of Kiev and Ingegarde
of Sweden. Sons of his second marriage were Philip and Hugh Magnus.
Hugh Magnus follows.

25 Hugh Magnus married Adele, or Adelaide, Countess of Vermandois and
Valois. Hugh was killed at Tarsus in Cilicia in 1102 and was buried in
the Church of St. Paul there. He became Count of Vermandois through
his marriage. He was prominent in the Crusades and participated in the
siege and capture of the cities of Nicaea and Antioch in 1096. In 1101
he made a second voyage to the East, but the crusading forces were
attacked by the Greeks under Alexius Commenus. Daughter Isabel married Sir Robert de Beaumont.

24 Isabel—consult Rurik the Viking chart, Isabel #24, and descend therefrom
unto #1, Marjorie Merriweather Post.

(References for House of Capet on page 310)

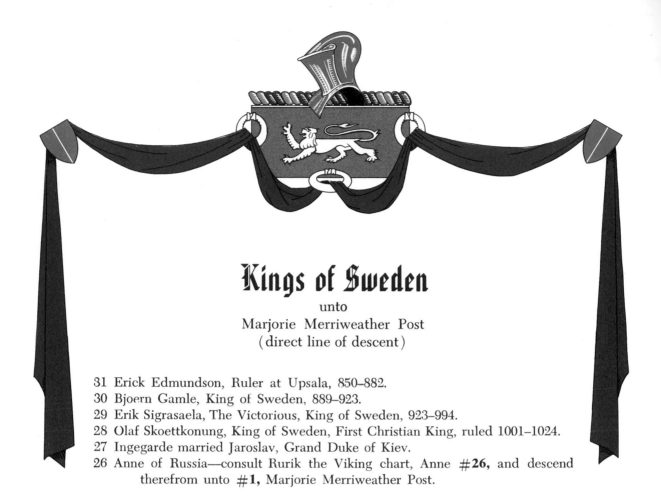

Kings of Sweden

unto
Marjorie Merriweather Post
(direct line of descent)

31 Erick Edmundson, Ruler at Upsala, 850–882.
30 Bjoern Gamle, King of Sweden, 889–923.
29 Erik Sigrasaela, The Victorious, King of Sweden, 923–994.
28 Olaf Skoettkonung, King of Sweden, First Christian King, ruled 1001–1024.
27 Ingegarde married Jaroslav, Grand Duke of Kiev.
26 Anne of Russia—consult Rurik the Viking chart, Anne **#26,** and descend therefrom unto **#1,** Marjorie Merriweather Post.

Counts of Vermandois

34 Pepin, son of Charlemagne, and 2nd wife (born 777, died 810) King of Lombardy.
33 Bernard, King of Italy, died 818.
32 Pepin, Seigneur of Peronne and St. Quentin.
31 Heribert I, Seigneur of Peronne, killed 902, Count of Vermandois.
30 Heribert II, Count of Vermandois, Troyes and Meaux, died 943, married Hildebrante, daughter of Robert, Duke of France.
29 Albert I, Count of Vermandois, died 987, married Gerberga of France.
28 Heribert III, Count of Vermandois, died 8.21.1000, married Hermengarde.
27 Otto, Count of Vermandois died 1045, married Pavie.
26 Heribert IV, died 1080, married Adele, daughter of Paoul III, Count of Valois.
25 Adele, Countess of Vermandois, married (1) Hugh Magnus, son of Henry I, of France.
24 Isabel—consult Rurik the Viking chart, Isabel **#24,** and descend therefrom unto **#1,** Marjorie Merriweather Post.

De Berkeley and Kings of Denmark

unto

Marjorie Merriweather Post

23 Harding, son of King of Denmark, died 1116, came to England with William the Conqueror, married Lyneda.

22 Sir Robert FitzHarding (de Berkeley) died 1170, obtained Lordship of Berkeley, married Eva de Estmond.

21 Maurice de Berkeley, died 1190, County of Middlesex, married Allce de Berkeley.

20 Thomas de Berkeley (1170–1243) married Joan de Somery, daughter of Ralph de Somery, Lord of Camden.

19 Maurice de Berkeley (1218–1280) married Isabel de Creoun.

18 Thomas de Berkeley (1245–1321) married Margaret called Joan de Ferrers.

17 Maurice de Berkeley—consult Rurik the Viking chart, **#17,** and descend therefrom unto **#1,** Marjorie Merriweather Post.

De Ferrieres [Ferrers]

25 Walkelin de Ferrieres of Normandy.

24 Henry de Ferrieres went to England with Norman invaders. Largest land-owner in Derbyshire, ninety Manors, Lord of the Castle of Tutbury.

23 Robert de Ferrieres, Earl of Derby, died 1139, crested Earl of Derby by King Stephen in 1138; married Hawise de Vitre, daughter of Andre.

22 Robert de Ferrieres, Earl of Derby, died before 1160, married Margaret Peverel.

21 William de Ferrieres, Earl of Derby, died in Syria before October 1190, married Sibyl de Braose.

20 William de Ferrieres (1172–1247) married Agnes de Kevelioc, Earls of Chester.

19 William de Ferrers, Earl of Derby, died 1254, married (2) Margaret de Quincy.

18 Joan de Ferrers—consult Rurik the Viking chart, Joan **#18,** and descend therefrom unto **#1,** Marjorie Merriweather Post.

Atwater of New England
unto
Marjorie Merriweather Post

9 David Atwater, died 1692; married Demaris Sayre, died 1691.

8 John Atwater, born 11.1.1654, died 1748; married (1) Abigail Mansfield, daughter of Moses Mansfield.

7 John Atwater, born 8.17.1683, died 3.11.1765, Cheshire; married 8.4.1713 Elizabeth Mix, born —, died 2.20.1758.

6 Stephen Atwater, born 9.8.1714, died 11.26.1806, Cheshire; married (1) 2.2.1744, Hannah Hotchkiss, born 1.10.1710, died 2.20.1758, daughter of Deacon Stephen Hotchkiss and Elizabeth Sperry.

5 Stephen Atwater, born 5.13.1758, Cheshire (Wallingford), died 11.26.1836, Crawford County, Pa., married 3.3.1780, Cheshire, to Anna Moss, born 11.29.1757, Wallingford, died 11.23.1801 (Granville, New York ?), daughter of Barnabas and Anna (Hollingsworth) Moss.

4 Betsey Atwater, born 12.9.1794, Cheshire, died 8.18.1861, Springfield, Illinois, married 3.19.1820, Granville, New York to Truman Post, born 12.11.1796, Cornwall, Vermont, died 10.29.1847, Waverly, Illinois. (see genealogy herein).

3 Charles Rollin Post, born 1.15.1826, Cornwall, Vermont, died 7.15.1919, buried Springfield, Illinois; married 10.10.1853, at Hartford, Connecticut, to Caroline Lathrop, born 11.27.1824, Ashford, Connecticut, died 10.17.1914, Fort Worth, Texas.

2 Charles William Post, born 10.26.1854, Springfield, Illinois, died 5.9.1914, buried Battle Creek, Michigan; married 11.4.1874, Pawnee, Illinois, to Ella Letitia Merriweather, born 9.18.1853, Springfield, Illinois, died 10.12.1912, Washington, D. C.

1 Marjorie Merriweather Post, born 3.15.1887, Springfield, Illinois.

(References for Atwater of New England on page 310)

Lathrop of New England

unto

Marjorie Merriweather Post

9 Rev. John Lathrop who came to New England with Rev. Thomas Hooker. Original Bible (published 1605 in England) is now in the Lathrop Room, Sturgess Library, Barnstable, Massachusetts.

8 Samuel Lathrop, born in England, died 2.29.1700, Barnstable; married 11.28.1644, at Barnstable, to Elizabeth Scudder.

7 Israel Lathrop, born October, 1659, Norwich, died 3.28.1733, Norwich; married 4.8.1686, at Norwich, to Rebecca Bliss, born 3.18.1663, Norwich, died 8.22.1737, Norwich, daughter of Thomas Bliss, Jr. and Elizabeth ———.

6 John Lathrop, born 10.2.1690, Norwich, died 5.5.1752, Norwich, married 4.7.1715, at Norwich, to Elizabeth Abell, born 10.—.1695, daughter of Joshua and (2) Bathiah (Gadger) Abell.

5 Azel Lathrop, born *ca.* 1730, died after 1785; married Elizabeth Hyde, born 4.11.1755, Norwich, died Ashford, 1835; she married (2) Ezra Huntington. She was the daughter of Phineas and Ann (Rodgers) Hyde. See Hyde Genealogy.

4 Erastus Lathrop, born 5.18.1784, Norwich, died 7.30.1851, Hartford; married 9.21.1807 at New London, Sarah Bailey, born 1.13.1791, New London, died 7.16.1856, Jacksonville, Illinois, daughter of Nathan, Jr. and Mary (Ward) Bailey.

3 Caroline Cushman Lathrop, born 11.27.1824, Ashford, Connecticut, died 10.17.1914, Fort Worth; married 10.10.1853 at Hartford, to Charles Rollin Post, born 1.15.1826, Cornwall, Vermont, died 7.15.1919, buried Springfield, Illinois

2 Charles William Post and Ella Letitia Merriweather.

1 Marjorie Merriweather Post.

(References for Lathrop of New England on page 310)

Meriwether - Merriweather

unto

Marjorie Merriweather Post

9 Nicholas Meriwether (1631-1678) who came to America, *ca.* 1652, lived James City, and Goochland County, Virginia, married Elizabeth (?) Woodhouse, who married (2) William Browne, Sr.

8 Nicholas Meriwether (1675–1744) married Elizabeth Crawford, daughter of David.

7 David Meriwether (1690–1744) died Louisa County, Virginia; married Ann Homes (Holmes).

6 Nicholas Meriwether (1719–1758) married Frances Morton, who married (2) Samuel Pryor. (She was a half-sister of John Morton Jordan).

5 Reuben Meriwether (1743–1794) was born in Louisa County, Virginia, and died Anne Arundel (now Howard) County, Maryland. Came to Maryland at the request of John Morton Jordan, was prominent in Maryland affairs; married Sarah Dorsey, 1769–1770, in Anne Arundel County, she was born 10.14.1747, Anne Arundel County, died November —, 1809, Anne Arundel County, daughter of Thomas Beale Dorsey and Ann Worthington Dorsey. Thomas Beale Dorsey was the son of Caleb and Eleanor (Warfield) Dorsey.

4 Nicholas Merriweather, born 6.14.1778, Anne Arundel County, Maryland, died 9.28.1872, Logan County, Ohio; married (1) Elizabeth Hood, on 12.12.1797, Anne Arundel County, she was born *ca.* 1779, died 1830 in Cincinnati; he married (2) in Clark County, Ohio, widow Caroline Lownes, on 11.3.1838, who died 4.3.1875, age 74.

3 John Hood Merriweather, born 7.2.1808, near Elkridge, Maryland, died 10.15.1863, buried Springfield, Illinois; married 3.5.1835, Clark County, Ohio, to Elizabeth Hummel, born 1813, Pennsylvania, died 8.18.1868, buried Springfield, Illinois.

2 Ella Letitia Merriweather, born 9.18.1853, Springfield, Illinois, died 10.12.1912, Washington, D. C.; married 11.4.1874, Pawnee, Illinois, to Charles William Post.

1 Marjorie Merriweather Post.

(References for Merriweather and Dorsey lines on page 310)

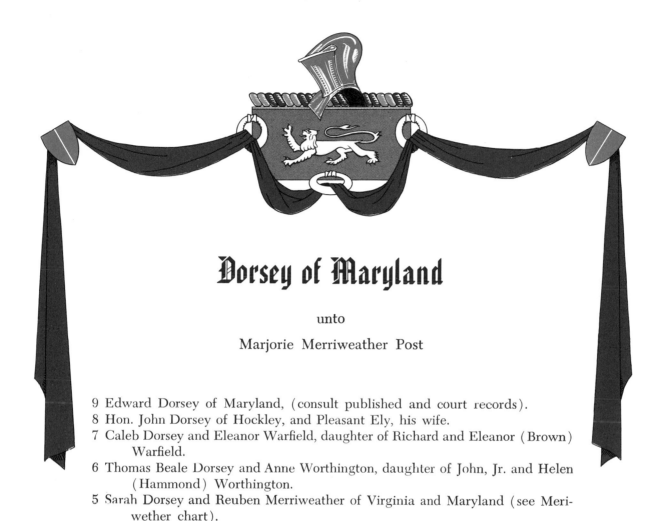

Dorsey of Maryland

unto

Marjorie Merriweather Post

9 Edward Dorsey of Maryland, (consult published and court records).

8 Hon. John Dorsey of Hockley, and Pleasant Ely, his wife.

7 Caleb Dorsey and Eleanor Warfield, daughter of Richard and Eleanor (Brown) Warfield.

6 Thomas Beale Dorsey and Anne Worthington, daughter of John, Jr. and Helen (Hammond) Worthington.

5 Sarah Dorsey and Reuben Merriweather of Virginia and Maryland (see Meriwether chart).

4 Nicholas Meriwether and Elizabeth Hood, daughter of John Hood, Jr. and Rachel (Howard) Hood.

3. John Hood Merriweather and Elizabeth Hummel (see Meriwether chart).

2 Ella Letitia Merriweather and Charles William Post.

1 Marjorie Merriweather Post.

REFERENCES OF CHARTED ANCESTRAL LINES

References for Rurik, The Viking Chart

Cokayne, 2nd ed., for de Quincy, de Ferrer, de Berkeley, la Zouche, Sutton, Blount.

Visitations of Shropshire, for Berkeley, Mainwaring, Sutton, Blount.

Visitations of Cheshire, for Cotton, Mainwaring, Charleston.

Norwich, Vital and Probate Records.

Ancestors and Descendants of Robert Abell, by A. & L. P. Abell, (1940).

National Society Daughters of the Barons of Runnemede, membership of Marjorie Merriweather Post May (proof filed with society).

References for the House of Capet

Genealogical Tables Illustrative of Modern History, H. B. George, 5th ed. No. XII.

Histoire généalogique et chronologique de la maison royale de France, P. Anselma.

La grande encyclopédie, Vol. XXVIII, pp. 738-39; *Ibid.* pp. 364-66.

Dictionary of Royal Lineage, C. M. Allstrom, Vol. II, pp. 276, 749, 750.

Trésor chronologie, L. de Mas-Latrie, p. 1662.

Bibliothéque de l'école des hautes études-sciences historiques et philologiques, Vol. LXXXVII, pp. 358-61; Vol. CXLVII, p. 201.

History of Russia, B. Pares.

Russia from Varangians to Bolsheviks, R. Beasley, p. 24.

L' art de vérifier les dates, N. V. de Saint-Allais, Vol. IV, Pt. 2, pp. 242-43.

References for Atwater of New England

Atwater Genealogy, by Frances Atwater, 1927, and prior editions.

N.B. The published genealogy must be supplemented with research in Connecticut Vital Records; probate matters will expand.

References for Lathrop of New England

The Lathrop Genealogy, pub. 1884, Huntington.

N.B. The published genealogy must be supplemented with research in Connecticut Vital and Probate Records; Bible information from original on file at Sturgess Library, Barnstable; no data available on Azel beyond letters of Caroline Lathrop Post who stated "after grandfather Lathrop died, grandmother married Mr. Huntington."

References for Merriweather and Dorsey Lines

*N.B. At this time, the compiler of this work is in process of preparing a Meriwether genealogy for publication. The above offered line is a preliminary presentation, but documented from Marjorie Post back unto Nicholas and Frances (Morton) Meriwether; prior data are in process of research.

*N.B. The Dorsey line will not be documented herewith. Maryland wills and deeds will verify claims given.

INDEX